CREATIVE MUSIC EDUCATION

CREATIVE MUSIC EDUCATION

*A Handbook for
the Modern Music Teacher*

R. Murray Schafer

SCHIRMER BOOKS
A Division of Macmillan Publishing Co., Inc.
NEW YORK

SCHIRMER BOOKS
A Division of Macmillan Publishing Co., Inc.
866 Third Avenue, New York, N.Y. 10022

Collier Macmillan Canada, Ltd.

Library of Congress Catalog Card Number: 75—30286

Printed in the United States of America

printing number
1   2   3   4   5   6   7   8   9   10

Library of Congress Cataloging in Publication Data

Schafer, R. Murray
    Creative music education.

    1. Music--Instruction and study. 2. School
music--Instruction and study. I. Title.
MT1.S29   780'.72   75-30286
ISBN 0-02-872330-9

The five parts of this book were originally published separately as:
THE COMPOSER IN THE CLASSROOM: Copyright © 1965 by BMI Canada Limited. Copyright assigned 1969 to Berandol Music Limited, Scarborough, Ontario.
EAR CLEANING: Copyright © 1967 by BMI Canada Limited. Copyright assigned 1969 to Berandol Music Limited.
THE NEW SOUNDSCAPE: Copyright © 1969 by BMI Canada Limited. Copyright assigned 1969 to Berandol Music Limited.
WHEN WORDS SING: Copyright © 1970 by Berandol Music Limited.
THE RHINOCEROS IN THE CLASSROOM: Copyright © 1975 by Universal Edition (Canada) Ltd.

Copyright Acknowledgments

Contents

A Note to the Teacher

The material in this volume was originally published in a series of five "booklets." It documents nearly fifteen years of teaching in Canadian and American schools, universities, and summer music camps, recording experiences with teachers, children, university students, and amateur musicians. In the past few years, as I have tried out similar teaching ideas in a dozen other countries on three continents, I have noticed a growing number of music educators moving out in similar directions. An encouraging sign, though the area is still rather bleak. And that, I would say, is the only justification for the reappearance of my "diary of personal experiences" in a format that looks suspiciously like a textbook.

If this is indeed a textbook, it is not laid out like a traditional one. It does not begin with a "March of the Middle C's." It does not progress stepwise to reach some deliriously systematic high note of accomplishment, after which, *basta*, it stops. I do not think this book ends at all, because it deals with the principles of ongoing musicianship.

The principal issues dealt with in the five "parts" of *Creative Music Education* are creativity, ear training, the soundscape, words and music, and music in relation to the other arts. *The Composer in the Classroom* deals primarily with creativity, perhaps the most neglected subject in Western musical education. *Ear Cleaning* expands traditional concepts of ear training in order to deal with both the newer forms of today's music and the acoustic environment at large. To refer to the acoustic environment, I use the word "soundscape." It seems to me absolutely essential that we begin to listen more carefully and critically to the new soundscape of the modern world. It is only by listening that we will be able to solve the noise pollution problem. Clairaudience in schools to eliminate audiometry in factories. Ear cleaning instead of ear muffs. Ultimately we may be able to design the soundscape, to improve it aesthetically —and that ought to interest every contemporary teacher.

In *The New Soundscape* the music class touches other subject areas: geography, sociology, communications, public affairs. So does the issue dealt with in *When Words Sing*, for it investigates the middle ground between music and poetry, an area which both contemporary composers and "concrete" poets are opening up to us. (It has been gratifying to learn that this section of the book has been used by departments of English literature to help students discover the potentialities of the human voice.) In the last section of the book, *The Rhinoceros in the Classroom*, I venture more strongly into territories of some other arts, particularly drama and the visual arts. We are searching today for a new integrity in life and art, and the music teacher cannot ignore the value of links with other subject areas, even if the matter is explored diffidently at first.

These are all large themes. I have only scratched the surface of each. I could have said more, and indeed in working sessions have developed the material further. (It will perhaps not be inappropriate to mention here that the little compositions I have written as illustrations are available from Berandol Music, 11 St. Joseph Street, Toronto, Canada.)

The main thing that will strike the reader of these pages is that they are a personal account rather than a method for slavish imitation. It is for this reason that my writing is descriptive rather than prescriptive. Nothing in this book says *"Do it* this way." It only says *"I did it* this way." It was all a little unusual at the time. Perhaps you will find that it still is.

CREATIVE MUSIC EDUCATION

Part I

THE COMPOSER IN THE CLASSROOM

The discussions and experiments reported in Part I came about as a result of two invitations to work with music students in schools.

In the summer of 1964 I was invited to join the teaching staff of the North York Summer Music School and under the loose heading of "Musicianship" I was given a free hand with two large classes of instrumental and vocal music students. The first four discussions took place at this time.

I was also fortunate enough to be one of fourteen Canadian composers chosen to attend a 1965 seminar, sponsored by The Canada Council and organized by The Canadian Music Centre, at which the relationship of the contemporary composer to school music was studied. Much of the time was taken up in visiting schools where we talked and worked with young people before receiving commissions to write music for them. The fifth and sixth discussions took place at this time. On both occasions, my work was facilitated by a very exceptional music educator: Mr. C. Laughton Bird, Co-ordinator of Music for the North York Board of Education. Everything would have been impossible without his inclination for adventure.

The following texts are condensed transcriptions of some of the sessions. The experiments were often used to reinforce points raised in discussions and seemed to grow naturally out of them. Except for the discussion "Mask of the Evil Demon," which involved elementary school students, I was dealing with high school students, aged about 13 to 17.

GETTING ACQUAINTED

OBSERVATIONS: As an outsider, anxious to work in an unorthodox manner with the students, it was first necessary to put them in a relaxed and discursive frame of mind. Hence the rather tentative quality of the opening discussion.

SCHAFER: I should like to get to know a little about you and your musical interests. As you know, I am not a regular music teacher, but rather a composer. I thought we might begin by making a list of the kinds of music you like and dislike. Everybody has a favorite kind of music and everybody probably has violent dislikes as well; I don't mean individual pieces of music, but rather categories—like chamber music or jazz. Call out your likes and dislikes and I'll put them up on the blackboard. Let's label your favorite kinds of music "OK Music" and the kinds you dislike "Non-OK Music."

Answers are called out and copied down. After a few moments the blackboard looks like this:

OK MUSIC	NON-OK MUSIC
Jazz	Folk Music
Popular Music	Opera
Chamber Music	Jazz
Opera	Modern and Electronic Music
Country and Western Music	Symphonic Music
Band Music	Country and Western Music
Musicales	
Light Concert Favorites	

SCHAFER: This is very interesting. I see a number of categories in both columns. What do you think this indicates?

STUDENT: It shows that everybody has different tastes in music.

SCHAFER: Do you think that is a good thing or a bad thing?

STUDENT: I think it is a good thing, because it shows that there are many different personalities and a special kind of music to suit each personality.

SCHAFER: Do you mean that everybody likes only the kind of music that reflects their own personality? Do you like only one kind?

STUDENT: I like Country and Western.

SCHAFER: Only!

STUDENT: I like band music too.

SCHAFER (to class): How many of you like only one kind of music from our chart? Hands?

No hands are raised.

More than one?

All hands are raised.

Good, Now let me draw a comparison for a moment. How many religious faiths do we have represented in the class?

It is discovered that a number of students are from varying Protestant denominations and others are of the Jewish faith.

Now let me ask you this: how many of you belong to more than one of those groups mentioned?

No hands.

Each of you espouses only one religious faith. Yet none of you restricted musical interests to one kind only. It is quite clear then that you can like more than one kind of music without having a crisis of conscience over it. This is a very important distinction between the appreciation of art and other kinds of intellectual activity. With religion—and the same is true of politics or philosophy—you accept the one system which seems to you to be most reasonable, but in doing this you automatically negate all other systems as being invalid. You can't be a communist and a capitalist at the same time any more than you can be Jewish and Christian at the same time. But art appreciation doesn't work this way at all; it's rather an accumulative thing, you keep discovering new things of interest, but these new things in no way negate the things you enjoyed before. Can anyone confirm this observation from personal experience?

STUDENT: Well, once I just liked jazz, and now I like Beethoven as well; but I still like jazz.

SCHAFER: Probably most of you have had similar experiences. In all art we recognize the fact that different people have different enthusiasms and opinions and we tolerate them. A whole world originally separated the two kinds of music you just mentioned. Beethoven's music was originally written as a diversion for the European aristocracy a century and a half ago, whereas jazz grew up as the musical expression of the enslaved North American negro. At first one form was for aristocrats and the other for slaves. Today we are neither slaves nor aristocrats and we can appreciate both kinds of music objectively. We do not declare war on nations because they like the wrong kind of music.

STUDENT: Different armies marching into war will have different national anthems.

SCHAFER: Ah, but they aren't making war because they can't agree on the melody of a national anthem. This is a case of music being used to support something that is outside music—in this case a political ideology. Yes, people will certainly fight over politics, but no one ever shot a piano player just because he or she was playing the wrong tune.

STUDENT: It sounds as if music isn't very important.

SCHAFER: And is it?

STUDENT: Well, I think it is.

SCHAFER: Does it necessarily follow that it is unimportant just because people don't fight over it?

ANOTHER STUDENT: Perhaps it's important just because of this. Perhaps it brings people together instead of separating them.

SCHAFER: Good! But what about these different opinions in music? How can you and I, for instance, be drawn together if I like chamber music and hate popular music and for you the situation is exactly reversed? What is . . .

STUDENT AT BACK (aside): Professors are supposed to like chamber music.

SCHAFER (overhearing): Someone at the back has made an assumption. Suppose I make one too. Teen-agers are crazy over the hit parade. How many of you listen regularly to the hit parade?

About 70% of the class raise their hands.

By the law of percentages my assumption is correct. Now you see what we've done here is to associate the hit parade with teen-agers just as our friend at the back associated professors with chamber music. Thus, certain kinds of music seem to be representative of certain classes of people, though I want you to bear in mind that this is an extremely broad generalization. Supposing I disliked teen-agers—and I hope you know that I don't; but supposing I did—what would be the effect on my musical tastes?

STUDENT: I think you would dislike everything about them including their music.

SCHAFER: Yes, probably. But has my dislike of teen-agers really got anything to do with music, which is after all, an abstract art?

STUDENT: It shouldn't have, but it probably does.

SCHAFER: We tend to associate certain kinds of art with certain people or groups of people and this undoubtedly affects our appreciation. I've often wondered whether it is possible at all to disassociate music from human beings and appreciate it clinically—in its pure form. I don't think it is possible entirely. But I think sometimes it is necessary to appreciate it this way if our musical tastes are to develop and change. In other words, let the music speak for itself, not through associations. I should never allow myself to become so blinded by prejudice that I refuse to listen to the hit parade; you should never allow yourselves to become so blinded by prejudice that you refuse to listen to chamber music. Music is not the private property of certain people or groups. Potentially every piece of music was written for all people.

I suppose what I really want to tell you is above all to be curious about music. Don't be content to stand still in your musical tastes, because as I said a few moments ago, you are not going to betray your old favorites by acquiring new ones. This horizon can go on expanding and expanding; all your life there will be new things to discover. Of course, I'm not saying you should like everything you come in contact with. Only a fool would react like that. I'm simply saying that if you're going to discover interesting music you will have to go out and find it.

It's just the same as going to a library. You may look through twenty books before you find the one you want to read, but if you hadn't looked through the twenty you'd never find anything worthwhile to read. And the strangest thing is that the book you choose this year will not be the same as the one you may choose next year. Time really forces us to go on acquiring new tastes. We don't go on reading comic books all our lives, do we?

STUDENT: Some people do!

SCHAFER: What would you think of someone who still read comic books at the age of forty?

STUDENT: I'd say that person was a case of arrested development.

Laughter.

SCHAFER: Right! And anyone who goes through life liking the same kind of music without acquiring any new enthusiasms is also a case of arrested development.

Someone once said that the two most important things in developing taste were sensitivity and intelligence. I don't think this is so; I'd rather call them curiosity and courage. Curiosity to look for the new and the hidden; courage to develop your own tastes regardless of what others may say or think. People who will risk being laughed at by others because they have individuality in musical tastes (and this will happen) show real courage. People who like things only because it is socially useful for them to do so we call snobs. Listening to music is a deeply personal thing and with society moving as it is today towards uniformity and conventionalism, it takes real courage to discover that you are an individual with an individual mind and individual tastes in art. Listening to music properly will help bring out the uniqueness in you.

The bell rings.

WHAT IS MUSIC?

OBSERVATIONS: A very large area of misconception is exposed in this discussion by asking a basic question. The interesting conclusion reached is realistic with regard to the musical scene today; and although it does not seem to be compatible with O.E.D. or pamphlets on music appreciation, it does seem that students studying the subject deserve the benefit of a useful and "living" definition of music. The class is asked how long they have been studying music. Several answers: two years, three years, four years, seven years.

SCHAFER: I remember a teacher I once had in school asking me to describe a circular staircase without using my hands—a very difficult thing to do, though of course not impossible. Well, today I am going to ask you a question that is also difficult to answer, though it is also not impossible. I thought we might discuss it together and see if we can establish a definition. The question is this: *What Is Music?* One of the worst things that can happen to us in life is to go on doing things without knowing what they are or why we are doing them. You have all been making music for a number of years, and we hope you will go on making music for many more years. But what is this thing you are spending so much time doing? Any definitions?

Hesitantly at first, then more vigorously, definitions are offered and are written down on the board:

> Music is something you like
> Music is sound arranged with rhythm and melody
> Music is sound pleasing to the ear
> Music is an art
> Music is a cultural activity concerning sound

SCHAFER: This is enough to start with. We can rework these as necessary. Let us look at them more closely. First: *Music Is Something You Like.*

Schafer goes to the record player and puts on the first record he picks up. It happens to be the "Raggedy Waltz" from Dave Brubeck's recording "Time Further Out."

SCHAFER: Is that music?

CLASS (puzzled): Yes!

SCHAFER: Would all those who don't like jazz please stand up.

Several stand.

SCHAFER (to one of those standing): You don't like jazz?

STUDENT: No, I hate it!

SCHAFER: But you agree that it was music you heard?

STUDENT: Yes.

SCHAFER: Something fishy here. Music is defined as *Something You Like*. We listened to some jazz. You agreed that it was music we listened to. But if you don't like jazz how can it be music?

STUDENT: There·is something wrong with the definition.

SCHAFER: Obviously it's unsatisfactory. There is something too personal about saying that music is something you like. The big question is: who is "you"—and what gives "you" the right to distinguish between music and non-music for the rest of us? Whatever music is, it is clear that it cannot depend on the pleasure of one person only. It must be something more general than that.

What about the third definition: *Music Is Sound Pleasing To The Ear*. Here we have eliminated the controversial "you" which was too personal and we have substituted a sort of collective ear—all listeners to music. What about it?

STUDENT: Well, there are certain sounds which are pleasing to everybody's ear and certain sounds that are displeasing. The sounds in the street aren't music.

SCHAFER: A car in the street screeches its brakes—is it music?

EVERYONE: No!

SCHAFER: Why?

A pause: no comments.

All right, we'll leave that for a moment and return to it later. But you all agree that noise can't be music.

Nods of agreement.

All right, let's see.

Schafer goes to the bass drum and strikes it rhythmically several times.
Is that music?

CLASS: Yes!

At the back of the classroom there is a large garbage can. This is also struck several times rhythmically.

SCHAFER: Is that music?

CLASS: No!

SCHAFER (surprised): Oh! There's a difference? Can you tell me what it is?

STUDENT: The drum sounds a definite tone but the garbage can is just noise.

SCHAFER: Can anyone tell me what the definite tone of the bass drum is?

BASS DRUM PLAYER: I think its "A."

SCHAFER: All right: (beating the drum) Class sing "A."

Confusion results. There are nearly as many different pitches sung as there are students.

SCHAFER: An odd "A" (Laughter). I think you've been misled into thinking the bass drum has a definite pitch. It is true that sometimes it seems to take on the tonality of the other instruments in the orchestra when it is played with them; but in fact it has no definite pitch itself. The sound it produces is "noise" just as that produced by the garbage can is noise.

A brief discussion of the difference between regular and irregular vibrations follows. It is pointed out that it is this which distinguishes sounds of definite pitch from mere noise. Following this Schafer again goes to the drum and the garbage can and strikes each in an identical manner.

SCHAFER: Now what about it? Do you still think one is music and the other not?

STUDENT: There are other instruments sometimes employed in the orchestra that produce noises just as the garbage can—for example the anvil.

SCHAFER: Right! Can you think of any others?

VOICES: Cow bells! Sandpaper blocks! Whistles! Sirens! Typewriters!

SCHAFER: Good! I want you to think of this question of whether the garbage can produces music or not for a while and we'll come back to it again. But let's continue looking at our definition of music: *Sounds Pleasing To The Ear.* To help us study this I'm

9

going to set you a task. Will you all take out your instruments and get ready for playing.

Each student takes an instrument. All the instruments of the orchestra are represented.

Here is your assignment. You have just been commissioned by Alfred Hitchcock to write the musical score for his most recent horror film. In the particular scene we are scoring today the victim is entering a darkened house. The murderer hides behind the door and at a certain point leaps out and stabs the victim. How shall we reinforce this dramatic scene with our music?

The students make a number of suggestions. To accompany the victim's entrance into the house the class decides on a soft, low tremolo in the strings which grows louder and then cuts suddenly as the victim opens the fatal door. As the murderer springs out the entire orchestra plays a sforzando chord. But what chord? This becomes a matter of some discussion. Someone suggests it doesn't matter as long as it is loud. G major is tried. The class rejects G major as too bright. Someone suggests G minor. The sequence is repeated again with G minor. The class is still dissatisfied. They find it "too conventional" and "not frightening enough."

SCHAFER: I think Mr. Hitchcock would agree with you. You all sense very clearly that in order to illustrate this tense and brutal situation we need a chord of utmost tension. May I make a suggestion? Let everyone check with their neighbor and see what notes they want to play and then choose a different one for yourself. Choose any note you wish, but make it as loud as possible. Ready, on my cue!

The class is amused at this suggestion but is eager to try it out. The results are striking; the sound produced is indeed terrifying.

SCHAFER: We also have a number of singers in the class and we haven't given them anything to do as yet. How can we include them?

STUDENT: I don't think we can include them. There is nothing they could sing that would fit in.

A SINGER: We don't know any frightening songs.

SCHAFER: Tell me, what would you do if someone jumped out from behind a door and waved a knife at you?

10

SINGER: I'd scream.

SCHAFER: Well?

The class looks up brightly.

SINGER: When you play the chord do you want us to scream?

SCHAFER: At the top of your lungs! Ready? Here we go!

The sequence is repeated, this time with the voices. The sound is so frightening that several girls cover their ears and shudder. Three people come rushing in the door crying "What happened?" Everyone is certain that Mr. Hitchcock would have been delighted.

SCHAFER: Now, no one was in any doubt as to whether that sound was agreeable to the ears; it certainly wasn't. But as a sound it was effective for our purposes. I am assuming it was a musical sound because it was a "musical" score we were asked to write for the film. But if that is so, what happens to our definition of music as *Sound Pleasing To The Ear?* Think about that until tomorrow.

The bell rings; the period has ended.

The following day:

SCHAFER: We are still trying to define *what is music.* Yesterday we wrote some music for a horror movie. Today I want to begin by playing you a recording. In it there is a narrator speaking and he is accompanied by an orchestra and chorus. He is one of the few survivors of the Nazi extermination of the Jews in the Warsaw ghetto. He is describing the scene as he remembers it.

Arnold Schoenberg's A Survivor from Warsaw *is played. The work, with its text of mixed pathos and hate, is intensely dramatic. At its conclusion the class, in which there is a large number of Jewish students, is obviously shocked and deeply moved. Only after the class has recovered somewhat is it possible to continue with the enquiry.*

SCHAFER: If there was any doubt as to whether our experiment yesterday was legitimate music, I don't think anyone will deny that what we just heard was a powerful and moving musical experience. Does anyone have anything to say about it?

STUDENT: I thought the music was effective in describing the tragedy. There were places where it illustrated the words perfectly. For example, on the words "moaning and groaning" the whole orchestra produced such a painful kind of sound that the words were made all the more forceful.

ANOTHER STUDENT: I thought that the accompaniment to the German officer was particularly effective. It made him into such a hateful creature.

A THIRD STUDENT: For me the most dramatic section was when the narrator thinks he hears the chorus of dead Jews singing and then they suddenly burst into song.

SCHAFER: That is certainly the turning point in the work. Before that it had been completely negative. You used the words "painful" and "hateful" to describe this piece of music. But when the chorus of dead Jews enters the positive element asserts itself; their singing has a tortured and haunting determination that is both frightening and yet very strong. It is as if the composer was saying "Even though you may kill the Jewish people you will never be able to kill the memory of them."

But what interests us here is placing that work beside our definition of music as *Sound Pleasing To The Ear*. I'm afraid they are incompatible aren't they? One of them must go.

STUDENT: The definition must go.

SCHAFER: Yes, I'm afraid so. A definition must include all the members of the family it proposes to define. It ties them all together. You can't have a definition which leaves something outside. Let's try another one of the definitions against *A Survivor from Warsaw*. *Music Is Sound Arranged With Rhythm And Melody*. What about that? Was there rhythm and melody in *A Survivor from Warsaw*?

STUDENT: I don't think you could say there was melody.

SCHAFER: What do you understand by melody?

STUDENT: Well, something you can whistle or hum.

ANOTHER STUDENT: I don't agree. I think there was melody there even if you couldn't whistle it. Maybe there can be painful melodies as well as pleasant ones. Maybe the accompaniment to the words "moaning and groaning" could be described as melody.

SCHAFER: It's all going to depend on our definition of melody isn't it? To begin with, what is a melody made of?

STUDENT: A series of tones.

SCHAFER: What tones?

STUDENT: It could be any tones.

SCHAFER: These tones?

He goes to the piano and plays five or six disjunct tones, different registers, different dynamics.

STUDENT: I suppose they could be, but it's not a very good melody.

Laughter.

SCHAFER: You're probably right. But remember, we're just trying to define the term; we're not trying to distinguish between good and bad melodies.

STUDENT: But doesn't a melody have to have some order to it if it is to express a certain emotion?

SCHAFER: I'm glad you mentioned that. The particular succession of tones the composer chooses—their range, dynamics and instrumentation—these things give a certain character to a melody and this in turn draws a certain emotional response from the listeners. The series of notes that accompanied the "moaning and groaning" of *A Survivor from Warsaw* had a certain emotional character, just as the choral movement of Beethoven's ninth symphony has quite a different emotional character because the composer's intention is different.

STUDENT: Does the same thing apply to rhythm?

SCHAFER: You can answer that.

Schafer taps a music stand in a steady manner; then he taps it in a seemingly haphazard manner.

Are they both rhythm?

STUDENT: They must be, but one is more organized than the other.

SCHAFER: Good! A rhythm can be any sequence of accents and we organize them or disorganize them as we wish, depending on the particular effect we want. We have certain ways of organizing them which we call metres (just like metres in poetry) and we have certain ways of disorganizing them such as tempo rubato (robbed time) syncopation, ritardando, accelerando, and so forth, or by superimposing different metres and thus confusing the simple decisive accents of individual metres. For a specific effect we may want to disorganize the accents completely. For instance, if I put a series of regular dots on the blackboard and told you that each of them is an accent—

●　　　●　　　●　　　●　　　●　　　●

—I could then confuse the regularity of those dots by adding a lot of other dots around them so that although the first series is still present, it would be difficult to distinguish.

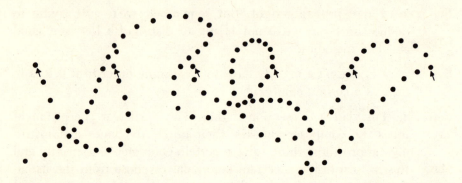

STUDENT: It seemed that *A Survivor from Warsaw* did that.

SCHAFER: To an extent it did. *A Survivor from Warsaw* is a rhythmically more complex piece than, say, a Beethoven symphony; but we should never confuse rhythmic intricacy with a lack of rhythm. A lack of rhythm is pure chaos—though even that can have its place.

So we can salvage the words rhythm and melody for our definition, as long as we remember to use them in the manner discussed. Melody is simply an organized sequence of tones; rhythm an organized sequence of accents. The key word to remember is "organized." The fact that a composer has thought it out makes it something very different from the noises we hear in the street, for example. But I would ask you always to remember too that this organization can sometimes create a very disorganized effect. Because even if we disorganize sounds we are still organizing them.

Thus the second definition on the board—*Music Is Sound Arranged With Rhythm And Melody*—would seem to be perfectly accurate as far as it goes.

Schafer then goes to the bass drum and beats it.

But what about that? Melody?

STUDENT: No, just rhythm.

SCHAFER: It can't be music then?

STUDENT: I . . . really don't know. The last time you hit it we said it was music, but now . . . I just don't know.

SCHAFER: Remember what I said a moment ago about making the definition stretch around the thing it is defining. Don't ever try to make the thing itself fit the definition. It must be the other way around. Follow your instincts.

STUDENT: Then it is still music.

SCHAFER: Still? So surprised? What would you say then about the definition?

STUDENT: I don't think it's wrong as it stands, but it seems that it's not absolutely necessary to have both rhythm and melody in order to have music.

SCHAFER: Let's make a provision for melody and rhythm in our model definition, but let's not make it absolutely necessary that they both always be present. Will that do?

CLASS: Yes.

SCHAFER: All right. Another question then: A man is hammering a nail into a board. Is he making music?

Thoughtful consideration by the class.

This is like our old question of the garbage can. If I beat it, am I making music?

Thoroughly pensive expressions.

A car screeches its brakes in the street. Is it music?

STUDENT (brightly): No sir, because the sound of the brakes isn't organized.

SCHAFER: Good! But that still leaves us with our hammering carpenter and our garbage can.

STUDENT: About the garbage can—we decided that it could possibly be used as a musical instrument, for special sound effects I mean.

SCHAFER: If I wrote a piece of music called *Garbage Can Polka,* and wanted to have a real garbage can struck during the piece, would the striking of the garbage can be music?

STUDENT: It could be, but I don't think it would be very interesting music.

SCHAFER: That's not the point. We are not distinguishing between good and bad music, but only trying to discover what music is. If under these conditions it could make music, why does it not make music when the garbageman dumps it into the truck?

STUDENT: He's not intending to make music.

SCHAFER: That's the answer we've been looking for! Go on.

STUDENT: Well you intended to use the garbage can as a musical instrument and the garbageman didn't. That's the only difference.

SCHAFER: Exactly! The operative word here is *intention.* It makes a great deal of difference whether a sound produced is really intended to be listened to or not. Sounds in the street are not intended to be listened to; they are incidental. If car manufacturers could make silent brakes for cars I am sure they would do so—though, of course, you must bear in mind that car brakes, just like car horns, are warning signals. That is to say, they are intended to be heard, though not for their own sake alone but rather because they signal us that danger is at hand. But what about a sound that is quite incidentally produced and has not this ulterior purpose; what about our carpenter?

STUDENT: He is not making music when he hammers, because he is not intending to. The sounds he is producing are just incidental; the important thing is to hammer the nails in.

ANOTHER STUDENT: But sir, what if the carpenter is whistling to himself in time to his hammering?

SCHAFER: You answer it.

STUDENT: I suppose his whistling is music even if his hammering isn't.

SCHAFER: This is getting a bit philosophical. In order to begin whistling the carpenter must have listened to the sound of his hammering. That was what suggested the whistling to him, even though the suggestion may have been a subconscious one. And so the hammering became a kind of music to him, and since it provides the rhythmic accompaniment to his tune, it becomes part of the music for us too.

16

STUDENT: If I am eating supper the sound of the cutlery on the dinnerware is not music, but if I fill a number of glasses with water after supper and strike them, this becomes music. Is that right?

SCHAFER: You answered it yourself. The intention makes all the difference. Now let's see where the word "intention" fits into our definition of music. We have decided already that music is "organized sound." We also know that music may include certain features such as rhythm and melody. Now we have concluded that music is sound "intended to be listened to." Would anyone like to try and unify these conclusions in a definition?

STUDENT: Music is . . . an organization of sounds . . . with rhythm and melody . . . which is intended to be listened to.

SCHAFER (COPYING ON THE BLACKBOARD): Let's put brackets around "rhythm" and "melody," since we already know that it is conceivable music could exist without both of these things; also that if we were going to give a complete definition we might have to consider other features of sounds.

Music Is An Organization Of Sounds (Rhythm, Melody, etc.) *Which Is Intended To Be Listened To.*

STUDENT: What about the other original definitions of music as *an art* and *a cultural activity concerning sound*?

SCHAFER: That's another matter again. To consider them we have to start all over again and ask "What is art?" and "What is culture?" And since the bell is going to ring in about three minutes, we'll have to leave that for another time. But at least we have reached a few conclusions and they have allowed us to form the basis of a definition, though later refinements would, no doubt, be desirable.

STUDENT: Sir, yesterday when you began this discussion, I went to the dictionary to see what definition was given for music. Their definition is different from ours.

SCHAFER: Did you copy it down? Can you tell us what it was?

STUDENT: Yes sir. It says: "Music—the art of expressing or stirring emotion by melodious and harmonious combinations of sounds; any pleasant sound."

SCHAFER: That's rather close to one of the definitions we eliminated isn't it? That should give you something more to think about. Let me just leave you with this thought: definitions define *things*. When the things change so do the definitions. Perhaps music has changed since your dictionary was written. Perhaps one of you will one day write a dictionary and you'll be able to bring the definition up to date.

STUDENT: Sir, that's too much to hope for.

SCHAFER: All right then. Let's just hope for this: that our little discussion has given you something to think about and that perhaps we're a little closer to understanding what it is we've been doing every time we enter this music room.

The bell sounds.

Was that music? Class dismissed.

DESCRIPTIVE MUSIC

OBSERVATIONS: The real purpose of this discussion was to discover a way of releasing whatever improvisatory gift the students had. It relied in the first instance on the trick of "imitating nature" to accomplish this. It seemed an expedient method to relax the students and prepare them for some of the more subtle improvisatory experiments to follow.

SCHAFER: As you know, I am a composer. I want to begin today by asking you why a composer writes music? Any ideas?

STUDENT: Because he wants to express something.

SCHAFER: Express what?

STUDENT: Feelings perhaps, or thoughts.

ANOTHER STUDENT: Perhaps there is a desire to describe something, or to imitate nature.

SCHAFER: Suppose the composer wanted to imitate nature by means of the various instruments of the orchestra. Can you think of anything a composer might imitate on a specific instrument?

STUDENT: A composer could imitate a waterfall on a harp.

SCHAFER: Yes indeed! Unfortunately we don't have a harp here to demonstrate this for us. Can you think of something else that we could imitate on one of the instruments in the class?

STUDENT: Machine-gun fire on a snare drum.

SCHAFER: Snare drummer, could you play us some machine-gun fire?

Rapid bursts of machine-gun fire follow on the drum. The class finds it rather amusing.

SCHAFER: Anything else?

STUDENT: An army marching into war on the trumpet.

SCHAFER: Trumpeter, could you describe it for us.

19

The trumpeter is reluctant. At this point a music teacher who has been standing in the back of the class springs up and calls out "Yeoman Bold—page 5." Fortunately the trumpeter is still reluctant.

SCHAFER: Is there any other instrument that could give us the kind of fanfare we are looking for?

TRUMPETER: The horn would be the best.

The horn players are less timid. One after another they improvise little fanfares.

SCHAFER: Good! Anything else?

STUDENT: The clarinet could imitate laughter.

The first clarinet player promptly plays a high "wah-wah-wah-wah," much to the amusement of the whole class.

SCHAFER: Clarinets, listen to the sound of the class laughing. Do you think you could imitate that as a group?

They try. A burst of shrill stridulations follows. The remainder of the class are beside themselves with amusement. The clarinettists are bewildered; they look for an explanation.

SCHAFER (To the rest of the class): Do you think they were successful in imitating laughter?

More laughter from the class.

STUDENT: I thought it was terrible. It was so disorganized.

Again laughter.

SCHAFER: Listen! Is that organized? Do we all laugh together in unison? Ha ha ha ha! Like that?

STUDENT: Well, no.

SCHAFER: We gave the clarinettists the assignment of imitating laughter with their instruments, nothing more. Did they do this effectively or not?

STUDENT: Well, yes.

SCHAFER: For the moment, we are not concerned with whether what they did was music or not, but rather merely with trying to use

20

musical instruments to imitate different things in nature. Can you think of anything else we might try out, and the appropriate instrument for it?

STUDENT: Bird-calls on the flute.

SCHAFER: Flautists?

Several flautists are asked to imitate bird calls—trills, ornaments, etc.—first one after the other and then together.

That was a fairly straightforward assignment. Could I ask you to try something a little more complex? A bird takes off, flies up into the sky; it sings to its mate while circling around, and then it slowly descends again to earth. The movement of the flight might look something like this:

The flautists are undaunted. Several attempt it, and with considerable success. In order to achieve the slow circling quality of the bird's ascent and descent the majority use a highly chromatic melodic idiom. Most sustain the improvisation for twenty seconds or more. At the end of each improvisation Schafer asks for suggestions and criticisms from the entire class. The seriousness with which criticisms are put forward soon devolves on the performers the necessity of meeting them with more concentrated effort. Gradually the whole atmosphere of the class begins to become one of intense seriousness.

SCHAFER (to flautists): That was extremely good. You realize, of course, that in those imitations of a bird you have actually—each of you —composed a piece of music for yourselves.

The flautists seem flustered at the suggestion.

You are accustomed to thinking of composers as people who died a long time ago—Bach, Beethoven, and so forth. Well, perhaps you realize now how false this is. The composition of music can be as immediate to us as anything else. You are still a long way from being Beethovens, to be sure, but what you are doing was exactly what Beethoven once did—you reacted to a suggestion and transferred it into original music.

Is there anything else we could try?

STUDENT: What about fog settling over the city?

SCHAFER: That may be a little difficult. How do you suggest we do it?

STUDENT: I thought on the lower brass and woodwinds—the tubas, trombones, baritones, saxophones, and bass clarinets.

The band is a large one containing at least two or three of each of these.

SCHAFER: What should they play?

STUDENT: They should play long, low notes, very softly.

SCHAFER: All right, let's try it!

TUBA PLAYER: Sir, what notes shall we play?

SCHAFER: For the moment just play any notes you wish, so long as they are low, long, and soft. We just want to create the texture of the fog, nothing more.

They try it. The sound is turbid and ominous. One bass clarinettist unintentionally doodles at something quite inappropriate.

SCHAFER: What did the rest of the class think?

STUDENT: The bass clarinet messed it up.

Others agree emphatically. The clarinettist is embarrassed and asks if they can try it again. They do and this time he settles down.

SCHAFER: Any more comments?

STUDENT: Usually when fog comes in it comes as clouds first and then gradually settles down over the city, and then moves off as clouds again. I think you might try to imitate this as well by playing some higher notes first, then lower, then higher again.

SCHAFER: All right. Follow my baton as I move it slowly across, down and up again.

As the baton moves, the sound takes on a more solid character.

BARITONE SAXOPHONIST: Sir, I wonder if we could add a fog-horn to the sound. I can imitate a fog-horn pretty well on my instrument.

SCHAFER: OK, let's have it.

The baritone saxophonist plays a low, soft note then lets it grow louder, finally cutting it off with a choked sforzando. The effect is quite realistic.

SCHAFER: Shall we add that? Everyone else play as softly as possible and out of the fog we'll hear the crescendo of the lonely fog-horn.

Graphically the resulting texture is like this:

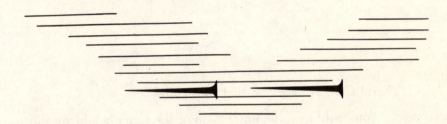

SCHAFER: That was quite an interesting sound. At least it did evoke some of the density and the mysteriousness of fog. Is there anything else we could try?

STUDENT: What about a forest?

SCHAFER: How?

STUDENT: I don't know exactly, but the wind blowing through the trees . . .

SCHAFER: Is it the wind you want to describe or the forest?

STUDENT: Both of them.

SCHAFER: Can you think of ways to describe the wind?

Numerous suggestions: glissandi in the strings, roaring arpeggios on the piano and harp, plaintive woodwind murmurs, etc.

Obviously we can suggest the wind in various ways depending on whether it is a spring breeze or a raging storm; but what about the forest—I'm concerned about the forest?

There are no suggestions.

Let's put the question more explicity.

Schafer draws on the blackboard.

There! Can we describe that musically?

STUDENT: You could give the impression of the tree's height by starting low in the orchestra and climbing to something higher and then falling again.

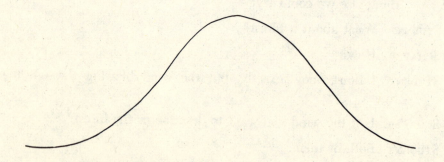

SCHAFER: Like that? How do I know that is supposed to be a tree and not, say a mountain—or a wave—or an ant hill?

STUDENT: You don't.

SCHAFER: We've reached an impasse here. Certainly there are some things that can be described in music with considerable accuracy provided the listener has some imagination; but there are also some things that are impossible to describe. In the few moments remaining we might attempt to classify them.

The first group would include natural events that have a unique sound of their own; for instance, a waterfall, or the sound of gun-fire, or a cuckoo's call. A second group would include those natural events which may have no definite sound of their own but still suggest an atmosphere that can be created—a specific kind of movement of a texture perhaps. This is where our bird flight comes in. There we had a fairly definite idea of the circling and gliding movement of the bird in flight. Also the fog; here there was no movement but a dense and murky texture was suggested which we could reproduce musically on a certain group of instruments.

But then we have all those static or inanimate objects. They suggest neither a movement nor a texture, and they make no sound that we can imitate. A stone, for example, or a telephone pole, or a tree. Here we are at a loss to know what to do. We can give some idea of the wind blowing through the leaves of a tree, or if the tree is in a dense forest, we might give some impression of the density of the forest by means of a certain orchestral texture, but we cannot describe the tree with any accuracy. It has never been done and it never will be done. Sometimes you might think this is being accomplished, but I think on closer inspection you will discover that the idea of the tree has been suggested to you *before* you listen to the music either in the title or in some descriptive program notes.

Some time you might try making a list of things which fall into each of these categories and for those that can be imitated or suggested you might indicate the instrumentation you feel would be most appropriate. Here is a little list to start on. Think about each of these things and put them in the right category.

A stormy sea

A sunset

A gentle breeze

The Empire State Building

A galloping horse

A horse standing still

A leaf

Wind in the leaves

A dog barking

An angry teacher

Children playing

A patriotic flag

The Rocky Mountains

An iron foundry

A babbling brook

A glass of water

The prospect of homework

Smoke

TEXTURES OF SOUND

SCHAFER: We have already talked about using our instruments to suggest or imitate various natural events. Now we are going to explore some of the raw material the composer uses to bring about different emotional responses in listeners. For instance, if I said "anger," what kind of musical sound would you think of?

STUDENT: Something loud.

ANOTHER STUDENT: Something loud and piercing.

SCHAFER: I wonder why these qualities?

STUDENT: Because an angry person yells in a loud and piercing voice.

SCHAFER: That could certainly be one reason. Loud and piercing or high have their opposite extremes in soft and low. Would a soft low sound suggest any emotion to you?

STUDENT: Melancholy.

ANOTHER STUDENT: Love?

SCHAFER: You don't seem too sure of it. Why do you say love?

STUDENT: Because the person in love speaks in a soft, soothing voice.

Titters from the girls.

SCHAFER: Yes, I think you have a point. At any rate you would never be reminded of anger by a soft low sound, or of love by a high loud sound, so you can see that these different extremes do have some quite definite power to stir our emotions, even though we may not all be able to agree on precisely what emotions they stir.

Now, as I said, soft and loud, high and low are opposites. Can you think of any other values in the musical vocabulary that are opposites to one another.

STUDENT: Long and short.

ANOTHER STUDENT: Fast and slow.

SCHAFER: Good! Perhaps this gives us enough to work on.

He writes them down on the board.

HIGH	LOW
LOUD	SOFT
SHORT	LONG
FAST	SLOW

SCHAFER: Now the composer uses basic values like these in creating a composition with a specific character. What I want you to realize is that these values have the power to affect the listener in very different ways. For instance, take your instruments and on my cue play me a high loud note—any note will do, we are just concerned with the texture of sound here.

A high, loud texture of sound is produced, frightening a few girls.

Now play on my cue again a very low, soft note.

A soft, low texture is produced.

Now you don't need me to tell you that those two sound sensations were very different; one was angry and frightening, the other was soothing or perhaps sad. It is the composer's job to use these materials to produce something meaningful and moving. Sometimes a composer chooses to restrict himself or herself to certain of these values only; just the same as a painter sometimes paints in what is called a "limited palette." That is, he or she purposely chooses to restrict the work to certain colors. Perhaps you have seen paintings by Picasso from his "blue" or "rose" periods; these were painted on a restricted scale of that kind. In the same way, if a composer wishes to create a certain atmosphere he or she may restrict their work to certain values— for example, the music will be "slow" and not "fast," or it will be "soft" and never "loud," and so forth. To illustrate this, I want to play for you parts of two works which employ this kind of "limited palette" in music. The first piece is by Claude Debussy and is entitled *Afternoon of a Faun.*

The first two or three minutes of the recording are played.

You can see that a quite definite mood is created here. Now the second piece creates another mood, again by restricting itself to specific musical values. It is entitled *Night on a Bare Mountain* and is by the Russian composer Modeste Moussorgsky.

The first two or three minutes of the recording are played.

Now would someone like to apply our table of values to those two compositions and tell us the difference?

STUDENT: The two pieces were completely different. The first used soft, low, long, and slow musical values, and the second used high, loud, short, and fast values.

SCHAFER: Yes, they contrasted with each other completely, didn't they? Perhaps you can begin to see the power these values have over the listener when the composer uses them imaginatively. Now in those two compositions we had a complete division of the values (writing on board) like this:

Debussy	*Moussorgsky*
SOFT	LOUD
LONG	SHORT
LOW	HIGH
SLOW	FAST

We might call these compositions "lyrical" compositions because they tend to use related values to create and sustain one mood. Now if a composer wanted to create a "dramatic" composition he or she would be more concerned with contrasting values, with abrupt changes, and surprises. Can you think of a composer whose music is full of this kind of drama?

STUDENT: Beethoven is always full of surprises.

SCHAFER: Beethoven is perhaps the best example we could mention. In Beethoven you are surprised constantly by some new turn of events. A soft passage is suddenly interrupted by a loud burst from the whole orchestra; or a loud *fortissimo* passage suddenly becomes a *pianissimo*. There are also numerous places in his music where a very slow section is followed immediately by a very fast and furious section. Thus if we were to study the music of Beethoven we would find that all the different extremes in our chart were brought together in violent juxtapositions, like this:

28

Debussy		Moussorgsky
SOFT ←	B E E T H O V E N	→ LOUD
LONG ←		→ SHORT
LOW ←		→ HIGH
SLOW ←		→ FAST

This is what makes Beethoven such a dramatic composer. Of course, I've oversimplified this whole thing a great deal in order to make a basic point quite clear to you.

Now in order to help you appreciate the emotional effect of different qualities of sound, I thought we might try a little experiment. I should like you with your instruments to illustrate the different qualities of sound we have been discussing and we will see (and feel) how they contrast with one another. We are not going to be playing any special notes or chords, but let us rather think of producing textures of sound. For instance, there is a difference between the texture of my corduroy jacket and my nylon shirt. I'd like you to think of texture in sound just the same way. So don't worry about what notes to play; I'll indicate to you the general pitch-level of the note—whether it is low, middle range or high—by the height of my hand as I give you the sign. Now I'm going to give you a number of signs with my hands and each of them is going to stand for a different kind of texture in sound.

Schafer explains and tries out the various signs he proposes to use. They are these:

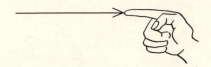

A soft note: a horizontal movement with the finger.

A loud note: a horizontal movement with the fist.

29

Crescendo: horizontal movement of the arms beginning with the fingertips and culminating in the fists.

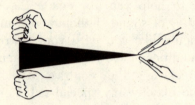

Descrescendo: horizontal movement of the arms beginning with the fists and culminating with the fingertips.

Short accented notes: punching fist indicates the rhythm desired.

Soft staccato notes: plucking finger indicates the rhythm desired.

Trill: fingertip indicates the tempo desired by oscillation from very slow to very fast.

All out: play anything as fast and as loud as possible. Violent movement of both hands before the body.

Schafer experiments with these signs and the students respond with their instruments. A deliberate attempt is made to build sequences of signs using the maximum amount of contrast possible, i.e., a short, soft sound followed by a long, loud sound, etc.

SCHAFER: Now we're going to add counterpoint to this sequence of sound-textures we have been producing. I would like one of you to come up and assist me in conducting, so that we can add another perspective to our experiment.

An assistant conductor is chosen and the orchestra is divided. Each half follows the cues of one conductor. The conductors stand so that they can see one another and attempt to create contrasts in sound textures, with each texture called forth by one conductor inspiring its opposite from the other. Eventually there are three conductors (all students now) and the orchestra is divided into three groups. The conductors stand in a semi-circle where they can see one another. Schafer moves back to listen to the sounds.

SCHAFER: Hold it just a minute! Before we go on let me ask you if you have any criticisms of the sound you are producing.

STUDENT: Sir, the sounds are too confused and muddy. Everybody is doing something different.

SCHAFER: Yes, it is too muddy. And the reason is that the conductors are not paying enough attention to one another. Each of you is being carried away with the sound of your own little group. You are paying no attention to the other conductors. You have forgotten your original assignment, which was to produce contrasts of sound. If everybody is playing all the time we just get a fat morass of sound. There is no drama there.

31

Try to appreciate it this way: there is nothing interesting about a solid wall without any windows in it. By means of windows we articulate the wall and we bring light to people inside the building.

We put windows into music by means of rests—silence. It is only when one part is resting that we see more clearly what the other parts are doing. Let's try it again and I want the conductors to listen to each other and watch each other. Don't just go piling things on top of one another. Think about the sounds your colleagues are producing and when you have an appropriate contrast to add, add it. But above all, listen, listen, listen!

The experiment continues and the longer it continues the more interesting and thoughtful the resulting texture of sound becomes. Later a small choral group is added and is given three vocables: "s," "m," and "ah." These three produce complete contrasts in sound since "s" is unvoiced, while "m" is spoken with the mouth closed and "ah" with the mouth open. Dynamics are added to these and also a relative indication of pitch by the height of the cue. The experimenting, which now inincludes four groups (three orchestral and one choral) under four conductors, continues with lively though not uncritical enthusiasm until the bell ends the period.

MUSIC AND CONVERSATION

OBSERVATIONS: On hand are five players of wind instruments—the standard wind quintet. The intimacy of this group makes it attractive for more challenging experiments. While the analogy used here between conversation in speech and improvisation in music is not quite as conclusive as it may be made to appear in the following discussion, it proved a valuable means for drawing an immediate response from the performers.

It is difficult to decide whether the real value of an experiment such as that to follow is in drawing out latent talent for improvisation or merely as an exercise in ear training. Probably it serves both uses. Certainly it was discovered that most students never listen at all to one another when they play in bands and orchestras where there are twenty clarinets or sixteen flutes all tootling away at the unison line of their Beethoven-Browns and Handel-Jacksons. Thus, to force students to listen, as was necessary here, would seem to constitute an important "breakthrough" in their musical education.

SCHAFER: Today I should like us to try some exercises in improvised music. As you know, not all music is written down—most jazz, for instance is not. Also in the past there have been periods where the performer was expected to improvise (actually to compose) part of the composition. This was the *cadenza* of the concerto and it was here that the performer could display both virtuosity and whatever creative gift he or she might have. Also many contemporary composers are beginning to rely on performers to improvise or compose parts of the music themselves. A real attempt is being made to break down the feeling of separation that has grown up between performer and composer in recent years.

Now, after those words of introduction, I'd like to give you a little problem which we are going to solve by improvised music —that is, music we make up as we go along. The problem is this: you are to converse with one another, but instead of voices you have only the instruments you are holding in your hands. Everything you wish to convey to your neighbor, all your thoughts, emotions and ideas, must be done by means of these instruments. Who would like to say something first?

Nervous laughter. Finally one by one they are persuaded to improvise little solos. The expedient is used of asking them to "say something sweet"—"say something angry," and so forth to inspire these. At first they are abrupt, self-conscious and formless; but within a few minutes they have become more extended and contain snatches of character.

SCHAFER: Now that each of us is getting adept at the monologue, we can move into the field of dialogue. This time I want you to follow each other immediately. When I point to you, you will begin and the first person will fade and drop out. But I want each of you to begin by picking up an idea from your predecessor and then to extend it from there. Just as in conversation when one person concludes a statement another person might start by saying "I know," or "I agree with you," before they go on with their own remarks? Will you try that? Come in whenever you feel like it after I point to you.

After several rounds of this Schafer is dissatisfied with the manner in which one player picks up from the other. The links are capricious and seldom if ever relate to what the first player had played.

SCHAFER: No, I'm afraid it won't do! You're not listening to each other! Let's just try some linking passages alone. First, one of you play a little motive, and then I want the rest of you, one after another to imitate it—not exactly note for note, but preserving the general character of the passage. All right, flute, oboe, clarinet, horn and bassoon, in that order. Ready?

It is still apparent that the performers are not listening to one another. A figure played by one instrument which might consist of five or six notes becomes an unrecognizable sequence of three notes in the next. It is necessary to simplify further.

SCHAFER: Let's just take two notes. A whole world of character can exist in the relationship between two notes. They can be soft or loud, high or low, short or long; and because there are two of them they can contrast dramatically with one another. Remember our experiment with contrasting textures the other day? Let me hear you each play a contrasting pair of notes on your instruments.

34

These follow. Considerable imagination is employed. If size = dynam-ics, height = pitch and length = duration, some of the examples played could be portrayed graphically thus:

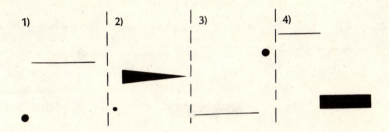

SCHAFER: Good! Now this time one of you play a group of two notes and the others will imitate it in succession—not necessarily the same notes, but the same outline of character.

This is executed well. The players are finally beginning to listen to one another. The exercise is repeated with three notes, then four notes.

SCHAFER: We are beginning to make order out of chaos at last! This time I'm going to ask you to introduce a little variation in the imitations. Just as if one person made a remark in conversation and another person repeated it with embellishments. Can you tell in what ways a composer can vary little two-note motives such as those you have been playing?

FLAUTIST: He can alter the rhythm.

SCHAFER: For example?

FLAUTIST: If the rhythm of the two notes was long and short he could change it to short and long.

An example is played.

SCHAFER: Good! What other ways?

OBOIST: By changing the notes and keeping the rhythm the same.

BASSOONIST: If one was loud and the other soft the composer could re-verse them.

FLAUTIST: The composer could turn them upside down or play them backwards.

SCHAFER: Yes, all of these things would be possible. Let me just note them down on the board.

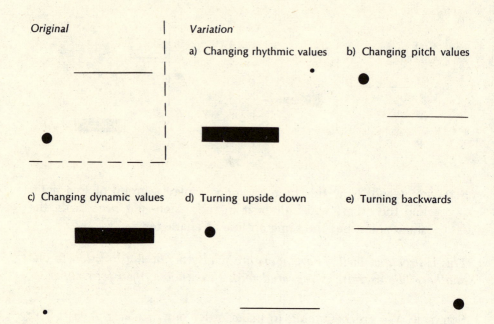

SCHAFER: These are some of the ways in which we can bring variations out of a little two-note sequence of notes such as you have been playing. As you look at that chart do you notice anything that would indicate a general principle of variation technique?

Silence.

Well, put it this way, what is to prevent me from writing, well, any two notes on the board and saying that it is a variation of the original pair?

BASSOONIST: They wouldn't have anything in common with them.

SCHAFER: Exactly, and there's your principle. In all of these variations you will notice that only one feature is changed—one time it is the rhythm, the next the pitch, then the dynamics, and so on—but the other features remain the same. You must have some features remain the same as the original or else it ceases to be a variation. Let's try all this out! We'll go back to the two-note motive and each of you will play a variation on it. Let's start with the horn player this time.

At first the playing is hesitant and the players feel insecure as to what is permitted and what is not. But soon the variation technique becomes clear to them and they begin to react more naturally to it.

SCHAFER: You should continue to do that among yourselves from time to time in order to learn to react quickly to the sounds others are producing. Now let's go back to our original cycle of solos. One starts playing, then another starts, and the first quietly retreats and drops out. But each time a new player begins he or she must pick up a little motive or a phrase from the predecessor and comment on it (i.e., either repeat it or vary it) before going on.

The results are much more effective this time.

SCHAFER: Let's go back to our comparison between what you are doing and a spoken conversation. You have been having a very orderly discussion; one person speaks after the other and each agrees with their predecessor before going on to say something of their own. That may be an ideal way to hold a conversation but I think it is a little unrealistic. The fact is that we are not all so patient in conversation with others. We don't always agree with them. Also the emotional pitch of a conversation can really work up to quite a fever. I wonder if we could apply these things to what we are doing here. Let's try conversing without my cuing you. Just come in whenever the mood strikes you. You may agree with your fellow conversationalists or disagree with them as you please.

They begin, but soon the texture is such a jumble that it is impossible to hear any instrument clearly.

SCHAFER: Wait a minute now! It is true that sometimes in conversation we all speak at once, but then no one understands what is being said. That was my impression in listening to you. We had five people speaking five different languages as fast as possible and no one cared what the others were saying. A very wise man once said: "The best conversationalist is the best listener." The person who refrains from any comment until just the appropriate moment and then says exactly the right thing is the person everyone respects for wit and intellect. Only a fool talks all the time. Now listen to each other and let's try again.

The resulting sound, though less verbose, is still by no means lucid.

SCHAFER: It's improving. But remember the importance of silence in music. Silence in music is like windows in architecture; it lets the light come through. Wait until you have an important comment and then add something to the texture; otherwise stay silent and listen to what the others have to say.

Again an improvement.

SCHAFER: It's getting much better. Let's look again at human conversation. Sometimes one person dominates a conversation completely and the others just seem to form a chorus of agreement. For example, think of the captivating political speaker; the audience simply follows the speaker's lead with a sort of sympathetic vibration. Let's try something like that in music. One of you, say the clarinettist, is the solo speaker on the platform. The rest of you merely accompany her quietly.

They try, but although the others play as quietly as possible, the mere movement of their playing detracts from the clarinet solo.

SCHAFER: Perhaps you yourselves felt, as I did, that you were covering up the soloist. I wonder how we could have you playing without letting this happen? Let me suggest something. If I were to draw that last episode on the board it might look something like this, with the heavy line denoting the clarinet and the thin lines the accompanying instruments.

Now you can see the jumble of the texture at once. But if I were to contrast the very athletic line of the clarinet solo with light and straight lines in the other instruments, the jumble disappears at once. Look at this:

In music the utmost clarity is achieved by contrasting different kinds of texture such as this. Let's try the solo again, this time with the rest of you playing soft slow notes. Together you'll produce chords and this will serve as a kind of harmonic mat for the soloist to stand on.

They try again and the striking change is immediately sensed by all.

SCHAFER: Now let's try to incorporate all the different things we have learned into a single spontaneous improvisation. I won't cue you. I want you to "feel" your way into the music yourselves and react as you wish. You may agree with the others or disagree with them as you wish, though I would ask you to bear in mind that agreement is more desirable in the long run if the conversation is to continue. Also I want you to remember the great value of silence in conversing. Comment only when you have something constructive to add to what the others are saying. Don't just doodle.

They begin. After a minute Schafer stops them to make an observation and they begin again. They are stopped again and more observations follow. And so it goes. Gradually their playing becomes more cohesive and lucid and one begins to sense a kind of intimate communion among the performers. Above all they are listening to one another. This was exemplified brilliantly at one point in the improvisation where the flute sounded a little descending figure and this was picked up immediately in the oboe, then the clarinet and the horn. The bassoonist reversed the motive and it passed quite spontaneously back up through the voices to the flute again. Such intimate counterpoint could never have been produced an hour before!

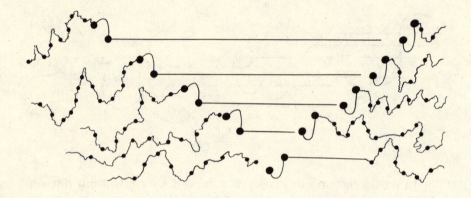

MASK OF THE EVIL DEMON

OBSERVATIONS: It is the duty of every composer to be concerned with the creative ability of young people. But one has to be quick to catch it. For our system of music education is one in which creative music is progressively vilified and choked out of existence. As the teacher of the high school band parades the splendid Beethoven-Browns and Bach-Smiths, he or she is galvanizing everything creative within the child into an unshatterable plethora. Any public school class will improvise uninhibitedly, but by the time they have reached grade 12 or 13 this ability has completely soured into nervous laughter at the prospect of playing four notes that weren't given to them, a situation we may trace directly to the teacher whose exclusive battle cry seems to be "Yeoman Bold, page 5!"

This last session took place in a public school (grade six, I believe). The pupils were being trained in the Orff method, a method where at least a modicum of creativeness is encouraged—alas, in the hands of poor teachers, none at all. But the teacher of this class was quite exceptional, otherwise we could not have achieved as much as we did that winter day when the students, refusing to break for recess, persisted in perfecting "our" little creation—*The Mask of the Evil Demon*.

TEACHER: As you can see, we encourage the boys and girls to make up their own music on the Orff instruments—ostinato forms at first and later rondo forms. Class, Mr. Schafer is a composer; he writes music for other people to play and listen to. I'm going to ask Mr. Schafer to speak to you now and perhaps he will compose something for you to play.

SCHAFER: That you, Miss ———. Since I notice that you are all composers too, for you are also making up your own music to play, I think it would be more fun if we made up a piece of music together, don't you?

The class is delighted. Looking about the class Schafer notices the walls are covered with things the class has made—drawings, cutouts, masks, etc. Spotting a particularly fierce-looking mask, Schafer has a poem by Bertolt Brecht spring to mind. Possibly something to build on.

Translated:

The Mask of the Evil Demon

On my wall there is a Japanese mask, carved in wood, painted with gold paint. It is a mask of the evil demon. O pity! I look at the swollen face muscles and realize how difficult it must be to have to be a mask of evil all the time.

SCHAFER: I'm just looking at all the fascinating things you've made and put up on the walls. And over there, look at that fierce mask—it's wonderful! Something occurred to me as I was looking at it. I was thinking how frightening it might be if you had that mask hanging in your bedroom at night. Suppose it was a mask of the evil demon; wouldn't you be afraid to look at it in the dark?

The children shiver and agree.

SCHAFER: Supposing we made a little poem up about it. "On my wall there is a Japanese mask carved in wood, painted with gold paint. It is a mask of the evil demon." Someone write that down on the blackboard for us. And while they are doing it let me ask you this: if you were saying that to a friend, how would you say it?

Two or three children recite it dramatically.

SCHAFER: That's very good. But supposing you really wanted to frighten your friend, how would you recite it then?

BOY: Well, I'd whisper it in his ear and then when I came to the "mask of the evil demon," I'd yell it in his ear.

SCHAFER: Let's try that. Let's all whisper it together and then when we say "mask of the evil demon," we'll all yell it out.

CLASS (Whispering softly): "On my wall there is a Japanese mask carved in wood, painted with gold paint. *It Is a Mask of the Evil Demon!*"

SCHAFER: Yes, let's really accent the word demon. Very soft at the first and then really getting loud; ready?

CLASS (Whispering very softly): "On my wall there is a Japanese mask carved in wood, painted with gold paint. *It Is a Mask of the Evil Demon!*"

SCHAFER: Good! I think that would really frighten him. Now tell me, what would you do if someone came up to you and whispered that in your ear and then frightened you?

GIRL: I'd scream.

SCHAFER: Can you all scream? Pretend you've just been frightened. Let's hear you scream.

CLASS: Aaaaaaaaaaiiiiiiiiiiieeeeeeeeee!

SCHAFER: Now let's recite our poem again and then after we cry "demon" we'll all scream.

CLASS: "On my wall there is a Japanese mask carved in wood, painted with gold paint. *It Is a Mask of the Evil Demon!*"Aaaaaiiiiieeeee!

SCHAFER: I notice that you all have instruments in front of you. If you wanted to express something really frightening on your instruments how would you do it?

GIRL: I could beat my drum really hard.

ANOTHER GIRL: And I could hit the wood block really hard too.

BOY: I could hit the xylophone hard too.

SCHAFER: Show us how.

BOY: Like this! (He hits two notes, one with each stick.)

SCHAFER: Is that the most frightening sound you can get from the xylophone? Can you think of anything else?

ANOTHER BOY: He could run the sticks over all the keys very fast; that really gives a scary sound.

The first boy tries it. He experiments and finally decides the best sound is produced by a glissando in contrary motion, thus:

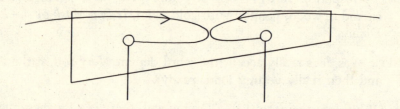

During this discussion the cymbal player has been edging to be called on for his contribution by holding up his cymbals poised to strike terror into the hearts of his class mates.

SCHAFER (Noting the cymbalist): Well, go ahead.

CYMBALS: Crrrrrrraaaaaaaaaashshshshshshshshshshshshshsh!

SCHAFER: What about those other instruments, say the glockenspiel and the metalophone?

The children experiment with these; glissandi and sharp attacks are tried. At length they conclude that these instruments are not so satisfactory for producing a fearful sound.

SCHAFER: All right, let's leave them out for a moment. Just the drums, the cymbals and the xylophones. Let's recite again and just after we scream we'll strike the instruments too.

CLASS (Whispering softly): "On my wall there is a Japanese mask carved in wood, painted with gold paint. *It Is a Mask of the Evil Demon!*" Aaaiiiiiiieeeeeee! Crrrrrrraaaaaashshshshsh!

SCHAFER: I'm sure even your teacher was frightened by that sound. But you know, when I look at this mask I also feel sorry for it; do you know why? Look at the swollen face muscles of the mask. The poor mask has to look like that all the time. It's awfully hard to make an ugly face and hold it for a long time isn't it? Have you ever tried? But that's what this poor mask has to do. Don't you pity it?

The class pitied the poor mask.

Let's add a phrase to our poem to show that we pity the mask. Let's say: "Oh pity, I look at the swollen face muscles and realize how difficult it must be to have to be a mask of evil all the time." Would someone like to write that on the board for us, and while they are doing it who would like to recite it?

Various students recite it and Schafer asks the others to criticize their recitations. At length one girl is found who gives the line just the right expressive and pathetic quality. The students decide she should recite it alone.

SCHAFER: Perhaps the rest of you could accompany the reciter on your instruments. How could this be done? Remember the mood. You are pitying the mask and feeling sorry for it. On what instruments could we express this? On the cymbals?

CLASS: No, not on the cymbals!

BOY: Perhaps on the metalophones and glockenspiels.

SCHAFER: How?

BOY: By playing very low notes slowly and softly.

SCHAFER: Let's try that with the reciter.

The metalophone and glockenspiel players seem almost to caress the keys with their sticks.

SCHAFER: That was very well done. Are there any other instruments we could add to that—the wood blocks perhaps?

CLASS: No, not the woodblocks, they're too loud!

A BOY: We could use the drums if instead of hitting them we just stroked or rubbed them softly with our hands.

SCHAFER: That's an interesting idea! Let's hear how it sounds!

The soft shuffling sound of the drumheads is added to the reciter and the idiophones.

SCHAFER: Is there anything else?

GIRL: Couldn't we sing something?

SCHAFER: What could you sing?

GIRL: Perhaps if we just sang "Oh pity" or something like that and made low moaning sounds, or weeping sounds.

SCHAFER: Let's try. Everyone sing "Oh pity" and make it sound like a moan. Just keep repeating it over and over very softly.

The soft web of vocal sound is added to the playing and the recitation.

GIRL: Mr. Schafer, I don't think the singing is very good.

SCHAFER: What's wrong with it?

GIRL: I don't like "Oh pity." It doesn't sound enough like a moaning sound and it's not pretty to sing.

SCHAFER: Can you think of anything else that would be better?

A number of suggestions come from several children. Finally someone suggests singing "Oh sorrow" instead because "it sounds more like moaning." The observation is very astute. Of course the long open vowels of "sorrow" are more suggestive of moaning than the short "i" of "pity." The class tried "Oh sorrow" and is satisfied with it. The reciter also makes the appropriate change in her lines.

SCHAFER: Now let's put it all together and see what we've got.

They assemble the whole work and repeat it several times. Each time several little changes or additions are made.

BOY: Sir, why couldn't someone pretend he was the evil demon. He could wear the mask and when we cry "evil demon" he could jump up with the mask on.

SCHAFER: That's a good idea; who wants to be the evil demon?

This little dramatic interlude is interpolated; and later it develops that the evil demon leaps up from behind the teacher's desk (note the symbolism) and dances a fierce dance, accompanied on the drums. When the reciter begins the second section he wilts to the floor.

As time goes on Schafer gradually recedes from the work and the class begins to take over by making continual suggestions for changes and additions. "This time you do this and I'll do this," and so forth. One could not say that the work was being brought to formal consummation by this process; in fact, the opposite often seemed to be the case. But like the art of all nonliterate societies, its vitality rested precisely on its state of constant revision. When this is the case, the form of the work must be considered nothing less than the total sum of the work's transformations. True improvisation is a quest for form without ever finding it, and that is why we are wrong if we ever expect an improvisation to shape itself into a performance. Its vitality is in its ability to transform itself; nothing more.

46

In all, two hours elapsed from the time the experiment began until the noon bell went and the class was dismissed. Looking out the window as the children went home one saw the whispering, the frightening screams, and the fierce dance of the mask carried right out into the schoolyard, down the streets, and into life.

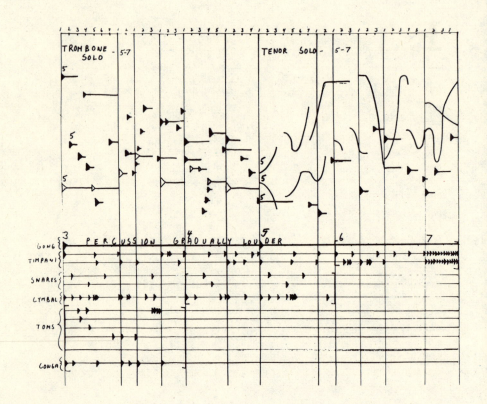

Part II
EAR CLEANING

The notes and exercises to follow formed part of an experimental music course offered to first-year students at Simon Fraser University. I felt my primary task in this course was to open ears: I have tried always to induce students to notice sounds they have never really listened to before, listen like mad to the sounds of their own environment and the sounds they themselves inject into their environment.

This is why I have called this a course in ear cleaning. Before ear training it should be recognized that we require ear cleaning. Before we train a surgeon to perform delicate operations we first ask him to get into the habit of washing his hands. Ears also perform delicate operations, and therefore ear cleanliness is an important prerequisite for all music listening and music playing.

The ear, unlike some other sense organs, is exposed and vulnerable. The eye can be closed at will; the ear is always open. The eye can be focused and pointed at will; the ear picks up all sound right back to the acoustic horizon in all directions.

Every teacher ought to be allowed his or her idiosyncrasies. It is my feeling that one learns practically nothing about the actual functioning of music by sitting in mute surrender before it. As a practicing musician I have come to realize that one learns about sound only by making sound, about music only by making music. All our investigations into sound should be verified empirically by making sounds ourselves and by examining the results. Obviously one cannot always assemble a symphony orchestra in the classroom to feel the desired sensations; so one makes use of whatever is available. The sounds produced may be crude, they may lack form and grace, but they are ours. An actual contact with musical sound is made and this is more vital than the most gluttonous listening program imaginable. Improvisatory and creative abilities — atrophied through years of disuse — are also rediscovered, and the student learns something very practical about the size and shape of things musical.

The lecture notes printed here offered me work-points over which to extemporize; and it would be my sincere hope that by printing them in this unaltered form, they might serve to suggest circles of thought in the reader's mind as well. The exercises printed after the lecture notes followed each individual lecture and were intended to test the validity of whatever we may have said during the lectures.

NOISE

Where should we begin?

We can begin anywhere. It is often useful to examine a negative in order to see the positive clearly. The negative of musical sound is noise sound.

Noise is undesirable sound.

Noise is the static on a telephone or the unwrapping of cellophane candies during Beethoven.

There is no other way to define it. Sometimes dissonance is called noise, and to timid ears this may be so. But consonance and dissonance are relative and subjective terms. A dissonance for one age, generation, individual, may be a consonance for another age, generation, individual.

About the earliest dissonance in music history was the major third (C to E). About the latest consonance in music history was major third (C to E).

Noise is any sound which interferes. Noise is the destroyer of things we want to hear.

Schopenhauer said man's sensitivity to music varies inversely according to the amount of noise he is able to withstand, or something to that effect. He meant as we grow choosy about the sounds we listen to, we are progressively distracted by sound signals which interfere (for instance, unruly audience behavior at concerts).

For the insensitive person the concept of noise is invalid. A sleeping log hears nothing. Machinery is indifferent to noise because it has no ears. Exploiting this indifference, wired background music was invented for earless humans.

On the other hand:

For a person who is truly moved by a piece of music even applause may constitute an interference. It would be like crying encore at a crucifixion.

For the sound-sensitive individual, the world is filled with noise.

You know what they say about silence.

Exercises

1. Try taping a classroom discussion. Afterwards, play back the tape. Concentrate on listening to the sounds you did not intend to record. What other sounds (noises) do you notice?
2. Question for discussion: If you do not like a piece of music is it noise?

3. The following text is to be read by a student at the front of the class in a normal voice. During the reading the teacher cues the class periodically to smother the reader with bursts of noise (roars, whistlings, hissings, gurglings, screams, shufflings, laughter, applause, etc.).

> My voice will at times be smothered by noises which are louder and more chaotic than my reading. At other times this noise will cease and my voice will be heard as the only sound in the room. The sound the others are making is noise because it is undesirable to a true comprehension of my reading. This is why at plays, poetry readings, concerts and lectures, the audience is asked to sit quietly.

Graphically, the above experiment may be shown thus:

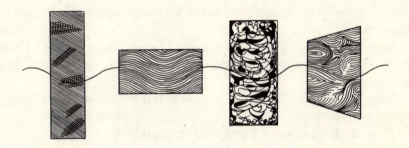

4. Take the noise inserts alone in a new context. They are now to represent a rowdy crowd, say during one of the scenes of Shakespeare's *Coriolanus*. Are they still noise?
5. In the light of our definition of noise as undesirable sound signal, consider the fate of the garbage can in the discussion entitled "What Is Music?" Part I.
6. Listen to the recording of John Cage reading his lectures on "Indeterminacy" (Folkways Records). Question: Are the sounds accompanying his voice sometimes noise, always noise, or never noise?

SILENCE

Silence, some say, is golden. It is merely a figure of speech.

In fact: Silence—the absence of sound—is black.

In optics white is the color containing all colors. We have borrowed from this term "white noise," the presence of all audible frequencies in one sound complex. If we filter through white noise, eliminating progressively larger bands of higher and lower frequencies, we eventually reach the single tone—the sine tone. If we filter this out too we have silence, total aural darkness.

Silence is a container into which a musical event is placed.

Silence protects musical events from noise. Musical events, being sensitive, appreciate this protection.

Silence becomes progressively valuable as we lose it to various kinds of noise exhibitionism: industrial sounds, sports cars, transistor radios, etc.

Because it is being lost, the composer today is more concerned with silence. He composes with it. Anton Webern moves composition to the brink of silence.

John Cage says, "There is no such thing as silence." (Pause 30 seconds and listen.)

If so, is silence noise? (Pause 30 seconds.)

Silence is a pocket of possibility. Anything can happen to break it.

Silence is the most potentialized feature of music. Even when it falls after a sound it reverberates with the tissue of that sound and this reverberation continues until another sound dislodges it, or it is lost from memory. Ergo, however dimly, silence sounds.

Individuals like to make sounds and to surround themselves with sounds. Silence is the outcome of the rejection of the human personality. Human beings fear the absence of sound as they fear the absence of life. There is nothing so sublime or stunning in music as silence.

The ultimate silence is death.

Exercises

1. A take-home assignment: Silence is elusive. Try to find it!
2. Try to pass a sheet of paper throughout the class silently. Everybody listen for the sounds of the paper being passed.
3. Just as in absolute darkness the tiniest light is an event of unique significance, in a container of profound silence even the dropping of a pin becomes uniquely important. Try this. Place pin-drops and other diminutive sounds in containers of profound silence.

4. As the students enter the class Schafer stands at the door motionless with a pile of paper in his hand and a sign pinned on his jacket reading: "Take paper. Write down the sounds you hear." The students entering take paper and record the sounds within and outside the room. A discussion follows to see how sound sensitive the students have been. Did they hear Schafer accidentally drop a kleenex on the floor? And so forth. Two girls have engaged in periodic chatter. They were asked to read out the list of sounds they had heard. While each had recorded the sound of other's voice, neither had heard her own voice. Pity.

The previous day the same text was given to three small children: Anthea, age 12, David, age 9, and Miranda, age 6. It is discovered that while many of the adult students failed to notice the most intimate sounds of all—the sounds of their own body, their breathing, their heartbeat, their voice, their clothing etc., David and Anthea were very sensitive to such sounds. Here are their lists:

David

Grownups talking	Me banging pencil and sniffing
Miranda talking	Miranda thumping
My pencil and paper moving	My teeth chattering
Mommy doing dishes	Me coughing
Clock ticking	Anthea talking
Grownups walking	The fan
Me scratching my head	A tap turning on

Anthea

The tick of the clock	The sound of the furnace
The sound of Miranda's quick running steps	Mommy washing the dishes
David banging his pencil	The turned-on tap
Miranda's breathing	The sound of water boiling
David's deep breath	Miranda's giggling
The sound of David's pencil	The crackle of the fire
The sound of David's paper	My breathing
Daddy's heavy steps	The sound of the pencil on the paper
Phyllis's soft steps	The sound of the fan
Daddy's whistling	Me taking off my hair-band

Miranda, who doesn't write, drew pictures of water-drops, a fire, and her own pencil moving.

TONE

The tone cuts silence (death) with its vibrant life.

No matter how softly or loudly, it is saying one thing: "I am alive."

The tone, intruding on the darkness and oblivion of silence, cuts a light into it.

Let us call the instant of sound-impact the "ictus." The accent of the ictus divides silence from articulation. It is like the dot in the painter's vocabulary, or the period at the end of a sentence.

This dividing of silence from articulation should be one of the most exciting experiences possible. In medicine the "ictus" refers to a stroke or sudden attack.

In creating an individual is given one free gesture. After that comes the discipline of establishing relationships. We are still on that point of free gesture. Only for that instant until we slice into sound do we feel terrifyingly free.

Sustaining past the ictus, the tone stretches itself out in a horizontal line at a constant altitude (frequency).

In language the tone is called a phoneme. This is the most elementary speech sound. The word phoneme itself, for instance, is a five-tone word: Ph-o-n-e-m(e).

But we are still considering one-tone compositions.

The single tone is two-dimensional. It is like a white line moving steadily across a black, silent time-space.

But there are distinct limits of interest in such behavior. How does the tone keep from boring itself?

Exercises

1. Assume you have been mute for a long time. Try to feel the vibrancy of cutting the air with pristine sound—the terrifying freedom of the ictus.
2. The class is given a single tone. How expressive can a one-tone composition be made merely by punctuating it with silence? The tone may be short or long, repeated rhythmically or arhythmically. Different students are asked to conduct the class in this exercise.
   With a finger the conductor creatively incises sound into silence.
3. Sustain the tone for a very long time, at least until total boredom overtakes it. The class must feel the unvaried tone dying a slow, slow death. Ask for suggestions as to how the tone can find new life. The class will find no difficulty in discovering the need for variations of amplitude and timbre. They may even discover antiphony.

4. Experiment with echo effects. Let part of the class sing loudly then cut to reveal other voices sustaining softly. The discovery of the potentiality of acoustic space is thus suggested.
5. Another way to help a tone live by using space: The class stands around the room. The student conductor with both arms outstretched slowly pivots so that only one portion of the class is heard singing the tone as it slowly moves about the room in a circle. Interest in the tone is sustained by using the total acoustic space available.

The full four-dimensional continuum of the soundscape has now been as it were subliminally suggested by considering the quest of a single tone to remain alive, and the student is prepared for the more intensive investigations of the dimensions of sound to follow in the next lectures.

TIMBRE

Tone color—overtone structure.

If a trumpet, a clarinet, and a violin all play the same tone, timbre is what makes trumpetness, clarinetness, and violinness.

Timbre is that characteristic overstructure of a tone that distinguishes one instrument from another at uniform frequency and amplitude. (Scientific explanations of how this is so can be found in all music dictionaries. Sometimes it is more valuable to think picturesquely.)

The tone is bored with its role.

Timbre gives it a colorful wardrobe of new clothes.

Timbre brings the color of individualism to music. Without it everything is a uniform and unvarying grey, like the pallor of a dying patient. Thus death is orchestrated in monochrome by the electronic organ.

By comparison, the colorful array of instruments in the symphony orchestra is an expression of *joie de vivre*.

Human speech expresses this same *joie de vivre* in the most vibrant manner. In speech timbre may change the sound of a word and also its meaning: sat, sit, seat, site, soot.

Every sound in speech has a different timbre, and hence the timbre change is constant and rapid. In music, where one instrument may be used more or less extensively, the changes are less rapid.

A warm sound gives the impression of moving towards the listener; a cold sound moves from him. (Suggestion of a third dimension.)

A real third dimension is brought to a sound by means of amplitude.

Exercises

1. A problem: Given one tone and the following text how do we make the text itself an example of the condition it is describing?

    "Timbre is the tone color of the note."

    After considerable discussion the class decides to divide the text into syllables, give each syllable to a different voice and by singing them one after another and sustaining them, a single line is produced which slowly changes color. Are there other solutions?
2. Another experiment along similar lines might be made with a group of instruments and voices so that each instrument or voice grows out of the last. Repeat this until the growing and dying of each individual combines to produce a line of unvarying amplitude.
3. Try moving this slowly around the room as before.

4. Name some instruments with a warm tone color. Name some with a cool tone color. Any differences of opinion?
5. The writer H. L. Mencken once described the music of Debussy as "a beautiful girl with one green eye and one blue eye." Do any composers suggest any particular colors to you? Why do you think this should be?
6. Each instrument has its own distinct timbre. But can different timbres be produced on one instrument? Various players try to produce different timbres on their instruments while the class, eyes closed, tries to guess which instrument has played.
7. If different singing or speaking voices sing or recite the same passages independently, the difference will be largely one of timbre. Eyes closed, have the class identify the different voices and describe the differences.

AMPLITUDE

Loudness—softness. Addition of the third dimension to the tone by the illusion of perspective.

Where does the loud sound appear in relationship to you, the listener? Where does the soft? A soft sound is instinctively thought to be behind a loud sound, hence the echo.

It is not accidental that shortly after Uccello and Masaccio began experimenting with perspective in painting Giovanni Gabrieli composed his *Sonata pian e forte* (to be sounded soft and loud) and thus introduced perspective thinking to music.

Does a loud sound imply any special movement, either in on the listener or down as if by the pull of gravity or in on itself?

Psychology shows that the loud sound is often thought to be concentric, i.e., vortical, though this is frequently interpreted as bearing in on the listener. (Note the experience of the single-note crescendo in Alban Berg's *Wozzeck*.)

A loud sound may also be characterized as carrying a heavy weight, and therefore the downward pull of gravity. Acute tensions arise when a forceful melody attempts to climb upward. A delicate line climbs upward effortlessly.

A soft sound is constantly dissolving, fleeing like mist, escaping from itself. It longs to fly over the horizon into silence. Hence we call it eccentric.

If amplitude is perspective in music, then the tone moves at the composer's will anywhere between the acoustic horizon and the eardrum.

Thus, to the fourth dimension of time, the three spatial dimensions are suggested. Every piece of music is an elaborate soundscape which could be plotted in three-dimensional acoustic space.

To speak of a soundscape, of course, is in no way to invoke program music. There is a difference in talking about space and attempting to fill that space with objects. The space to which we refer is empty save for the sounds cutting through it.

There is no "land" in a soundscape.

Exercises

1. Take a single tone. Appoint a student conductor. The conductor works out hand signals to indicate to the class the different dynamic qualities of tone desired. By means of dynamic shading—loud,

soft, slow or rapid growth and decay, rapid changes, echo effects etc.—the conductor shapes the tone creatively.

2. It will be observed that the extremities of loudness and softness are rarely if ever heard. Everything is medium-loud to medium-soft. It is at this point that the playing of the famous single-tone crescendo from Alban Berg's *Wozzeck* will be helpful. A brief résumé of the dramatic situation may be desirable. Wozzeck has just murdered his mistress Marie for her unfaithfulness. The curtain comes down and in darkness a single tone is heard, growing, growing as the whole orchestra gradually joins in, still growing, until the listener is literally pulverized by the force of this single elemental sound—then it breaks suddenly, the curtain rises and we move immediately into a gay tavern scene. The effect of this exercise is immediately noticeable as the class returns to the production of their own single-note crescendos.

3. So much for loudness. How soft can music be made to sound? Various students are called to the front of the class and asked to hum a note as softly as possible. The class closes their eyes. When they hear the note they put their hands up. The amplitude of the sound must now be progressively reduced until one by one the rows of hands stay down and only one or two students at the front directly before the singer raise their hands. This, then, is the effective limit to which a pianissimo may be pressed, the point just before the sound disappears over the acoustic horizon into silence.

4. In music we usually recognize three grades of softness: *P, PP, PPP*, and three levels of loudness: *F, FF, FFF*. How many distinguishable grades of softness can you produce with your voice? With your instrument? How many of loudness?

5. How interesting can the single-tone composition be made by employing amplitude, timbre, and silence as coloring and shaping devices? Several students are asked to try filling a one-minute container of silence with an interesting one-tone composition.

6. Divide the class into three or four groups and separate them, each with its own conductor, in different parts of the room. Repeat the former exercise. This time each conductor must listen to the others in order to lead his own group in a contrasting manner. Maximum respect for silence must be encouraged as providing an opportunity for listening to what the others are doing.

Note: Bearing in mind the relationship that has been drawn between perspective and dynamics, it may be pointed out to the class that the sonic tensions they are producing figuratively dissolve the walls of the classroom as they reach back to the horizon of sound (pianissimo) and even beyond the horizon to silence; and then plunge forward again (fortissimo). A distinction may be made here between what we call "real space" and "virtual space"—for the sonic tensions of a soundscape exist in a virtual space which pushes through the walls of the classroom and stretches back to the acoustic horizon in all directions.

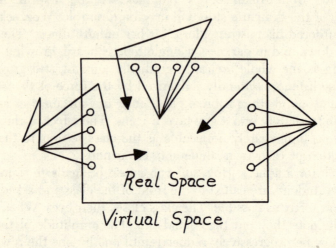

Real Space

Virtual Space

7. Problem: Illustrate the qualities of amplitude by setting the word "amplitude" to music as a one-tone composition. After much discussion the following was produced as showing many different features of amplitude—pianissimo, fortissimo, sforzando, crescendo, and descrescendo.

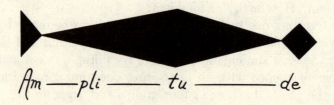

Am —pli —— tu —— de

MELODY

A melody, to paraphrase Paul Klee, is like taking a tone for a walk.

To achieve melody we must move the tone to different altitudes (frequencies). This is called changing the pitch.

A melody can be any combination of tones. There are beautiful melodies and unbeautiful melodies, depending on the purpose for which they are intended. Some melodies are free and others are rigidly organized but this does not make them any more or less beautiful.

Speech uses sound in a continuously gliding fashion, and we speak of the melody in speech as inflection.

Musical melodies are usually limited in their movement by fixed points (pitches). Need they be?

When we indicate the general shape of a musical melody by a curved line we could be more precise and draw a series of horizontal lines (tones) moving to different altitudes (pitches).

Amplitude, timbre and silence, to name but three things, can enhance a melody-line. For instance:

1. A melody moving in freedom
2. The same enhanced by amplitude
3. The same broken by silence

Melodies may be made to move through the realms of the cosmos. Through custom, Western man has come to associate higher melodies with the heavens and lower melodies with the earth (or hell). This need not be so but many classical composers have felt this way. Thus we have the following examples:

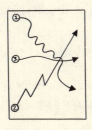

1. A melody falling from grace
2. A melody with a bold, aspiring spirit
3. A phlegmatic, unadventurous melody (bourgeois melody, wired background music, wallpaper music; the object of such melodies is not to interfere with one's digestion)

Exercises

1. Instrumentalists or vocalists are given two tones and allowed freedom to treat them as expressively as possible in brief improvisations. Then three tones are given, then four, etc. But every care must be taken in these initial stages to ensure that the full expressive potential of, say, two given notes is exploited before the student is given new notes. The full effects of amplitude, silence, rhythmic articulation, phrasing, etc., must be realized. The effects of timbre change may be obtained by giving the same two notes to two or three voices or instruments to improvise in consort.

Some typical note series:

2. Individual students are asked to improvise, vocally or instrumentally, free melodies suggested by the following words: (1) high swinging, (2) deep and sad, (3) light tripping, (4) "that strain . . . had a dying fall," (5) cold getting warmer, (6) agony to laughter, (7) heavy to light, (8) it flees into the distance, (9) thick, (10) help!

Analyze the characteristics of the different melodies produced.

3. Try combining some of these individual flights of expression with the foregoing exercises in which single tones are sustained and shaped expressively by the entire class.

4. The class is asked to discuss how they would set each word of the following Latin sentence to music.

> Deposuit potentes de sede et
> (He hath put down the mighty from their seats and
>
> exaltavit humiles.
> exalted the humble and meek.)

The phrase is rich in emotional qualities and each word demands special attention. The communal setting might be notated on the board in notes or merely by means of curved or angular lines. Only after the psychographic curve of each word has been discussed in detail does the instructor play a recording of Bach's setting of these words from the *Magnificat in D*. Compare the settings in relationship to the heaven-hell concepts introduced in the foregoing lecture.

TEXTURE

The texture produced by a dialogue of lines is called counterpoint. *Punctus contra punctum* (point against point) is the original Latin term from which this word is derived, suggesting quite rightly that dynamic tensions are now in operation.

At first there was no counterpoint in music. Then there was parallel movement of lines (called *organum*).

Perhaps the greatest single discovery in music was the discovery of oblique or contrary movement of lines. In the occident this happened around the end of the eleventh century.

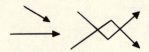

Counterpoint is like different speakers with opposing points of view. There is evident pugilism in all counterpoint, a delight in opposition for its own sake, but not at the expense of lucidity.

Perhaps it is more than coincidental that this development took place at a time when the independent power of the medieval cities and guilds was coming to challenge feudal fealty.

Many musical lines in combination (say 40) produce a dense texture (solid mass). You do not hear very much detail in such a texture.

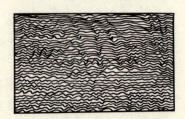

Few lines (say 2) produce a clear texture—like a Matisse drawing.

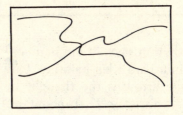

Except for special effects, cleanliness is always desirable in music. The skillful composer tears away; the clumsy composer thickens up.

The object is that you should hear what is happening.

Exercises

1. The class is asked: If we wanted to produce the most opaque texture possible, how would we do it? Many solutions are tried out before it is realized that if every student sings a different note the desired maximal thickness will result.
2. And the most transparent texture possible? "One voice alone," someone says. But can one voice be a texture? What is the minimum number of voices required for a texture? Should the voices be close together or separated widely to produce the desired effect of maximal transparency? Experiment with different intervals.
3. Two texts are given which are to be set to music by the class in such a way that they illustrate the textures they express:

   This is a very opaque texture.

   This is a very transparent texture

4. Listen to some *organum*. Listen to some many-voiced renaissance choral music—for instance, Thomas Tallis's forty-part motet. Listen to a Wagner score. Listen to a Webern score. Comment on the textural differences.
5. The text "punctus contra punctum" is given. Using different voices or groups of voices and dividing the phrase in any way desirable, work out an illustration of the contrapuntal tensions implied by the words.

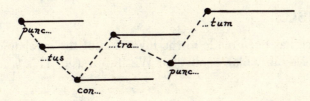

RHYTHM

Rhythm is direction. Rhythm says: "I am here and I want to go there."

It is like the arrow in a Paul Klee painting. Paul Klee says of the arrow: "The father of the arrow is the thought: how do I expand my reach? Over this river? This lake? That mountain?"

Originally "rhythm" and "river" were etymologically related suggesting more the motion of a journey than its division into articulations.

In its broadest sense rhythm divides the whole into parts. Rhythm articulates a journey like footsteps (dividing the whole walk into parts) or any other arbitrary division of the journey. "Rhythm is form cut into time as design is determined space." (Ezra Pound)

There may be regular rhythms and nervous irregular rhythms. Whether they are regular or not has nothing to do with their beauty. The rhythm of horseback riding may be irregular, but this form of travel is enjoyed by many.

Just as we have spoken of real space and virtual space, so we may speak of real time and virtual time.

A regular rhythm suggests the chronological divisions of real time —clocked time (ticks). It lives a mechanical existence.

An irregular rhythm stretches or compresses real time giving what we may call psychological or virtual time. It is more like the irrational rhythms of life.

Music may exist in either clocked or virtual time though it prefers the latter in order to avoid monotony.

A clock, says William Faulkner, slays time.

We do not have much polyrhythm in Western music because we are spellbound by the audible ticking of the mechanical clock. It is possible, therefore, that those societies which show the greatest rhythmic aptitude (African, Arabian, Asian) are precisely those which have been left mostly out of touch with the mechanical clock.

Because rhythm is pointing an arrow in a certain direction, the object of any rhythm is to reach home (the final chord).

Some rhythms reach this destination and others do not.

Rhythmically interesting compositions keep us in suspense.

Exercises

1. Reference has been made to the invention of the mechanical clock and the way in which it affected Western music. This is not an

original idea, even if it has occurred to few people. The simple fact is that all previous means of measuring time (water clocks, sand clocks, sundials) were *silent*. The mechanical clock is audible. For the first time in history duration was divided into proportionate time-cells which *sounded*. Our traditional method of quantitative rhythmic notation—which came into existence with the so-called *Ars Nova* composers, who lived in the fourteenth century, shortly after the invention of the clock—divides notes into time-cells, each in a proportionate relationship to the others. It is quite otherwise with the qualitative rhythms which preceded the mechanical clock and the qualitative kinds of rhythmic notation beginning to be used in contemporary music, now that the clock has outlived its usefulness. It is interesting that while we have always lived under the totalitarian spell of the clock, we make poor clocks ourselves. Human beings really aspire to the fluid concept of what we have called virtual time. This can be illustrated in a simple exercise which several students may be asked to perform: Moving your arm in a clockwise direction describe an absolutely steady circle of an arbitrary duration—say thirty seconds—arriving at the starting point on time! Can it be done? See our demonstration of this to follow in Transcript Two on page 87.

2. The text "polyrhythm" is given to the class. By reciting the word in different ways, build up a chorus of polyrhythms. For instance:

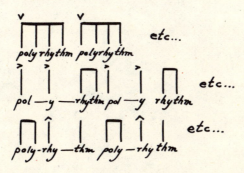

Try adding the following body movements to emphasize the different rhythms:

Snap fingers	V
Clap hands:	>
Stamp feet:	∧

3. Rhythmic training in the West has lagged far behind melodic training. There are many excellent exercises by Hindemith and others designed to improve our puny rhythmic skills. Here is a good elementary exercise, suitable for class use, designed by Gabriel Charpentier—who, incidentally, must also be credited with the invention of the clock exercise.

First the exercise must be mastered by the class in unison. Then it may be treated canonically by different groups.

1 = 1 shout	1234	1324	1342
2 = 2 foot stamps	2341	2314	2143
3 = 3 finger snaps	3412	3124	3142
4 = 4 hand claps	4123	4213	4312
	1432	2134	1423
	2431	1243	2413
	3421	3214	3241
	4231	4132	4321

Thus: "Ah," thump, thump, snap, snap, snap, clap, clap, clap, clap, etc.

4. Another useful exercise in asymmetrical rhythm is to construct messages in Morse code which must then be clapped rapidly in unison. Each student may also make up a "signature rhythm" on his own name. Polyrhythm can be created by coupling these "signature rhythms," some double speed, half speed, etc.

THE MUSICAL SOUNDSCAPE

We can now combine all the expressive potentials of which we have spoken and think of them as interacting within a cone of tensions.

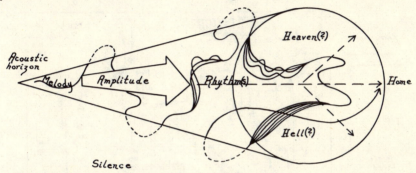

A musical composition is a journey back and forth through this cone of tensions.

Exercises

1. Take several of the preceding vocal exercises and try to fashion them into a little choral composition. Different groups may perform different exercises in different orders to create contrapuntal and formal interest.

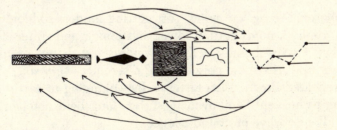

2. Another way of seeing the dynamic tensions of a soundscape is to study the implications of a schema such as that shown following.

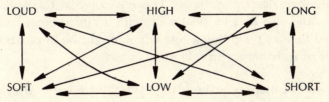

To create a mobility of expression try having different students sing or play little exercises combining these characteristic potentials in all possible ways, i.e., loud-high-long followed by short-low-soft, etc.

3. A third way might be to read at random from a chart such as the following. Each effect should be clearly distinguishable from the others.

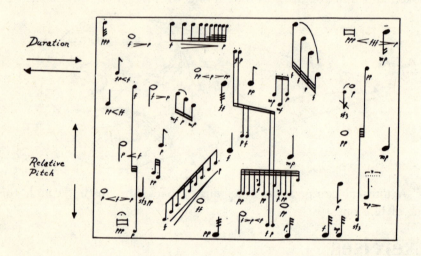

4. Another way: To give the same groups or individuals verbal descriptions to interpret in sequence:

High piercing—long low notes, soft getting louder—suddenly loud and short—high notes getting lower and longer and softer—full melodious curve—dying, swelling, swelling and dying—driving and swinging upwards—now poised in calm serenity—very soft, short notes repeated slowly, then faster—a line plunging to earth—a line aspiring to heaven—flamboyant gestures—long held note softly and slowly dying away—profound silence.

5. For the painter Paul Klee a line drawing was like going for a walk. The following description is his. It is obvious that the walk with a pencil could also be a musical walk with an instrument and it is included here as providing a text which might be improvised by a number of instruments in solo and consort.

. . . act of motion beyond the dead point (line). After a short time we pause to draw breath (broken line, or if repeated, rhythmically interrupted line). A backward look to see where we have gone (counter movement). A river . . . (wavy movement). Higher up there is said to be a bridge (series of arches) . . . We meet someone with the same ideas. At first we are united in joy (convergence). Then gradually differences intervene (two lines moving independently). A certain excitement on both sides (expression, dynamic and psyche of of line). We cross . . . a dense forest. Another river is lost in fog . . . Basket weavers are going home with their cart (the wheel) . . . Later it becomes muggy and nocturnal. A flash of lightning on the horizon (zigzag line). Over our heads the stars are still apparent (series of dots) . . . Before we fall asleep much will recur in our memory, for even such a brief journey is full of impressions.

6. Here is another unusual text which has been used as the basis for a composition (improvisation) by a group of instrumentalists and vocalists. The students were presented the text in segments and asked to work out a short section illustrating it; then the segments were joined together. In interpreting it an attempt should be made to make the calculated things *sound* calculated and the spontaneous and surprising things sound spontaneous and surprising. This implies that the completed composition may be a combination of ordered and unordered segments.

> Cold calculation, random spots of colour, mathematically exact construction, . . . now silent and now strident, painstaking thoroughness, colours like a flourish of trumpets or a pianissimo on the violin, great, calm, oscillating, splintered surfaces.
> Wassily Kandinsky: from a catalogue, 1910.

7. A class of instrumentalists is divided into groups. As many as eight groups are possible if the class is large. Each group selects a leader who will act as its conductor. The following assignment is given to all groups: find an interesting sound.

The groups are given ten minutes to experiment (preferably in separate rooms). No restrictions are placed on them, except that their sound should involve all the performers in the group. It may be consonant, dissonant, short, long—whatever they wish. The instructor may as well be warned to expect some very unusual sounds. On one occasion, for instance, brass players produced curious effects by removing some of the tubing from their instruments.

The groups return. They perform their sounds. The other groups act as critics. If the sound produced does not interest them, the group in question is sent out again to find a better one. When all the sounds have passed the acid test, the class is given a second assignment: find a contrasting sound.

This should be as complete a contrast as possible. Again no other restrictions. After ten minutes the second series of sounds is brought back to class and they are performed, discussed, criticized. Often it is felt they do not contrast sufficiently with the first sound and several groups are sent out to find better sounds.

The above exercise is repeated until each group has five sounds, each substantially different from all the others; for instance, one high-loud sound, one low-soft sound, one melodious sound, one harsh sound, etc.

The groups are now separated around the room with their backs to the center as shown. The conductors stand before their respective groups facing the center. The instructor, as master conductor, stands in the center of the class.

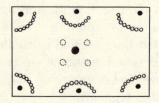

The master conductor may now alert any of the subconductors with his left hand by indicating with raised fingers, which sound he wishes produced (1 - 5). With his right hand he cues the subconductors to begin or to stop playing. As soon as the subconductors see these cues they communicate them to the respective groups. Any number of sounds may be piled up or stripped away. A mobility of sound should be created by constantly cuing different groups in and out. After a little practice the master conductor will soon learn which sounds go well together and which do not.

Stage two calls for a small group of three or four soloists to come forward and seat themselves around the master conductor facing him—that is, with their backs to all the other musicians. Now the original sounds are to be regarded as a harmonic background to solo improvisations. The master conductor signals a soloist to begin by tapping him on the shoulder and to stop by tapping him a second time. The soloists must produce sounds which contrast significantly with whatever ensemble sounds are sounding in order to preserve their identity as soloists. This does not mean, of course, that they should merely play louder than the others, but that they must produce sounds that are so strikingly contrasted with whatever they hear at a given instant that they will be heard without difficulty. Several times during the experiment the music is stopped. If everyone in the room does not hear the soloist(s) performing at that moment, something is wrong and discussion should determine what it is.

The object of the experiment is to keep the sound as fluid as possible. The ensembles and soloists must be in a state of constant interaction. At times everything may be stripped away and one soloist may have an unaccompanied *cadenza*; at other times the entire group may engage in a furious *tutti*.

By placing the musicians in different locations in space with their backs to one another, herd instincts are discouraged and the performers are encouraged to use their own minds and their ears.

Transcript I
CHARLES IVES
AND PERSPECTIVE

NOTE: Although the first of these transcripts originated not at Simon Fraser University but with a class of grade 11, 12, and 13 string players at the North York Summer Music School, it is included here for its relationship to some of the issues raised in the preceding text. It is similar to the kind of "bull sessions" that frequently punctuated our work in the "Ear-Cleaning" course, where ideas were pulled off the shelves and tested empirically.

OBSERVATIONS: The class has just spent two or three sessions discussing Charles Ives, this remarkable man and his remarkable music. A lot of Ives music reflects the composer's life in New England. He was fond of incorporating the sounds of his native environment into his music—a country fiddle tune, a church choir, a village band. In the second movement of *Three Places in New England*—"Putnam's Camp" —Ives incorporates not one but several bands. The atmosphere is one of a Fourth of July picnic, with all the bands from miles around out in festive garb and in sporting competition with one another. The scene can be imagined easily enough. The class has just listened to a recording of "Putnam's Camp."*

SCHAFER: Well, what did you think of that?

A STUDENT: Very exhilarating.

ANOTHER STUDENT: I enjoyed it. At times it was awfully confused, but there were a lot of tunes I recognized in it and I could follow them along quite easily.

A THIRD STUDENT: At first I thought it was rather funny—like Haydn's *Toy Symphony*. What appealed to me most were the rhythms; they were very complex and very modern. The whole thing sounded so fresh. I liked it.

ANOTHER STUDENT: At the end the sounds were so clashing and con-

---

* From: Henry Cowell, *Charles Ives and His Music,* New York, 1955, p. 106. The next quote, *ibid.,* p. 66n.

fused that they seemed to cancel one another out. Instead of everybody coming together at the end the opposite thing happened. It seemed as if everybody was playing something different.

SCHAFER: They were. Ives was once in the audience when this piece was played. Afterwards someone apologized for the scrambled effect, which they assumed was the fault of the orchestra. But Ives said: "Wonderful how it came out! Every man for himself— just like a town meeting."

Laughter

STUDENT: But that's just what I disliked in the music. Everything was so complicated that you couldn't sort anything out. I just thought it was funny.

SCHAFER: Is there anything wrong with humor?

STUDENT: No, but when a thing is that confused no one can understand it.

SCHAFER: First of all, let's be careful when we say no one. You are perfectly entitled to dislike any piece of music you wish as long as you don't pretend you are speaking for all of us. Only music critics are arrogant enough to think they can do this. We should be more humble. We speak for ourselves only.

If you prefer clarity in music so that you can understand everything that is happening, you are perfectly entitled to this preference. I admire your intellectual zeal. Others, however, are content to simply listen to a piece of music, perhaps letting themselves become immersed in it completely, understanding nothing, just experiencing sound. I am inclined to think that what goes on in a piece of music is the composer's business and that although you may understand very little, it will be enough for you to know how to respond. Let me try to give you an analogy. For instance,

Taking a telephone bill on a punched IBM card from his pocket —

can anyone tell me what the holes in this card mean?

Heads shake

I can't even tell myself, yet to the telephone company quite literally a whole wealth of information is contained here. It is enough for me to know that I have to pay the bill. It is true that in Charles Ives compositions a lot is happening at once and his music seems to be in constant collision with itself. Perhaps he doesn't want you to concentrate on anything in particular, but just to be smothered in textures of sound.

But let us look more closely at this confusion. How is this sensation of total chaos produced? Did Ives just take a dozen different marches, tear them up and paste them on top of each other, and then have them all played together?

STUDENT: It's not that confused! I didn't know that several different pieces of music could go so well together. If I chose three or four marches it would sound like a complete mess all the way through. There were points in the piece where everything seemed to come together and then they separated again. Sometimes we heard only one or two bands and we could tell which was which.

SCHAFER: What happened to the others?

STUDENT: I don't know. I guess they went around the corner!

Laughter

SCHAFER: That's not such a crazy idea as you may think. You're on the right track.

STUDENT: Well, if you were standing at one place, say, at an intersection and the bands were marching all around, the sounds would be fading in and out. At the very end it seemed as if all the bands converged on the intersection right under your nose . . .

ANOTHER STUDENT: . . . and had to play all the louder to try and keep from getting lost.

Laughter

SCHAFER: You make it very descriptive, and I think you are absolutely right. This is a picturesque piece of music. Can you think of a word that would describe the situation we have in this piece of music with some things going on in the foreground and other things going on in the distance?

STUDENT: Perspective.

SCHAFER: Exactly. And how does a composer create this illusion of perspective? By . . .?

STUDENT: . . . volume control.

SCHAFER: This is a very important devise in music isn't it? When a composer wants something to come out he makes it louder than the rest of the music. In a sense we might say it is like putting something in the foreground where it will be noticed. A soft sound in the background where it will not be apprehended so clearly. It was the renaissance painters who discovered perspective as a device for distinguishing between important and unimportant events in their paintings. If you look at a medieval painting it is often very difficult to decide which are the important things and which are unimportant because they all seem to exist together in the foreground. In music if we make something loud we thrust it forward and if we make it soft we draw it back into the distance where it will be less conspicuous. Do you think all music possesses perspective?

STUDENT: Almost every piece of music has loud and soft passages.

SCHAFER: Let me play you another piece of music. This one is a march for band dating from the time of Napoleon.

The record is played. As a military march it is almost consistently loud from start to finish.

SCHAFER: Now about this question of perspective—present or not?

STUDENT: I don't think so. It was pretty well always loud.

SCHAFER: Rather like a high-school band? (Laughter) Everybody out for himself. Everybody determined he is going to be heard regardless of whether he has a leading role to play or not. Listening to that last recording you probably had the impression that the whole band was standing square in front of you, almost on top of you. Like this:

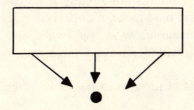

What about the Ives?

STUDENT: There is movement, marching about, into the distance and then back again.

SCHAFER: More like this, perhaps:

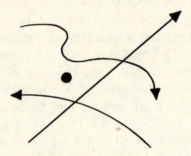

STUDENT: But they weren't really marching about were they? This was only the impression they gave because different sections appeared to get louder and softer at different times.

SCHAFER: It is just an illusion, of course, created by an intelligent use of dynamics. You know, however, from some of our previous experiments that sounds could quite literally be moved around the room by transferring them from one musician to another. Perhaps one might even have the musicians move about themselves. Ives only suggested possibilities along these lines and it has been up to other composers to experiment more fully with them.

With these things in mind I'd like to try an experiment with you. It has a double relationship to the things we have been discussing, which you will see presently. We are going to compose a little piece of descriptive music. Here is a text which will paint the scene for you:

A Sunday morning walk. . . . We walked in the meadows along the River and heard the distant singing from the Church across the River. The mist had not entirely left the river bed, and the colors, the running water, the banks, and trees were something that one would always remember.

What are the points of interest in the description?

STUDENT: The river with the mist rising, the church on the other side, the colors in the morning light.

SCHAFER: Suppose we were to reconstruct the geography of the scene in this classroom and then set it to music. I will be the narrator walking by the river. The front of the classroom will be my side of the river. Where could the church be?

STUDENT: At the back of the room.

SCHAFER: Good. What does that make of the rest of you?

STUDENTS (whimsically): We're the river!

SCHAFER: You have no choice, unfortunately. Now how do you suggest we fill in the sounds of this scene?

STUDENT: It's simply to represent the church and the choir. We could just play hymns.

A couple of hymnbooks are located and Schafer suggests a string quartet be chosen to play the four-part harmony. They are asked to leave the room, choose a hymn, practice it, and come back ten minutes later ready to perform it.

SCHAFER: Now as for the river; how do you think we could imitate this lazy river with the mist rising?

STUDENT: Obviously we should play something slow—soft murmuring sounds. Everybody might take two different notes and play them softly like slow wavy figures.

SCHAFER: Let's try it.

They do. Afterwards Schafer asks them if they are satisfied with the sound or whether they feel they can improve it in any way.

STUDENT: I think the violins could play very high and slow sliding effects to give the impression that the mist is slowly rising and curling around. The lower strings could continue to produce those slow trills to represent the deep water of the river.

They repeat the sound observing these suggestions. The soft veil of the strings does indeed seem to suggest the misty river. Meanwhile, the other students have returned with their hymn.

SCHAFER: I'm sure you are all curious, as I am, to put it together now.

They begin. The river flows. Then the quartet is cued to begin the hymn. After the performance comments are solicited.

STUDENT: The hymn was too loud. If it was really coming from across the river it should sound as though it were in the distance.

SCHAFER: Yes, the quartet *was* too loud. The impression I had was not that the river separated me from the church but that the church separated me from the river.

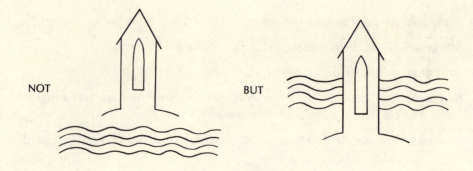

NOT BUT

STUDENT: Wouldn't it be better too if the strings on the one side of the class began and then gradually the others were added to give the impression of the river flowing across the scene?

SCHAFER: That's a good idea. Let's do it again that way. I will move my arm slowly across the class and you can begin as I point to you. And remember, in the string quartet, you are on the other side of the river, not my side. Play with a full tone, but quietly.

The experiment is repeated. The sensation is a curious one indeed. The muted, lethargic dissonances of the river through which are heard the filtered harmonies of a distant, diatonic hymn. Everyone is impressed with the sound as an atmospheric illustration of the text.

SCHAFER: Now I think I should identify the text for you. It is by Charles Ives. It is the way he described the inspiration he had for the third of his *Three Places in New England* entitled "The Housatonic at Stockbridge." The Housatonic is the river; Stockbridge is the little town with its church. You have just orchestrated this scene for yourselves. It's time to see what Ives does with it.

Schafer takes out the record and puts it on the turntable as the class waits with curiosity for the music to begin. . . .

Transcript II
MUSIC FOR PAPER AND WOOD

OBSERVATIONS: One begins by listening to sounds. The world is full of sounds and they can be heard anywhere. The most obvious kinds of sounds are the most frequently missed, and the ear-cleaning operation, therefore, concentrates on them. Once students have cleaned out their ears enough to hear the sounds around them, they can go a stage further and begin to analyse what they hear. It should be possible to reconstruct synthetically, or at least effectively imitate, a sound one has heard, provided the analysis has been accurate. This is the point where ear cleaning gives way to ear training.

Several sheets of paper are given to each student. Schafer begins to write a meaningless message on the board.

XOMYBAF ABND FERITOOM YBLLL ZIVP . . .

At least one student will have invariably begun to copy it down. Schafer suddenly whirls around.

SCHAFER: Why are you copying it down?

STUDENT: I don't know. I just thought that . . .

SCHAFER: You just thought it natural that a sheet of paper should be covered with writing, however meaningless. But supposing I told you that this piece of paper (holding it up) was not meant to be covered with words at all. This piece of paper is a musical instrument.

CLASS: ?

SCHAFER: Have you ever thought of a piece of paper as a sound-producing mechanism?

STUDENT: No, not exactly.

SCHAFER: Here's your chance. Everybody take a sheet of paper and experiment with it as sound. How many different ways can you think of to make sounds with it?

Many different ways are discovered. Some students crush their paper slowly, others quickly, some tear it slowly or quickly, some fold it, some blow across it or flick it with a finger or pencil, others stroke it, etc., etc. The class is given several minutes of liberty to discover paper as sound.

SCHAFER: I think I could hear some very ingenious sounds there, but of course, as all of you were experimenting at once, it was rather confused. Suppose we take another sheet and each of you produce your own sound independently.

The class repeats the sounds one at a time. One of the sounds—a stroking of the paper with the fingertips—is exceedingly subtle.

SCHAFER (To students at far side of room): Could you hear that?

STUDENTS: No.

SCHAFER: Then that's your own fault; you weren't quiet enough. Stop breathing if necessary; close off everything but your ears. Try again.

The girl's fingertips stroke the paper with seismographic delicacy.

SCHAFER: Hear it now?

STUDENT: I can just make it out; it's very quiet.

SCHAFER: Indeed! But so is a whisper. All the more reason for trying to hear it. A whisper is secret and privileged information. That is why we strain our ears to overhear it. It is a similar privilege to hear any delicate sound; most people never do.

Now could we try an improvisation with our paper instruments? As I point to you at random I want you to make a sound with your paper that is substantially different than that produced by the preceding person. This will tax your ingenuity and alertness more because you won't know what your predecessor is going to do until he does it.

This improvisatory exercise is performed with a kind of amused solemnity for several minutes until the class runs out of paper.

SCHAFER: By giving the paper a voice we have exposed its sound-soul. Every object on the earth has a sound-soul—or at least every object that moves, sounds. This is not to say that every sound is enchanting, but merely that it can be heard if we put our ears to work.

I want now to introduce you to another fairly simple sound. (A set of bamboo wind chimes are produced from a brief case.) Do you know what these are?

STUDENT: They are Japanese wind chimes. You hang them outside somewhere and the wind blows through them producing a clattering sound.

ANOTHER STUDENT: Weren't they originally used to ward off evil spirits?

SCHAFER: You may be right about that. It would certainly seem possible, because if one strikes them hard the clattering sound is really rather frightening.

The wind chimes are struck rapidly with the hand and then held suspended allowing them to strike against one another until they return to a calm position.

SCHAFER: It's a rather interesting sound isn't it? Now I have a request to make of you. I want you as a class to imitate the sound of these chimes with your voices. How are you going to do it?

STUDENT: It's hard. The sounds have no clear pitch. I don't think we could imitate them exactly.

SCHAFER: As closely as possible then.

STUDENT: Well, it's a very dry sound, kind of hollow. We could probably make clicking sounds with our tongues.

SCHAFER: That's a start. Would you like to come up and try it out with the class? Just tell them what you want to do and let's hear it.

The student comes up and instructs the class to make clicking and clacking sounds with their tongues. He signals them to begin:

The clacking disintegrates into laughter.

SCHAFER: Did the chimes laugh? If not, your laughter is spurious. Just imitate the chimes. Can't you come any closer than that? Here, listen again to the original sound.

STUDENT: I think there are some sounds of speech that come close to that, for instance the sound of "k."

SCHAFER: Yes, you really mean "k" as a phoneme and not as a letter of the alphabet, don't you?

STUDENT: Yes, "k" as it might appear in "kick."

SCHAFER: Interesting. (Writing the phonetic alphabet on the board). Which of these sounds do you think come closest to the bamboo chimes?

CLASS: "d"
 ... "g"
 ... "t" ...

SCHAFER: Again as phonemes, that is the way they might appear in words such as "did," "got," or "tack." What would happen if you added these to your clacking sounds?

A new conductor comes to the front. He asks some of the students to continue with the clacking while others add the phonemes.

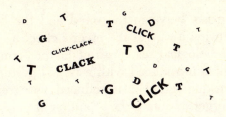

SCHAFER: Well?

STUDENT: I think it's an improvement. It gives more variety just as bamboo produces a variety of different sounds depending on which rods are striking together.

SCHAFER: We're beginning to get somewhere then. But we've only begun. Listen to the sound again and think of some of its characteristics. What is missing in our interpretation?

STUDENT: After you hit it the sound gradually dies away until there are just a few faint clicks at the end.

SCHAFER: The sound decays gradually until it dies away completely. What about the beginning?

STUDENT: Very abrupt. From absolute silence there is a sudden explosion of sound.

SCHAFER (pointing): Would *you* like to repeat the sound observing these facts?

The new student comes to the front and explains that as he shapes a tapering envelope with his hands the class is to let the sound fade away. But the opening attack? The student stands with his arms outstretched and pokes at the air. Nothing happens.

SCHAFER: Are you measuring something or conducting? Excuse me for interrupting, but I feel I must draw your attention to the relationship that exists between the mind and the body. A good conductor is always aware of the precise effect his gestures will have on the psychological responses of his performers. A calm, flowing passage is introduced with a lyrical gesture of the hands. A sudden brusque sound is introduced with real flourish. Above all, don't forget to obtain the attention of your performers before you begin. You have told us that the opening was explosive, percussive. Don't introduce it as if you were poking the air. Be prepared, be firm, attack it.

The student comprehends. He signals the class to attack the sound with his fists clenched; and then with a tapering movement of the arms he allows the sound to decay into silence.

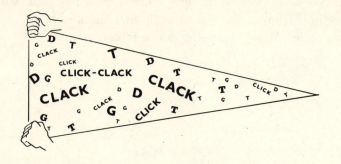

SCHAFER: Bravo! Now listen to the original sound again and see if you notice anything more specific about this decay.

The chimes are clashed again. Everyone listens. Nothing is noticed. Schafer asks the conductor to repeat the imitative sound and the class does so.

SCHAFER (Observing his watch): Eleven seconds from start to finish. How long was the original sound, did anybody notice?

No one noticed.

SCHAFER: Would you care to time it as I strike it again?

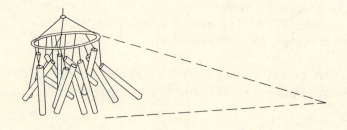

SCHAFER: How long?

STUDENT: Twenty-three seconds.

SCHAFER: Interesting. In our eagerness to get the opening flourish right we diminished the duration of the original sound by more than half. In the heat of our performance we thought we had duplicated the duration of the original sound, but you can see how inaccurate we were. This is the difference between real time or clocked time and virtual time, that is time as it appears to us. When it comes to the accurate measurement of time we are often careless and inconsistent. The truth is as human beings we make very bad clocks. I think I can illustrate this for you. Here is a problem: With your arm moving in a clockwise direction describe an absolutely steady circle of an arbitrary duration (say, 30 seconds) arriving at the starting point on time! Anyone care to try it?

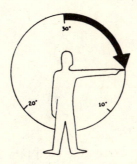

Several students try it while they are "clocked" by the class. None succeeds though some come very close. At length:

STUDENT: Can you do it?

SCHAFER: I can try.

He tries. He fails, arriving at the starting point two seconds too soon.

SCHAFER: The truth is it is almost impossible to accomplish because we tend to feel duration rather than to think about it logically as the accumulation of little time-cells called seconds.

But coming back to our original problem, you can see how it is necessary to be as objective and scientific as possible in analysing a sound if you wish to reproduce it accurately. You didn't analyse the sound properly or you would have observed its duration and, allowing for a small margin of error, you would have been able to duplicate this feature along with the others.

But there is still another feature of the original sound that I feel has escaped you. Listen again and use your ears.

The bamboo chimes are struck again. Everyone listens.

STUDENT: I don't think we should have divided ourselves into two groups with one producing the clacking sounds and the other the speech sounds. I think everyone should be free to choose whatever he wants to produce.

SCHAFER: Try it.

The new student conducts. Everyone is free to choose his own sounds.

SCHAFER: Better, but still I'm not satisfied. You are missing a very important point here, or at least you are not taking full advantage of it. Do the chimes vibrate in such a regular fashion—clack, clack, clack? Listen again and watch the rods.

STUDENT: No, they are quite free. They vibrate in a random fashion.

SCHAFER: Precisely! I always had the feeling when you tried to imitate them that you consciously tried to ignore this fact. No matter what a variety of sounds you made, each of you still uttered them in a pretty regular fashion—you imposed an organized rhythm on a sound which is not organized.

STUDENT: Couldn't we disorganize the sounds then? Everyone should utter his sounds in a completely free way without any recognizable rhythm.

The experiment is repeated one final time.

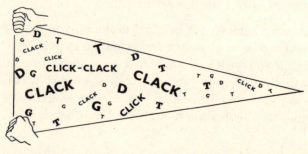

SCHAFER: Very good! I think we are now about as close to the original as we can come with human voices. We have tried to consider the duration of the sound, its dynamic shape, its tone color and its rhythmic texture. From this last we discovered that the bamboo chimes really produced a piece of arhythmic or "chance" music. Moreover, that if you want to produce the feeling of surprise and confusion of chance you will never do it by organizing your sounds. This leads us directly into the whole philosophy of chance music, and I think we might go on tomorrow to discuss this.

And they did.

FOUR POSTSCRIPTS

OBSERVATIONS: Everything we did in the course was calculated either to sharpen the ears, or to release latent creative energy, or both. Conciseness has been thought more desirable than verbosity. Here are some brief notes on a few more things we did and discussed in class. The reader will be able to fit them into context easily enough.

I

When the class was told of John Cage's statement to the effect that there is no such thing as silence, everyone was quiet. They were listening for silence. The only sound to be heard was the swish of one student's pencil as he copied down: "There is no such thing as silence."

II

One day an assignment was given: Bring an interesting sound to class. Some students are flustered. Schafer: "If I asked you to bring an interesting book to school you could do that couldn't you? Well, just go home and find an interesting sound. It's a lot lighter than a book."

One student brings a balloon, fills it up with air, then lets it out gradually—zzzzzzzzzzhzhzhzhzheeeeeeeesssssssshshshsh. When asked why it was interesting she said it was so because it was unpredictable. One never knew when it was going to go zhzhzhzh and when shshshsh.

A boy brought a metal clacker. He said it was interesting because all his life he had been hearing it but this was the first time he actually had ever been asked to listen to it.

Another girl brought a music box. It was interesting to her because the sounds were so mysterious; she had always marvelled that so many sounds could get locked up in such a tiny box.

A boy got up and said "animal" about a dozen times. He explained that it was interesting because the more often you repeated it the less it seemed to fit the thing it was supposed to represent. The sense was lulled to sleep and only a curious sound-object remained from which all meaning had vanished.

III

Everyone knows that our attitude towards music—the sounds we feel are significant and worth recording—is conditioned by the environmental sounds of our century, generation, and geographical position in the world. An interesting study could be made of the environmental sounds of different centuries, generations, and geographical areas.

One day the class was asked to look at a painting by Pieter Brueghel the Elder—"The Battle Between Carnival and Lent"—and to record all the sounds and potential sounds in it—everything from the lame man's crutch on the cobblestones to the sound of the lute.

Secondly, they were asked to go down to the corner, set up a tape recorder and tape ten minutes of contemporary environmental sounds.

Then they were asked to compare the sounds to be heard in the sixteenth century with those to be heard in the twentieth century, for instance, the number of human sounds and the number of mechanical sounds.

The same experiment could be worked with an number of paintings, poems or dramas from different periods in history or from different civilizations.

IV

One day someone wrote a poem which gave the class something to think about:

SOUND-POEM
If there is silence and sound—
Silence emptied of silence is sound
Silence filled with sound is sound
Sound emptied of sound is silence
Sound emptied of silence is sound
Silence emptied of sound is silence
Sound filled with sound is sound
Sound filled with silence is silence
Silence filled with silence is silence
Silence emptied of sound is sound
Sound filled with silence is silence

If there is no such thing as silence—

Silence emptied of silence is sound
Silence filled with sound is sound
Sound emptied of sound is sound
Sound emptied of silence is sound
Silence emptied of sound is sound
Sound filled with sound is sound
Sound filled with silence is sound
Silence filled with silence is sound
Silence emptied of sound is sound
Sound filled with silence is sound

And a final question:

"Why do men hear less when they
are yawning?"

(Aristotle, Problems Book I, XI.)

Part III

THE NEW SOUNDSCAPE

Overheard in the lobby after the première of Beethoven's Fifth: *"Yes, but is it music?"*

Overheard in the lobby after the première of Wagner's Tristan: *"Yes, but is it music?"*

Overheard in the lobby after the première of Stravinsky's Sacre: *"Yes, but is it music?"*

Overheard in the lobby after the première of Varèse's Poème électronique: *"Yes, but is it music?"*

A jet scrapes the sky over my head and I ask: "Yes, but is it music? Perhaps the pilot has mistaken his profession?"

YES, BUT IS IT MUSIC?

MUSIC: Art of combining sounds with a view to beauty of form and expression of emotion; sounds so produced; pleasant sound, e.g. song of a bird, murmur of a brook, cry of hounds.

> The Concise Oxford Dictionary, Fourth Edition, 1956

It was one of my first days in the music room. In the interest of finding out what we were supposed to be doing there, I set the class a problem. Innocently I asked: "What is music?"

We spent two solid days groping around a definition. We found that we had to reject all the customary definitions because they weren't inclusive enough, and you can't have a definition that doesn't embrace *all* the objects or activities of its class. The definition we did come up with and the transcript of our thinking-path is reported in Part I, *The Composer in the Classroom*. Numerous thoughtful people have pointed out inadequacies in that definition. I agree with their criticisms.

The simple fact is that as the growing edge we call the avant-garde continues its explorations along the frontiers of sound, any definition becomes exceedingly difficult. When John Cage opens the door of the concert hall and encourages the street noises to intersect his compositions he ventilates the art of music with fresh and seemingly shapeless concepts.

Nevertheless, I did not like to think that the question of defining the subject to which we are devoting our lives was totally impossible. I did not think John Cage would think so either, and so I wrote him and asked him for his definition of music.
His reply:

> *Music is sounds, sounds around us whether we're in or out of concert halls.*

The reference is to Thoreau's *Walden*, where the author experiences in the sounds and sights of nature an inexhaustible entertainment.

To define music merely as "sounds" would have been unthinkable a few years ago, though today it is the more exclusive definitions that are proving unacceptable. Little by little throughout the 20th century all the conventional definitions of music have been exploded by the abundant activities of musicians themselves. First, with the huge expansion of percussion instruments in our orchestras, many of which produce nonpitched and arhythmic sounds; then through the introduction of aleatoric procedures in which all attempts to organize the sounds of a composition rationally are surrendered before the "higher" laws of entropy; then through the opening out of the time and space containers we call compositions and concert halls to allow the introduction of a whole new world of sounds outside them. (In Cage's 4′33″ *Silence* we hear only the sounds external to the composition itself, which is merely one protracted caesura.) Finally in the practices of *musique concrète* it becomes possible to insert any sound from the environment into a composition via tape; while in electronic music the hard-edge sound of the tone generator may be indistinguishable from the police siren or the electric toothbrush. Today all sounds belong to a continuous field of possibilities lying *within the comprehensive dominion of music.*

> Behold the new orchestra: the sonic universe!
> And the new musicians: anyone and anything that sounds!
> There is a shattering corollary to this for all music educators.
> For music educators are the custodians of the theory and practice
>   of music.

And the whole nature of this theory and practice is now going to have to be completely reconsidered.

The teaching of traditional music has its special targets: the technical mastery of instruments such as the piano, the trumpet or the violin for the performance of a literature existing back over several hundred years. For the purpose of understanding the shapes of this music a theoretical vocabularly has been developed enabling the student to gloss any piece of Western music written between the Renaissance and our own time.

There is nothing permanent or perfect about this practice or theory, of course, and the music of the Middle Ages or of China cannot be measured by the rules of Classical theory any more than it can be performed on the instruments of the classical orchestra. The historical and geographical cultural sweepout that characterizes our time has made us very conscious of the fallacy of controlling the temperament of all musical philosophies by the same tuning fork.

The new musical resources I shall try to bring into focus in the following pages will require quite new attitudes of study-stress. New studies are needed in the curriculum and they will carry us far out into the shifting contours of interdisciplinary knowledge.

The new student will have to be informed in areas as diverse as acoustics, psychoacoustics, electronics, games, and information theory.

It is these last-named together with a knowledge of the form-building and form-dissolving processes as observed in the natural sciences that will be necessary to register the shapes and densities of the new sound-configurations of today's and tomorrow's music.

In the classroom in 1964.

More music is heard today by means of electro-acoustic reproduction than in its natural form, which leads one to ask whether music in this form is not perhaps the more "natural" to the contemporary listener; and if so should not the student understand what happens when music is so reproduced?

The basic vocabulary of music will change. We will perhaps speak of "sound objects," of "envelopes" and "onset transients" instead of "triads," "sforzando" and "appogiatura." Single sounds will be studied more attentively with attention paid to the formants of their overtone spectra and to their onset and decay characteristics.

Students will perhaps be trained to describe music in terms of exact frequencies or frequency bands rather than in the limited nomenclature of the tonal system. Dynamics too might better be described in relation to some standard reference such as the phon (loudness) or the decible (intensity) rather than in terms of a few ancient Italian intuitions on the subject.

The psychology and physiology of aural pattern perception will supersede many former musical studies in which musical soundings were rendered mute by paper exercises. (Traditional theory books deny all life to sounds, considering them as stationary cadavers.) Ultimately somewhere work might begin on a much-needed history of aural perception to show us how different periods or different musical cultures actually hear *different* things when listening to music.

One of the purposes of this part is to direct the ear of the listener towards the new soundscape of contemporary life, to acquaint him or her with a vocabulary of sounds one may expect to hear both inside and outside concert halls. It may be that the listener will not like all the tunes of this new music, and that too will be good. For together with other forms of pollution, the sound sewage of our contemporary environment is unprecedented in human history.

This brings me to my other purpose. In recent years the science of medicine has seen a dramatic shift of emphasis from the curing of disease to its prevention. This shift is so pronounced that the term "preventative medicine" needs no explanation. I am about to suggest that the time has come in the development of music when we will have to be concerned as much with the prevention of sounds as with their production. Observing the world sonograph, the new music educator will encourage those sounds salubrious to human life and will rage against those inimical to it. It will be more important to know about pain thresholds than to be concerned whether the devil still inhabits the tritone. It will be more in his or her interest to take up membership in the International Society for Noise Abatement than in the local Registered Music Teachers' Association.

If this suggestion strikes the reader as a joke I can only hope that the remainder of Part III will have a sobering effect. I have come to regard the whole matter of sound prevention as inevitable and urgent.

Part III isn't technical. It consists of some preliminary thought-excursions along the lines of the questions I have just raised. From time to time some of my first-year university students may get into the act. Why not? They are around me as I write.

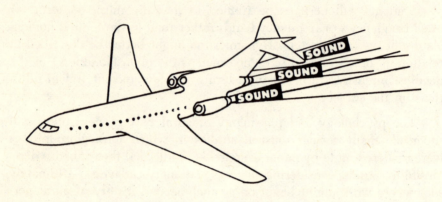

THE SONIC ENVIRONMENT

Anything in our world that moves vibrates air.

If it moves in such a way that it oscillates at more than about 16 times a second this movement is heard as sound.

The world, then, is full of sounds. Listen.

Openly attentive to whatever is vibrating, listen.

Sit quietly for a moment and receive.

The class had done this for four days running, ten minutes each day, chairs turned to the wall, receiving sound-messages.

On the fifth day they were asked to describe what they had heard. Everyone had by that time heard quite a lot of sounds—footsteps, breathing, chairs moved, distant voices, a bell, a train, etc. But were they describing what they had heard? Was it not merely a list of common words? Everyone knows what a footstep or a cough or a bell sounds like. But the difference between my footsteps and yours, or his cough and hers, how were we to describe that? One or two tried to express the difference by drawing pictures. Not too helpful.

If the new orchestra is the sonic universe, how do we differentiate between the instruments? How could we write the complete biography of a footstep in such a way that we would know it was your footstep's story and not mine?

One determined girl went down to a street corner on Saturday and tried to work out a descriptive notation for the different feet of the passers-by. She watched and listened to the choreography of the feet and noted the size of shoe or boot; the pitch of its step, high or low; the timbre of its sound, metallic, shuffling or clodhoppery; and the tempo of its movement from the deft tick-a-tack of heel points to the muted drag of vagrant feet.

The sounds of the universal orchestra are infinitely varied. Everyone was asked to spend ten minutes a day listening at home, in a bus, on the street, at a party. Lists of sounds heard were prepared. More lists were turned in, still underscriptive.

But one thing we discovered we could tell. The sounds heard could be divided into sounds made by nature, by humans, and by electric or mechanical gadgetry. Two students catalogued the sounds. Did people always hear the same sounds as we do? To make a comparative study, everyone was asked to take a historical document and note down all the sounds or potential sounds in it. Any document would do: a painting, a poem, a description of an event, a photograph. Someone took *The Battle Between Carnival and Lent* by Pieter Brueghel the Elder and gave us the sounds of a 17th century Dutch townscape. Someone else took a passage from an Arnold Bennet novel and gave us the sounds of an industrial North-of-England city in the 19th century. Someone else took a North-American Indian village, another a biblical scene, and so on.

We only sampled at random, of course, but perhaps certain conclusions could be drawn. For instance, we found that at first when people were scarce and lived a pastoral existence the sounds of nature seemed to predominate: winds, water, birds, animals, thunder. People used their ears to read the sound-omens of nature. Later on in the townscape people's voices, their laughter and the sound of their handicraft industries seemed to take over the foreground. Later still, after the Industrial Revolution, mechanical sounds drowned out both human and natural sounds with their ubiquitous buzz and whirr. And today? Here are some of our tables:

	Natural Sounds	Human Sounds	The Sounds of Tools and Technology
Primitive Cultures	69%	26%	5%
Medieval, Renaissance and Pre-Industrial Cultures	34%	52%	14%
Post-Industrial Cultures	9%	25%	66%
Today	6%	26%	68%

CONCERNING
SILENCE

With the intensity of the sound barrage going on all around, it has become fashionable to speak of silence. Therefore, let us speak of silence.

We miss it.

In the past there were muted sanctuaries where anyone suffering from sound fatigue could go into retirement for recomposure of the psyche. It might be in the woods, or out at sea, or on a snowy mountainside in winter. One would look up at the stars or the soundless soaring of birdcraft and be at peace.

It was understood that each human being had an inalienable right to stillness. It was a precious article in an unwritten code of human rights.

> Leaning on our stout oaken walking sticks,
> our sacks on our backs, we climbed the
> cobbled road that led to Karyès, passing
> through a dense forest of half-defoliated
> chestnut-trees, pistachios, and broad-
> leafed laurels. The air smelled of incense,
> or so it seemed to us. We felt that we had
> entered a colossal church composed of sea,
> mountains and chestnut forest, and roofed
> at the top by the open sky instead of a dome.
> I turned to my friend; I wanted to break the
> silence which had begun to weigh upon me.
> "Why don't we talk a little?" I suggested.
> "We are," answered my friend, touching my shoulder lightly.
> "We are, but with silence, the tongue of angels."
> Then he suddenly appeared to grow angry.
> "What do you expect us to say? That it is
> beautiful, that ours hearts have sprouted wings
> and want to fly away, that we've started along
> a road leading to Paradise? Words, words, words.
> Keep quiet!" [1]

Even in the hearts of cities there were reservoirs of quiet. Churches were such sanctuaries, and libraries too. In the concert hall even now a hush comes over the audience when the music is about to begin so that the music may be affectionately placed in a container of silence.

As long as these traditions existed the concept of silence was real and had dignity. Silence was thought of figuratively rather than physically, for a physically silent world was as highly improbable then as it is now. The difference was that the average ambient sound level was low enough to allow a person to contemplate without a continuous recital of sonic incursions into his or her thought-stream. (The sentences of our thoughts have undoubtedly grown shorter since the invention of the telephone!)

But to contemplate an absolute silence, that is a negative and terrifying thing. Thus when the infinity of space was first suggested by Galileo's telescope, the philosopher Pascal was deeply afraid of the prospect of an infinite and eternal silence.

> Le silence éternal de ces espaces infinis m'effraye.[2]

When one goes into an anechoic chamber—that is, a completely soundproof room—one feels a little of the same terror. One speaks and the sound seems to drop from one's lips to the floor. The ears strain to pick up evidence that there is still life in the world.

When John Cage went into such a room, however, he heard two sounds, one high and one low.

> When I described them to the engineer in charge, he informed me that the high one was my own nervous system in operation, the low one my blood in circulation.

Cage's conclusion:

> There is no such thing as silence. Something is always happening that makes a sound.[3]

Cage had detected the relativity of silence and in choosing *Silence* as the title for his book he emphasized that henceforth any use of this word must be qualified or assumed to be ironical.

The myth of silence has been exploded. From now on in traditional music, for instance, when we speak of silence we will not mean absolute or physical silence, but merely the *absence of traditional musical sounds*.

In the psychology of visual perception one talks of the alternation between figure and ground, either of which can become the visual message for the eye depending on what it wants to see. In certain drawings the identical forms combine to produce two subjects either of which may be seen in relief against a neutral ground. For a long time we may see only one image, then with a sudden flicker the relationship is reversed. Similarly, the sound engineer speaks of the difference between signal and noise, the wanted sounds from the unwanted. Behind every piece of music lurks another piece of music. The minuscule world of sound events which we have carelessly assumed to be "silent." The moment these events flash into the foreground we call them noise. Any reappraisal of music will have a good deal to say about noise; for noise is sound we have been trained to ignore.

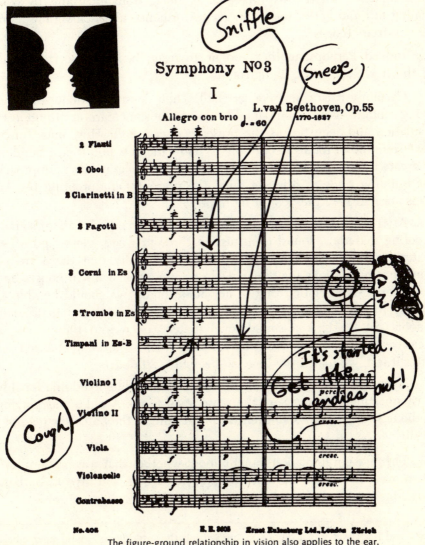

The figure-ground relationship in vision also applies to the ear.

If one listens carefully to the spaces between the cyclopean chords that open Beethoven's Eroica symphony, he or she will discover a dense population of quite "unheroic" sound events—coughs, shufflings, record scratches, or whatever. Like the distinction between figure and ground in a drawing, we may also now distinguish between figure and ground in music listening. Try, for instance, to listen to a musical performance focusing not on the music itself but on all the extraneous nonmusical sounds that surround the music and crowd forth during its momentary pauses. My class did this. It is a strangely sensitizing exercise to refocus the ear.

But we began by speaking of quiet sanctuaries, a student reminds us. Should we not try to protect great music from intrusions by continuing to build better rooms for its performance and demanding more scratch-free records?

Indeed. Perhaps, another student suggests, the new concert hall will be the stereo set in the living room.

Certainly it is a new concert hall. Then doesn't it follow that our living room or music room should receive the same careful attention to insulation and acoustics as the present concert hall? How many of us have soundproof rooms in our houses? How much would it cost builders to create them? And so we found ourselves an assignment: to approach the building trade to discover what the present soundproofing regulations are and how they could be improved.

After our investigation we found we had learned a lot about soundproofing materials, sound transmission through wood, glass, and other materials. We discovered, for instance, in our city that there are no minimum regulations for the acoustic treatment of walls in houses and apartments. We decided that in our "ideal home" we should be able to specify to the builder what noise level we were prepared to tolerate indoors. So we took a sound level meter* deep into the woods to measure the quiet there. At first, peace; then an airplane buzzed us. After it left, we took a reading: 20 decibels (20 db).

Then we went to the home of Jeff B., who said he lived in a terribly noisy apartment, to measure the noise level there. A radio was playing in the next apartment. Children were shouting in the hall. Our reading: 64 db.

Then we got into an argument about whether that was noise or not. There were five of us: Barbara, Donna, Jeff, Doug, and myself. Barbara liked the music on the radio . . . .

---

* A sound level meter is a device for measuring the intensity of sound in decibels with 0 db established as the threshold of hearing.

A NEW DEFINITION OF NOISE

We walked around for a while talking about noise. Doug carried the sound level meter, measuring, measuring. At a residential street corner (35 db) we stopped and I asked Jeff why he regarded his neighbor's radio as noise.

JEFF: Because it goes on all day, and I don't like their choice of programs.

BARBARA: Well I didn't find it disagreeable (at 40 db).

SCHAFER: Well then, how would *you* define noise?

BARBARA: Ugliness.

A bus passed by (80 db).

SCHAFER: Did you find it ugly?

BARBARA: What?

SCHAFER: That bus.

BARBARA: Well, it was loud but not nearly as ugly as the sounds in that piece you played to us the other day. (We had been listening to Edgar Varèse's *Déserts*.)

Jeff thought that was very funny and laughed (68 db).

SCHAFER: What makes a sound ugly?

Just then we were passed by a motorcycle going all out (98 db).

JEFF: That's a Harley-Davidson, sixty-two horsepower. What a beauty!

SCHAFER: Ugly?

JEFF: No, *beautiful!*

SCHAFER: Oh!

For a while we talked without speaking. Turning a corner we entered a park and sat down (35 db). From the distance the sawtooth sound of a lawn mower proceeded towards us pushing the meter up to 75 db. I began to think of the many confusions surrounding the word noise. Was it a matter of dissonance, of loudness, or simply of personal displeasure? The great nineteenth-century physicist Hermann von Helmholtz had little difficulty in distinguishing "music" from "noise." This is what he says in his famous book *On the Sensations of Tone*:

> The first and principal difference between various sounds
> experienced by our ear, is that between noises and musical
> tones . . . . We perceive that generally, a noise is accompanied by
> a rapid alternation of different kinds of sound . . . . Think for
> example, of the rattling of a carriage over granite paving stones,
> the splashing or seething of a waterfall or of the waves of the
> sea, the rustling of leaves in a wood. In all these cases we have
> rapid, irregular, but distinctively perceptible alternations
> of various kinds of sounds, which crop up fitfully . . . . Those
> regular motions which produce musical tones have been exactly
> investigated by physicists. They are oscillations, vibrations or
> swings, that is, up and down, or to and fro motions of sonorous
> bodies, and it is necessary that these oscillations should be
> regularly periodic. By a periodic motion we mean one which
> constantly returns to the same condition after exactly equal
> intervals of time.

Then he formulates his definition:

> The sensation of a musical tone is due to a rapid periodic motion
> of the sonorous body; the sensation of a noise to non-periodic
> motions.[4]

You can see this easily enough on an oscilloscope, an instrument for presenting sound pictorially to assist in its analysis. There is a branch of mathematics known as "harmonic analysis" which is concerned with the problems of analyzing the curves which appear on an oscilloscope to determine the ingredients of a sound. In a "musical tone" all the harmonics are proportionate to its fundamental and the pattern produced on the oscilloscope will be regular and periodic as in the first illustration. A "noisy" sound (to retain Helmholtz's distinction) is much more complex, consisting of many fundamentals, each with its own harmonic superstructure and these sound in disharmonious competition with each other. In its oscillographic picture a whole riot of lines results in which it is difficult or impossible to see any regularity or pattern.

But is this a satisfactory definition? Have we not already examined enough problems and paradoxes to force a re-examination of Helmholtz's classical proposition?

For instance, by Helmholtz's definition, the motorcycle we heard could not be considered noisy at all but rather "musical" for as a mechanical machine it must be periodic. You don't get very far on a non-periodic machine. And can we ignore amplitude in examining noise? The motorcycle was 98 decibels by our own reading. Colloquially speaking, a lot of people would call that "noisy." On the other hand many percussion instruments such as drums are non-periodic and yet we find them in symphony orchestras.

We seem to be in trouble. Scientifically, of course we cannot dispute Helmholtz's division of sounds into those which are periodic and those which are non-periodic. The problem is merely semantic and arises because he chose to call one "musical tone" and the other "noise." When music was still considered a collection of harmonically related sound events, noise automatically referred to disharmonious sound events. Percussion instruments were introduced into the orchestra in audacious acts by composers interested in breaking new sound barriers. Beethoven was as audacious when he gave a solo part to the timpani in the scherzo of his ninth symphony as was George Antheil when he introduced airplane propellers and sirens into his *Ballet méchanique*.

In the past people thought less of the intensity or loudness of sounds probably because there were far fewer brutally loud sounds in their lives. It was not until the Industrial Revolution that sound pollution came to exist as a serious problem.

It was the beginning of the present century that the Italian futurist composer Luigi Russolo, recognizing that "noises" dominated our lives anyway, suggested that they should be completely incorporated into music. In 1913 he wrote a manifesto entitled *L'arte dei rumori* (The Art of Noises) in which he pointed out that since the invention of the machine, man was gradually being conditioned by these new noises, and that this conditioning was changing his musical sensibilities. He called for an end to the banishment of "noise" to the realms of unpleasantness and demanded that people open their ears to the new music of the future. Now that this is precisely what is happening, the hitherto little-known Russolo is emerging as something of a prophet.

This then is the essence of our revised definition of noise. The communications engineers have given it to us. When someone is transmitting a message *any* sounds or interferences which impair its accurate transmission and reception are referred to as *noise*.

Noise is any undesired sound.

This makes noise, to be sure, a relative term; but it gives us the flexibility we need when we refer to sound. In a concert if the traffic outside the hall disturbs the music it is noise. But if, as John Cage has done, the doors are thrown open and the audience is informed that the traffic constitutes part of the texture of the piece, the sounds cease to be noise.

We may still speak of periodic and non-periodic sounds to distinguish between two quite different qualities of sound; but we must reserve judgment as to whether they are *music* or *noise* until we determine whether they constitute part of the message intended to be heard or are miscellaneous interferences to it.

Noise is any undesirable sound.

A few days later a popular music band was playing on the mall of our school full out with guitars and amplifiers. Jeff measured it at 101 db. "How can you stand it?" I screamed at a girl standing beside me. "Huh?" she replied. "Never mind," I said. "I can't hear you," she replied.

SOUND SEWAGE: A COLLAGE

NOISE: ANY UNDESIRED SOUND

The building is on a military installation somewhere in the
United States . . . . Inside are nightmares.

In one of the large laboratory rooms, two physicists and a
biologist stand about a heavy metal table. They wear thick
ear pads. On the table is a dial-covered device about the size
and shape of a television set, with a trumpet-like horn protruding
from its face. The device is a kind of siren, designed to produce
high-frequency sound of outrageous intensity. The scientists
are studying the effects of this sound on materials, animals and
men. They are wondering if sound can be used as weapon . . . .

One of the physicists begins the demonstration by picking
up a wad of steel wool with a tonglike instrument on a long
pole. He holds the steel wool in the invisible beam of sound
that issues from the horn. The steel wool explodes in a whirling
cascade of white-hot sparks . . . .

The biologist has brought a white rat into the room in a
small cage. The rat is running around the cage, looking unhappy
about all the noise. But his worries don't last long. The biologist
lifts the cage into the sound field. The rat stiffens, rises up to
the full stretch of his legs, arches his back, opens his mouth wide,
and falls over. He is dead. An autopsy will reveal that he had
died of instant overheating and a massive case of the bends.
There are bubbles in his veins and internal organs.[5]

The National Aeronautics and Space Administration wants to
know what loud rocket noises do to people around a
launching-pad, and why such noises occasionally cause nausea,
fainting, and epileptic-like fits.[6]

Scientific tests . . . reveal that changes in the circulation of the
blood and in the action of the heart take place when a person
is exposed to a certain intensity of noise. Even snatches of
loud conversation are enough to affect the nervous system and
thereby provoke constrictions in a large part of the blood
circulation system . . . . Workers in a boiler factory, for

instance, thus suffer from a constantly impaired circulation in the epidermis.[7]

Professor Rudnick and his colleagues built the most powerful siren ever conceived to that date. It made what was, as far as anybody knew, the loudest, continuous sound ever heard on earth up to that time: 175 db, some 10,000 times as strong as the ear-splitting din of a large penumatic riveter. The frequency range of this enormous howl was from about 3,000 cycles per second (near the top range of a piano) to 34,000 cps, in the ultrasonic range.

Strange things happened in this nightmarish sound field. If a man put his hand directly in the beam of sound, he got a painful burn between the fingers. When the siren was aimed upwards, 3/4 inch marbles would float lazily about it at certain points in the harmonic field, held up and in by the outrageous acoustic pressure. By varying the harmonic structure of the field, Professor Rudnick could make pennies dance on a silk screen with chorus-like precision. He could even make one penny rise slowly to a vertical position while balancing another penny on its side. A cotton wad held in the field would burst into flame in about six seconds. "To satisfy a skeptical colleague," reports Professor Rudnick, "we lit his pipe by exposing the open end of the bowl to the field." [8]

Researchers at the Max Planck Institute in West Germany want to know why workers in noisy places such as iron foundries have more emotional and family problems than those in quieter places.[9]

But of all the noises of Mexico City the loudest and most individual was made by the mechanical pile-driver opposite the Opera House. Thud-shriek, thud-shriek; it worked day and night; the hammer fell, the compressed air escaped and the great tree trunks sank foot by foot into the soft sub-soil. While, in the general slump, other major works were at a stand-still, this infernal machine pounded on incessantly, dominating a whole quarter of the city.[10]

The silence of sound began to get some attention during World War Two with the development of military applications such as sonar (Sound Navigation and Ranging) for tracking enemy vessels at sea. In the 1950's studies of other sonic phenomena began to disappear one by one behind a cloud of military secrecy—perhaps the most sincere honor that can be granted to any research project.[11]

. . . the effort now being made by the aeronautical industry to persuade us that we shall enjoy the din of supersonic airliners. Public relations machinery and techniques are working on an unsuspecting public with the slogan "learn to live with the boom." [12]

James Watt once rightly remarked that to uneducated persons noise is suggestive to power. A machine which operates silently or without vibration is obviously far less impressive than a noisy one.[13]

There are people, it is true—nay, a great many people—who smile at such things, because they are not sensitive to noise; but they are just the very people who are also not sensitive to argument, or thought, or poetry, or art, in a word, to any kind of intellectual influence. The reason of it is that the tissue of their brains is of a very rough and coarse quality. On the other hand, noise is a torture to intellectual people.[14]

The familiar exclamation . . . "quiet please" can be translated into scientific terminology as follows: "My work demands great concentration and I must therefore preserve the connective functions of my cerebral cortex. I cannot afford to weaken the inhibitory processes and I have to preserve the working capacity of my nervous system." [15]

If you cut up a large diamond into little bits, it will entirely lose the value it had as a whole; and an army if divided up into small bodies of soldiers, loses all its strength. So a great intellect sinks to the level of an ordinary one, as soon as it is interrupted and disturbed, its attention distracted from the matter in hand; for its superiority depends upon its power of concentration— of bringing all its strength to bear upon one theme, in the same way as a concave mirror collects into one point all the rays of light that strike upon it.[16]

Advancing civilizations will create more noise, not less. Of that we are certain. In all probability the noise level will grow not only in urban centers, but, with increasing population and the proliferation of machines, noise will invade the few remaining havens of silence in the world. A century from now, when man wants to escape to a quiet spot, there may be no place left to go.[17]

But just over ten years ago organizations were set up in a number of European countries to wage campaigns against the spread of noise. These bodies . . . decided to unite their action

and in 1959 formed the International Association Against
Noise . . . . Since its directorate has always comprised a
physician, an engineer, a specialist in acoustics, and two jurists,
the International Association is in a position to give prompt
and authoritative opinions on questions of international
scope within its field.[18]

The most inexcusable and disgraceful of all noises is the
cracking of whips—a truly infernal thing when it is done in the
narrow resounding streets of a town. I denounce it as making
a peaceful life impossible; it puts an end to all quiet thought . . . .
No one with anything like an idea in his head can avoid a
feeling of actual pain at this sudden, sharp crack, which
paralyzes the brain, rends the thread of reflection,
and murders thought.[19]

Motorcycles are our present problem. There is one motorcycle
or motorscooter for every 12 persons in our city . . . . In
Cordoba, we have studied some of the psychological aspects of
noise offences. Why, for example, do drivers, and especially
motorcyclists, remove or modify the mufflers on their vehicles?
Is it because a personality defect makes them enjoy excessive
noise? Or does the noisy urban environment give them a
kind of "thirst for noise"?[20]

There is something even more disgraceful than what I have just
mentioned. Often enough you may see a carter walking along
a street, quite alone, without any horses, and still cracking
away incessantly; so accustomed has the wretch become to it
in consequence of the unwarrantable toleration of this practice.[21]

In 1964 we set up Argentina's first Noise Abatement Council. . . .
Firstly, our new anti-noise municipal regulation distinguishes
between "unnecessary" and "excessive" noise. It classifies over
15 unnecessary noises which can be penalized without recourse
to noise level measurement or analysis.

Since the application of the anti-noise law we have
classified as unnecessary noises all public address systems that
can be heard outside enclosed premises, including music,
publicity, and speeches.[22]

Ling Electronics of California makes a noise generator whose
gigantic howl, loud enough to tear electronic equipment apart,
is used to test the toughness of space-flight hardware.[23]
How many great and splendid thoughts, I should like to know,
have been lost to the world by the crack of a whip? If I had
the upper hand, I should soon produce in the heads of these

people an indissoluble association of ideas between cracking a whip and getting a whipping.[24]

The growth of motor transport in the past 20 years has led many countries to revise their traffic codes—sometimes in the face of public opinion. The decision to forbid the use of motor horns in Paris was one such controversial move, and motorists in particular predicted that street accidents would increase. In practice the measure was remarkably successful. With a show of self-restraint that surprised the Parisians themselves the honking and blaring of horns was stilled from one day to the next. Paris now wonders how it ever managed to endure such a futile and nerve-racking din.[25]

With all due respect for the most holy doctrine of utility, I really cannot see why a fellow who is taking away a wagon-load of gravel or dung should thereby obtain the right to kill in the bud the thoughts which may happen to be springing up in ten thousand heads—the number he will disturb one after another in half an hour's drive through the town.[26]

Another of our findings is that well-educated people (scientists, scholars, artists and members of the liberal profession) are far more susceptible to the noise of traffic than relatively uneducated people.[27]

In August 1956 the use of motor horns was made illegal in Moscow and the noise level in the streets immediately dropped by eight to ten phons.[28]

France forbids the playing of transistor radios on rail, bus, and metro transport as well as in streets and public places such as parks and beaches. Nor is their use tolerated in restaurants and similar establishments.[29]

A New York skyscraper completed last year proved that buildings can be constructed quietly. People working in offices near the new 52 storey building reported that power lawn mowers buzzing around their suburban homes were more disturbing than the construction job. Blasting was muffled by special steel mesh blankets weighing several tons each. Spread over the blast site by cranes, they absorbed most of the sounds of the explosions, and also kept flying debris safely within a confined area. All the joints on the 14,000 tons of steel in the frame were welded silently to eliminate the hideous, shattering racket of conventional riveting or bolting.[30]

The aim of technical development should be to serve man, to make his life more agreeable and enrich it. So logically, technical progress should lead to less noise, not more.[31]

Still, superscreams are now being generated in military labs. Robert Gilchrist, president of Federal Sign and Signal tells us of tantalizing rumors that have circulated in the noisemaking business over the past few years. "We just heard about a siren of some kind, supposedly intended for Vietnam," he says. "It's said to produce something like 200 decibels." That would be several hundred times as powerful as Professor Rudnick's monstrous screamer.[32]

A sudden, very loud noise, such as gunfire, lasting only fractions of a second, may damage a person's hearing mechanism and produce a lasting loss of hearing or partial deafness. But exposure to noise levels quite common in industry—and indeed characteristic of certain branches of heavy industry such as forging and metal cutting—leads, progressively to "perceptive deafness," depending in each case on the intensity of the noise and duration of exposure. Once a hearing defect of this kind has set in, nothing can be done. Protective devices can help to postpone it and to slow down its development, but once the damage is done, it is irreparable.[33]

In the U.S.A. it is estimated that approximately 1,000,000 workers have serious hearing loss due to high noise levels in their places of work.[34]

Dear Students:
It is time to get acquainted with a new subject: Forensic Acoustics, the study of the growing number of noise-nuisance and ear-damage cases taken to court. Your old teacher hopes that you may also be interested in learning about the work of your local noise abatement society, or, if your community does not yet possess one, that you might yourselves form such a society. Address of the international Society Against Noise: Sihlstrasse 17, Zurich, Switzerland.

THREE THRESHOLDS OF THE AUDIBLE AND ONE OF THE BEARABLE

One day we spoke of clavichords. Clavichords make such tiny dulcet sounds that you can scarcely hear them. Heads cocked over the strings we listened to its tremulous vibrato.

BARBARA: Ssh.

No one dared breathe as out of the eggshell box a tiny musical message was whispered to us.

DOUG: And you say Bach actually preferred this to the organ and the piano?

SCHAFER: He did.

DOUG: Why?

SCHAFER: It was more subtle and he was a sensitive man.

DOUG: But it is so soft you have to listen so hard.

SCHAFER: Yes.

DOUG: Perhaps they had more acute hearing in Bach's days.

SCHAFER: Perhaps. They did seem to be more satisfied with soft and moderately loud sounds. One of the interesting things we discover from history is that music keeps getting louder. All of the famous old violins by Stradivarius and other craftsmen were strengthened during the 19th century so that they could produce stronger sounds. The piano replaced the harpsichord and the clavichord largely because it produced stronger sounds. Today, as the electric guitar and the contact microphone demonstrate, we are no longer content with natural sound at all, but want to boost it up to "bigger than life" size. Amplifiers are now available of sufficient strength to push sounds right past the threshold of pain.

BARBARA: What's that?

SCHAFER: That's when the sound pressure becomes so strong on the ear drums that it gives you physical pain or may even make your ears bleed. Ultimately you grow deaf.

Everyone looked a bit puzzled and scared. The amplifier as a lethal weapon through which music could conceivably destroy the human organism instead of bringing pleasure to it? But with the memory of our recent dance band still causing the adrenalin in my ears to bubble, I realized how close we were in fact coming to the pain threshold of bearable sound, which is around 120 decibels.

There has always been a certain malevolent streak among composers to "shock" the audience, a certain tendency toward pugilism bordering at times on brutality which is evident in composers as diverse as Beethoven, Berlioz, Stravinsky, and Stockhausen. I recalled that the critic Susan Sontag, speaking of the theatre of Happenings, noted that its most striking feature was its abusive treatment of the audience. During the Middle Ages the Pied Piper of Hamlin lured his victims off to their destruction by the irresistibly sweet tones of his flute. Today's sadist with his amplifier can kill his victims on the spot.

My class reacted suspiciously to my remarks. I *was* getting carried away. But I did not think (and as I write this, still do not think) that my pessimism and fear were unjustifiable. That extremely loud noises seem to glut the brain's sensation-receiving capacity making it impossible for the human being to function, is known by police departments which now use sirens to bring riots to a standstill. Deafness, of the kind found in the iron foundry, may indeed soon cease to be merely an occupational disease. At any rate, a society which experiments with sounds of humanly destructive intensities in the military lab cannot seriously expect the nastier of its private citizens not to participate in these vengeful amusements in whatever ways are at hand.

There is one threshold of the bearable and there are three of the audible. We can have sounds so soft they cannot be heard by the human ear. For instance, if we strike a tuning fork and listen, the sound soon seems to die away although we can see the fork vibrating; and if we amplify it by placing the fork on a table top we can hear it again, proving that it was still generating sound all along even though the sound was, before the resonance given it by the table, below the threshold of audibility for the human ear.

We also have sounds so high or so low that they cannot be heard.

At about 16 cycles per second we cease to hear low sounds and begin to feel them as massive vibrations which may shake the room. At 20,000 cycles per second or less, high sounds disappear as they pass out of the human hearing range. These things can be demonstrated with an oscillator, and young people are always a little proud when they discover that they can hear sounds somewhat higher than old people—a purely physiological fact resulting from youth. Many animals can out-hear people, of course, both in their sensitivity to very soft sounds and in their ability to hear higher frequencies. The cat, for instance, can hear sounds as high as 60,000 cycles.

We can draw a chart showing the perimeter of the humanly audible. The orinate shows the intensity of the sound in decibels with 0 db fixed at the threshold of audibility; while the abscissa shows the frequency range.

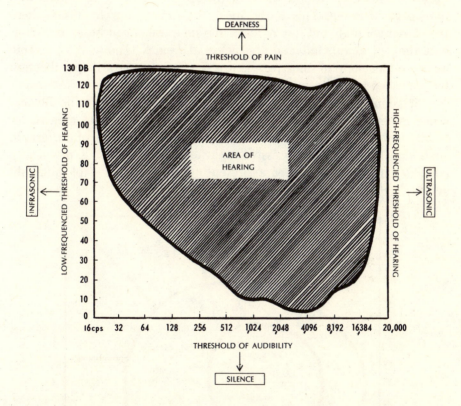

History shows that music is constantly getting louder. In reaction it has been getting softer too. Anton Webern wrote dimutive pieces in which there are sounds bordering on the threshold of audibility, (they are so soft). And you can speculate on how soft Morton Feldman intends the sound to be when he instructs a percussion player to play chimes and vibraphone with the fleshly part of his fingertips.

The same thing has happened to the pitch range of music. It has been pushed out gradually to the limits of perceptibility. Up to the Renaissance vocal music predominated and since the human singing voice from bass to soprano (excluding harmonics) extends roughly across the frequency range from 100 cycles to 1,000 cycles, most music was confined to this central frequency register. As instruments were invented which were more versatile in performance this range was extended greatly. We now have electronic sounds which take us right to the audible limits in both directions, or as close to them as our recording and reproduction equipment permits us to go.

It is easy to see that those instruments we call warm or lyrical (the cello, the viola, the horn, the clarinet) are precisely those which most closely approximate the range of the human voice. But if a composer wishes to suggest a sublime or superhuman event or sensation he or she makes considerable use of those instruments which lie far outside the human vocal range. This is the most evident in church music where the extremely high and low notes of the pipe organ can be used to suggest the voices of God and the celestial beings. Today if electronic music sounds eerie to some people it is partly because of its predilection for "transcendental" extremities in the frequency range.

Speaking approximately, we may say that while up to the Renaissance, or even up to the 18th century, music occupied an area in intensity and frequency range such as that shown in the core of our graph, since that time it has progressively pushed out so that it is practically coincidental with the shape representing the total area of humanly audible sound!

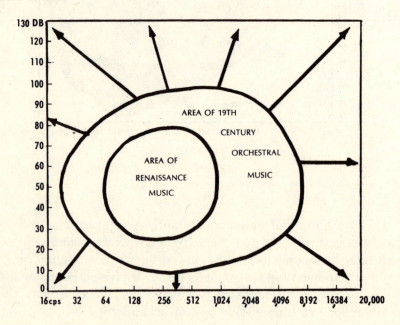

The composer can now journey anywhere throughout the sound-scape of the audible.

We tried to sense this by following various pieces of recorded music through this graph of expressive potentials with the tip of our pencils, registering all the fluctuations in pitch and dynamics. Then by drawing an enlarged version of the graph on the board and using a number of different sound-producers we tried to follow a moving pointer in order to reproduce these sensations at least in a general way.*

By jumping the pointer from one extreme position to another on our chart (say, loud and high to very soft and low) we led ourselves into the whole matter of *contrast*.

Any theory of music will sooner or later develop a sweeping series of studies dealing with contrast. Traditional tonal music had many kinds of contrast, of which that produced by the flickering alternation (I nearly wrote altercation) between consonance and dissonance inspired the most theorizing.

Every dissonance demanded its resolution in a consonance. Every consonance demanded a dissonance to disturb its boring life. The two were intimate enemies.

In the early days of atonal music it was thought that dissonance had murdered consonance and had imposed itself as the absolute despot of music. We realize now that this was an illusion and that sounds are only relatively consonant or dissonant depending on their context.

Dissonance is tension and consonance is relaxation. Just as the

---

* At the moment, of course, this is a horribly inexact exercise, for none of us have much feeling for pitch recognition based on the frequency scale or loudness recognition based on the decibel or phon scale. This would have to be learned. The new theory of music will have to develop some descriptive method of identifying and measuring perceived sound and it would seem natural that one conforming to the scientific measurement of sound would be the most appropriate, for it would give us the necessary flexibility for describing our perceptions of all sounds, which the traditional vocabulary of music theory does not do. After all, there is nothing sacred about a few Italian intuitions on the subject of dynamics or a handful of alphabetical symbols to designate pitch.

To have perfect pitch would then be to have perfect frequency, i.e. to know the difference between 440 and 466 cps. Sound clusters could be learned by their approximate band widths.

Frequency might also give us the clue to measuring tempo and rhythm, for frequency tells us the number of cycles per second. If the second were adopted as the basic temporal module in the new *solfège*, we could quickly speak of rhythmic octaves (doubling the speed), and the ratios between would give us all the rhythmic nuancing necessary.

The advantages of working out a solfège along the lines I am suggesting would be that all sounds could thereby be described and these descriptions could be checked quickly and accurately with electronic test equipment.

human musculature tenses and relaxes alternately, you cannot have the one activity without the other. Thus, neither term has absolute meaning; each defines the other. Anyone who does not realize this should try clenching his fist tightly for the rest of his life.

Consonance and dissonance are like two elastics, one stretched more tightly than the other. Their relativity is clarified by the addition of a third elastic, stretched more tightly than the first two. Now describe the role of the middle elastic vis-à-vis each of its neighbors.

No matter what happens to music the words consonance and dissonance will still be central to our theoretical vocabularly and they will apply to any set of opposites, not just tonal contrasts. A short sound, for instance, is dissonant by comparison to a sustained one. If you want some neutral words try Yin and Yang but you will always need some vocabulary to describe and measure contrast, for that is inevitable. But if we stick with the words consonance and dissonance we must expand the strictly limited meanings they had when applied to tonal music only. For instance, a single example:

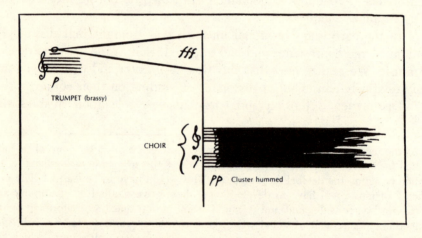

Quite contrary to what the traditional theorist would say, this single brazen trumpet sound with its asymmetrical harmonics is a dissonant event which finds its resolution in the soft velvet of the vocal tone cluster. Try it and you will hear this immediately. If you analyze some recent music in terms of its dissonances and consonances, tensions and relaxations, your instinct will show how desperately the textbooks need revision.

Thus, to conclude, we can make three important observations:

1. The concept of the threshold now becomes important for musicians because it divides in a very real sense the audibly possible from the audibly impossible.

2. We need to develop a new means for describing the sounds we perceive . . . I suggest this might be in line with the acoustic measuring standards of electronic instruments, which we could use to check our subjective sensations.

3. Any sound complex can be analyzed in terms of its relative consonance and dissonance within its acoustic neighborhood. Consonance and dissonance refer to variations in intensity, pitch, duration or tone color anywhere within the perimeters of the audibly possible.

The class was pensive. I began to feel like a theory teacher.

BEYOND THE AUDIBLE

DONNA: What about the audibly impossible? We saw what happened if you went beyond the pain threshold. What about the other directions?

SCHAFER: OK, we need an interlude, so let's indulge in some wild speculations. If you go very low, below about 16 cycles you no longer have a sensation of pitch but rather of vibratory tremblings. We call this the infrasonic range, as distinct from the range above about 20,000 cycles which we call the ultrasonic. You know the experience when a very deep pedal note on the organ gets the whole church vibrating. You could possibly imagine a kind of massage-music resulting from these very deep frequencies, for this is the area where the sense of hearing and the sense of touch overlap. I've known some young composers who became interested in this land of musical massage and they claim to have composed pieces using only these deep frequences.

DONNA: What are they like?

SCHAFER: I've never felt them.

DOUG: It must be something like the 'feelies' that Aldous Huxley talks about in *Brave New World*.

SCHAFER: Certainly various parts of the body resonate at various frequencies, some in the audible range and some below or above.
For instance, it has been discovered that the average human anal sphincter resonates at about 77 cycles. If it resonates hard enough it can no longer be controlled. Police have experimented in the control of mobs by employing very loud sounds of this frequency. An intriguing use of infrasonic waves forms the basis of a piece of music by the American composer Alvin Lucier. This uses the alpha waves of the brain as its sound-generating source. Alpha waves occur when one closes one's eyes and indulges in non-visualizing thought. A low-voltage brain-wave current, the alpha-wave signal is about 10 cycles. In Lucier's piece the performer has electrodes implanted on the skull to pick up these waves. You may imagine how theatrical the performance preparations could be! The waves are then amplified and fed to a number of loud-

speakers before which are placed some musical instruments such as gongs which resonate sympathetically with these very low signals.

DOUG: Now that's a piece I'd really like to hear!

SCHAFER: What you really hear are the harmonics of the gongs. You can't hear the alpha waves themselves; they are too low. Perhaps, as I just mentioned, the most interesting aspect of the performance would be the fascinating spectacle of a solo performer sitting on the stage with electrodes on his or her skull, closing and opening his or her eyes to start and stop the sounds, for alpha waves are only present when the eyes are closed—and sometimes not even then, to the misfortune of some attempts to perform the piece.

DONNA: What about high-frequency sounds, beyond 20,000 cycles?

SCHAFER: You remember we mentioned that cats could hear sounds up to 60,000 cycles, which gives them quite an edge on us. It may seem a little bizarre, but it's conceivable that compositions could be created in these upper frequency bands and performed on electronic generators exclusively for the appreciation of cats and their friends. Using electronic instruments you could easily write a symphony for cats that would be completely inaudible for us, and I suppose some day someone will have the bright inspiration of doing just that, though the indifferent cats will probably not make very good patrons of such music. Many animals can hear much higher sounds than we can.

Barbara, perhaps for tomorrow you could try to find out something about the hearing ranges of some of these animals and insects. Jeff, you and Donna see what you can find out about music under the microscope. I was talking to Dr. E. J. Wells in the chemistry department about this the other day. I think he may have something interesting to tell you in connection with his recent research. Then maybe Doug could find out something about the Music of the Spheres . . . .

DOUG: The what?

SCHAFER: The music of the Spheres. Have a look in some music history books. Then try some books on astronomy.

DOUG: Sounds wild!

SCHAFER: It is a bit. See you tomorrow.

Tomorrow. All were present, shuffling their notes, clearing their throats, anxious to begin.

SCHAFER: Barbara?

BARBARA: One of the most interesting kinds of hearing ability in the—
what did you call it?—the ultrasonic range is that of the bat. Bats
use ultrasonic echoes .at about 50,000 cycles to fly around obstacles without crack-ups. They bounce cries off obstacles and
thus are warned to beware of them. They do this at an amazing
rate of 50 echoing ultrasonic cries per second.

I also found something about the hearing of grasshoppers. Some
of them have little circular membranes like ears on their forelegs.
The females are courted by the males who chirp or sing to them.
If a male chirps into a telephone, a female at the other end can
be made to jump up and down even without seeing him. Sex
appeal among the grasshoppers definitely seems to have to do
with hearing rather than seeing.

SCHAFER: Charles Darwin thought that even our music was nothing but a highly developed form of the mating call.

DONNA: There are a lot of love songs in all music.

SCHAFER: Jeff, what did you find out from Dr. Wells?

JEFF: We listened to nuclear music in his laboratory.

SCHAFER: You tantalize us. What does it sound like?

DONNA: It makes little pinging sounds, very clear little pings, sharp at first then dying away. I've never heard anything quite like it before.

SCHAFER: Did Dr. Wells explain to you how he was producing it?

JEFF: Yes he did, and then he wrote out a little account. Perhaps I could read it. It's called Nuclear Music.

All matter is composed of molecules. Molecules are built from atoms. An atom consists of a very small nucleus carrying a positive charge, and a much larger charge cloud built of electrons, so that the total atom is electrically neutral. The atoms in a molecule are held together by chemical bonds, which are nothing more than directional electron clouds. Thus a molecule resembles a plum pudding—the nuclear plums are immersed in an electron cloud dough.

Now some nuclei spin on their own axis like tops. Those that do (the nuclei of the atoms of hydrogen, fluorine and phosphorus are examples) then behave like tiny magnets. As such they can be lined up in a large magnetic field, just as a small compass needle is aligned in the magnetic field of the earth. However, the alignment of the axis of spin of a single nucleus with the magnetic field is not perfect. It turns out that for a single spinning nucleus, the axis of spin rotates about the field direction with a frequency proportional to the field strength. The motion is called *precession* and the frequency is the *precessional frequency*. For a given field strength, this frequency is a natural, well-defined nuclear frequency.

Now in a good strong laboratory magnet different kinds of nuclei precess in different frequency regions scattered through the radio-frequency spectrum. In an electromagnet with a field strength of 14,000 gauss the nuclei of hydrogen precess at about 60 million cycles per second, those of fluorine at about 56 million cycles, and those of phosphorus at about 24 million cycles. Moreover, the characteristic frequency of a single kind of nucleus is modified slightly by two subtle types of interaction with the surrounding electron cloud. It is found that the nuclear frequency depends slightly on the density of the electron cloud surrounding the nucleus, i.e. on the thickness of the dough around each plum in our pudding model. This effect is of interest to chemists since all chemistry is due to the electron dough. Then if a molecule contains several nuclei of the same type, but in different architectural positions within the molecule, these will have precessional frequency characteristics of their position, and the molecule has a characteristic fingerprint *nuclear magnetic frequency spectrum.*

If you want to hear a guitar you pluck the string. When it is plucked it is removed briefly from its undisturbed position of equilibrium. In doing so it emits its own characteristic note or frequency, which depends on the string tension, and the loudness of the note is damped, or decays in time, due to the frictional losses from the vibrating string to the surrounding air.

Returning to our molecules, the nuclei acting in concert also can be 'plucked' away from their low energy orientation along the magnetic field by a short pulse of radio-frequency with frequency close to the natural nuclear frequency. From this high energy state the nuclei return to equilibrium and in doing so they emit their own damped characteristic precession frequency as a radio signal. The damping process here is quite different from that of the guitar string, but the result is quite similar. By standard radio-frequency techniques it is possible to heterodyne out the high radio-frequency carrier signal, and to make audible the small frequency differences between the various nuclei in our sample.

In general the more complicated the molecule the more complicated is the nuclear frequency spectrum, and hence the more complex and more audibly interesting the modulated envelope of the time spectrum. This modulation envelope is a pure molecular property, and in a very real sense the method which produces 'nuclear music' provides a new vehicle for impressing a unique characteristic of a molecule on the ear. And since understanding comes from the complete human interaction, any method which increases the number of senses that can be brought to bear can give new illumination.

DONNA: What does "heterodyne" mean? I got lost in Dr. Wells' notes somewhere around there.

SCHAFER: It refers to a practice of combining frequencies in the radio-frequency range in such a way as to produce beats whose frequencies are the sum and difference of the original frequencies. In the audio range this phenomenon is also well known, producing what are called *difference* and *summation* tones. It would take us well off course to go into the mathematics of this, but a good book on acoustics will explain it to you. It's enough to understand that the difference tone between two frequencies of, say, 1,000 cycles and 100 cycles would be 900 cycles, and the summation tone would be 1,100 cycles. Many difference tones can be heard quite easily with the naked ear; summation tones are usually rather more obscure.

Remember that the precessional frequencies of Dr. Wells' molecular nuclei are in the radio-frequency range; they oscillate at a speed of millions of cycles per second. He has made them audible by plucking them with another radio pulse of almost, but not exactly, the same frequency, thus producing a difference tone in the audio range. He has found it useful to store these sounds on recorded tapes for later analysis.

We might have thought that the world under the microscope would be a silent one, but even here we find that we can, with the aid of electronic equipment, discover sounds.

So much, then, for the microcosmic world of molecules. What about the macrocosmic world of stars and planets? Doug, what did you discover about the Music of the Spheres?

THE MUSIC OF
THE SPHERES

DOUG: The Music of the Spheres is a very ancient theory; it goes back at least to the Greeks, particularly to the school of Pythagoras. It was thought that each of the planets and stars made music as it travelled through the heavens. Pythagoras, who had worked out the ratios between the various harmonics of a sounding string, found that there was a perfect mathematical correspondence between them, and as he was also interested in the heavens and noted that they too moved in an orderly way, he conjectured that the two things were merely aspects of the same perfect mathematical law which governed the universe. If this was the case then obviously the planets and stars must make perfect musical sounds as they moved just as the vibrating string gave off perfect harmonics.

BARBARA: Did he ever hear the Music of the Spheres?

DOUG: He is supposed to have heard it, according to his disciples. But no one else ever heard it.

BARBARA: But I don't understand how the stars made music.

SCHAFER: You've all seen children's tops so you know that when you spin them they give off a certain tone. If you spin them harder what happens?

BARBARA: The pitch rises.

SCHAFER: And if I had a large top and a small top and spun them both at the same speed what would be the difference?

BARBARA: The large one would produce a lower sound.

SCHAFER: Then you should be able to determine the sound any spinning body sends out if you know its volume and the speed at which it is revolving. And as the heavens consist of millions of planets and stars, all different sizes and spinning at different rates, you can see how the Ancients thought there must be a whole symphony of such sounds. If you had enough planets spinning around on themselves and in different orbits so that from wherever you

130

listened they would constantly be changing their speed and distance from you, you would have a celestial harmony in stereo that was forever changing.

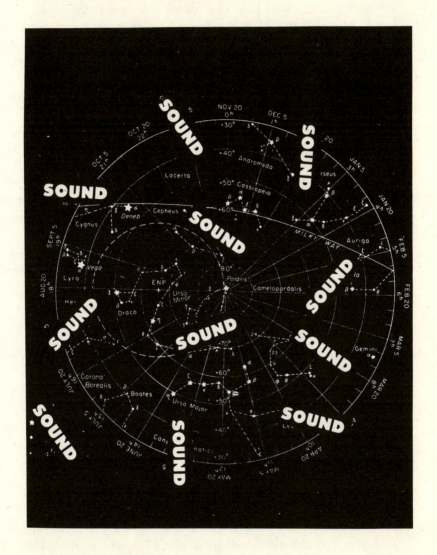

BARBARA: But I don't hear it. How can we hear it?

DOUG: Ssh! Listen!

(Long pause)

BARBARA: You're just fooling. I don't hear anything.

DOUG: Well, apparently you're not supposed to be able to hear anything. I don't know exactly why. But almost everyone in ancient times seems to have believed there was a Music of the Spheres. I was reading about this in a medieval writer, Boethius, who lived from 480 to 524 A.D. He said there were three kinds of music: vocal music, instrumental music, and Music of the Spheres. Here is what he said about the Music of the Spheres:

How indeed could the swift mechanism of the sky move silently in its course. And although this sound does not reach our ears, as must for many reasons be the case . . .

. . . though he doesn't give his reasons.

. . . The extremely rapid motion of such great bodies could not be altogether without sound, especially since the courses of the stars are joined together by such a natural adaptation that nothing more equally compacted or united could be imagined. For some are borne higher and others lower, and all are revolved with just impulse, and from their different inequalities and established order of modulation cannot be lacking in this celestial motion.[35]

I also came across a reference to it in Shakespeare's *Merchant of Venice:*

Look how the floor of heaven
Is thick inlaid with patines of bright gold;
There's not the smallest which thou behold'st
But in his motion like an angel sings . . .
Such harmony is in immortal souls;
But, whilst this muddy vesture of decay
Doth grossly close it in, we cannot hear it.[36]

SCHAFER: The astronomer Kepler was a contemporary of Shakespeare. Did you find any reference to Kepler's interest in the Music of the Spheres? He was infatuated with it.

DOUG: That's the best part. I was saving it. Kepler tried to compute the various sounds given off by the different planets depending on their rate of velocity and their mass—just like the tops. He actually came up with some tones for each of the planets. Here they are: [37]

132

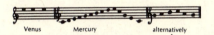

Everyone was anxious to hear these sounds, so we played them on the piano.

BARBARA: Is that all that Kepler heard? It's very disappointing.

SCHAFER: I don't think he actually heard it. He merely computed it mathematically and conjectured that if you could hear the planets they might sound like that.

BARBARA: But didn't anyone hear them? Why can't you hear . . . .

JEFF: Because there is no air in outer space and sound waves need air in which to travel.

SCHAFER: What would music sound like on the moon?

JEFF: It wouldn't.

SCHAFER: Because there is no atmosphere there. Sound waves need a physical medium in which to move. You must have done the experiment in high school physics where you put a tuning fork in a jar and then pumped out all the air. You can't hear the tuning any more.

But I've often wondered whether there isn't another reason too. Let me try to explain without getting too technical.

If we want to speak of the most elementary sound possible we will have to consider what is called the sine wave. The mathematician Schillinger has described this eloquently: 'One sine wave is the limit of simplicity in action.' The sine wave is the wave formed by a pure tone without any harmonics. It is the sound of the tuning fork and looks like this on an oscilloscope:

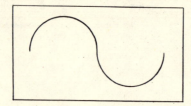

According to the French mathematician Fourier, any periodic sound, no matter how complex, is capable of being resolved into a number of these absolutely elementary sine waves; and the process of this investigation is called harmonic analysis. But Fourier also stated that the perfectly pure (mathematically defined) sine wave exists as a theoretical concept only. Because the moment you switch on the generator or strike the tuning fork you create little distortions called *onset transient distortions*. That is to say, the sound first has to overcome its own inertia to be set in motion, and in doing this little imperfections creep into it. The same thing is true of our ears. For the ear drum to begin vibrating it too has first to overcome its own inertia, and accordingly it too introduces more transient distortions.

BARBARA: Couldn't you get rid of them by starting the sound a long time ahead?

SCHAFER: Well, we're speaking purely speculatively today. The question is, how far ahead? In order to get rid of onset transient distortion completely you'd have to start the sound before you were born. The universe started before any of us were born. Maybe there are mathematically perfect sounds in the universe which have always been sounding. And if so, perhaps we could never hear them just because they are so perfect. All the sounds we hear are imperfect; that is to say, they start and they stop. And so they have tiny transient distortions in them. Is it not possible that there might indeed be some kind of Harmony of the Spheres which we can't hear because we are imperfect beings?

DOUG: That's just what the medieval writers thought.

SCHAFER: We have for a long time dismissed this as a foolish thought. But sometimes it seems people have mysteriously intuited an idea without knowing exactly why it should be valid, and only later has it been rehabilitated and validated by science. What I'm saying is merely what these ancient scholars believed, that a perfect sound would be perceived by us as silence!

There was a moment of quiet as that crazy idea sank in.

SCHAFER: If something is with you all your lives you take it for granted because you can't get outside to measure it. For instance, we've all been breathing air since birth, but what is the smell of air? It seems perfectly natural and odorless to us because we can't get away from it. All we can smell is the impurities in it. Well, perhaps it's somewhat the same with the Music of the Spheres. It is perfect and our music is just an imperfect human attempt to recreate it.

DONNA: It sounds religious.

SCHAFER: Is that bad?

JEFF: But there have been unidentified sounds picked up from outer space, haven't there?

SCHAFER: Tell us about them.

JEFF: I don't really know except I've heard people mention that mysterious radio signals have been picked up from outer space.

SCHAFER: There's an observatory in town. Why not phone up an astronomer and ask him about it?

Jeff did this and fifteen minutes later he was ready to report back.

JEFF: Astronomers have picked up signals from outer space but they are electromagnetic radiations, not sound waves. Electromagnetic radiations do not require a medium for their propagation and thus can pass across the vacuum of space. They are of much higher frequency than the sound waves you have been talking about, impossible for the human ear to hear. But they are still the longest of an entire range of radiations progressing through microwaves, radiant heat waves, infra-red, visible light, and ultra-violet waves, then to the X-ray spectra and finally to cosmic waves which are the shortest and highest frequency yet known to exist. All these waves move with the speed of light and are about 100,000 times faster than sound waves.

In 1955 the first radio waves were heard from Jupiter and those were the first heard from any planet in our solar system. They seemed to be organized but according to astronomers this does not mean that they were transmitted by outer space creatures. In fact, they are believed to have been caused by disturbances in the atmosphere of Jupiter similar to our thunderstorms. They sounded just like bursts of static on the radio.

SCHAFER: We certainly covered a lot of ground in our fanciful quest for music under the microscope and beyond the telescope. Are there any questions before we break up?

BARBARA: How does the radio work? I mean, I've always wondered how it's possible to have someone talking in one place and being heard in another without wires.

The rest of our session that day and the next consisted of an enquiry into how the radio worked. When we got confused we invited a radio technician to the class to straighten us out. It wasn't music, but it was fascinating.

SCHIZOPHONIA

We left the radio on. The voice of a disc jockey puffed along:

> Hey men, the Big Boss with the hot sauce's gotta secret!
> It's the Stevie Pinkus giveaway time (*blip-bloop-bleep*).
> Yessir, Big Stevie's giving away free, free prizes again!
> Hold on men, we might be calling youhoo (*fanfare*).

SCHAFER: Schizophonic.

GROUP: Schizo-what?

SCHAFER: Schizophonic. It's a word I invented. You know that *phono* pertains to sound. The Greek prefix *schizo* means split or separated. I was thinking of Barbara's wonder at how a voice or music could originate one place and be heard in a completely different place miles away.

> ... And now for all the buddies on the buddy-line here's
> the number one song in the nation at 4:10 p.m. "Wah
> Wah Wah"....

SCHAFER: Mind if I turn it off? (They did but I turned it off anyway.) The radio and the telephone have not always existed, of course, and before they did this miracle of the instantaneous transmission of sound from one place to another was quite unknown. Your voice only travelled as far as you could shout. Sounds were tied indissolubly to the mechanisms that produced them. In those days every sound was an original, repeated only in its immediate vicinity.

Now all that has changed. Since the invention of electronic equipment for the transmission and storage of sound, any natural sound, no matter how tiny, can be blown up and shot around the world, or packaged on tape or record for the generations of the future. We have split the sound from the makers of the sound. This dissociation I call schizophonia, and if I use a word close in sound to schizophrenia it is because I want very much to suggest to you the same sense of aberration and drama that this word evokes, for the developments of which we are speaking have had profound effects on our lives.

Let me suggest some of the drama of schizophonia by telling you a story which is supposed to be true. But even if it is apocryphal it won't matter.

You have all heard about Dracula, the vampire. This is supposed to be the origin of that legend:

At the end of the nineteenth century a Rumanian count went to Paris and fell madly in love with a young opera singer there. The young lady was quite famous and had made some recordings of operatic arias. But to the count's great grief she died quite suddenly and he despondently returned to his castle in the Carpathian mountains with a few recordings of her remarkable voice as his only souvenir. He had a statue of the lady sculpted in white marble and placed beside the fireplace of his drawing room, where in solitude each evening he played the recordings. The count had many peasants on his estate. These peasants, who, of course, had never heard a record player, peered into the windows on hearing a woman's voice, but saw only the count alone before the shadowy statue, and they were terrified. The count immediately became known as Dracula—*dracul* in Rumanian means "devil." All the other evil associated with the name springs from this simple misunderstanding.

You musn't imagine Dracula with a hi-fi set. He probably had very poor quality cylinder recordings, for although the phonograph was invented in 1877, just a year after the telephone, it took many decades before its quality had improved and the records sounded anything like natural. Radio is even more recent. It dates from the invention of the triode amplifier tube in 1906, and it also took many years before it was in everyday use and you could listen to it without earphones and without making complicated adjustments. In spite of that, some people soon realized its possibilities: the first public amplification of a political speech occurred in 1919, undoubtedly to the great satisfaction of politicians everywhere, whose plangent voices could now reach limitless numbers of voters.

Modern life has been ventriloquized.

Through broadcasting and recording the binding relationship between a sound and the person making it has been dissolved. Sounds have been torn from their natural sockets and given an amplified and independent existence. Vocal sound, for instance, is no longer tied to a hole in the head but it is free to issue from anywhere in the landscape. Now we can tune in on sounds originating from all over the world in our homes, in our cars, in the streets, in our public buildings, anywhere and everywhere. And as the cry broadcasts distress, the loudspeaker communicates anxiety.

To catch and preserve the tissue of living sound is an ancient ambition of man. In Babylonian mythology there are hints of a specially constructed room in one of the *ziggurats* where whispers stayed forever. In an ancient Chinese legend a king has a secret black box into which he speaks his orders, then sends them around his kingdom for his subjects to carry out, which I gloss to mean that there is authority in the magic of the captured sound.

BARBARA: Writing is also a kind of captured sound. In ancient times only priests and monarchs knew its secret.

JEFF: And precisely because of this they managed to hold their power.

SCHAFER: Perhaps something similar has happened in music. As musical notation became more and more precise the composer became more and more powerful. The composer of the early part of the 20th century tended to regard even the performers as push-button automata; everything was specified exactly in the score. The pages of such scores are black with editorializing.

Today we have the means for achieving even greater precision: recording. So important is the recording of music that it has come to replace the manuscript as the authentic musical utterance. Igor Stravinsky recognized this when he decided a few years ago to record all his music as a documentary guide to future conductors.

But no recording is an exact reproduction of living sound. Distortions are introduced in both its production and its playback. Even on the simplest home equipment there are devices for influencing the sound. By twisting the volume control knob the diminutive sound of the clavichord can be made to bulk up to the dimensions of a full orchestra; or an orchestra may be reduced to the whisper of the grass. Most hi-fi setups also have filters for reducing or boosting bass or treble frequencies. In these ways selectivity is introduced into the act of music listening and the listener is able to influence and control matters which in the past conformed to natural laws and were quite beyond his control.

What makes such a development spectacular is this: it is more natural for us today to listen to electrically reproduced music than to listen to live music, which begins to sound unnatural.

With tape recorders many other kinds of sound manipulations are possible which may lead to unrecognizable transformation and distortion of original sounds. Cutting and splicing tape, varying speed and frequency range, reversing sounds, and so forth; these are the techniques and they can be performed on most tape recorders.

We spent about an hour experimenting with sound in this way trying to discover the creative possibilities of the tape recorder.

First we had someone record an extended "sh" very close to the microphone with the speed of the machine at its highest setting. Playing it back at its lowest speed we discovered we had produced the sound of an enormous steam engine. Then we recorded someone biting into an apple at the same high speed and discoverd at a slower speed we had a perfect imitation of a large tree falling in a reverberant forest.

Recording the middle and lower notes of a piano in such a way that the volume control was turned up only after the note had been struck, we were surprised at the organlike or clarinetlike tones we had on tape.

Reversed sounds gave the group other surprises. On the whole they did not like them. A reversed sound has no natural reverberation; it expands backwards to burst in an echoless explosion. Without reverberation such sounds resemble those heard in an anechoic chamber, sounds which drop lifelessly to the floor. I have concluded the reason human beings find such sounds disconcerting is that they imply a world without air.

Have you ever heard your voice recorded and played back to you? Try it. It's surprising and educating. You can get outside yourself and critically inspect your voiceprint. Is that stammering and quirky sound really me, you say? You are a little more conscious of the way you speak afterwards.

Through recording we can freeze sounds for study. Great progress has been made in the analysis and synthesis of sound since the invention of recording. Before this, pursuing sound was like trailing the wind.

At this point I put on a sound-effects record and asked the group to describe what they heard.

BARBARA: Several knocks.

DONNA: Knocking.

JEFF: About a dozen knocks on a wooden door.

DOUG: Ten knocks on a heavy door.

If, as in the past, there was no way of repeating that sound we would have to be satisfied with these descriptions, but today—listen again.

Listening again we agreed that the sound consisted of six light, rapid knocks on a solid wooden door, followed by a short pause, then three louder knocks. The ability to repeat the same sound pattern not only helps us to study more accurately, but also to study our own process of pattern perception.

Throughout our discussion one factor had been consistent: the cutting free of sound from its natural origins; and it is this which I called schizophonia.

DOUG: Are you worried about it?

SCHAFER: We are living with it, aren't we? Perhaps it will only be possible to come back at a later date and determine whether it did us good or ill. But one matter does concern me. I wonder if I can explain it. Throughout previous life there has always been a correspondence between the physiological activity of producing sound and the psychological qualities we attribute to it. There is a big energy output in a loud sound, a tensing in a high sound, a relaxing in a low sound and so forth. This is true whether you use your vocal chords or a musical instrument. I would say this has helped us to feel into the depths of sounds with our muscles and nerves. And since we produce these sounds with our bodies we have an instinctive sympathetic feeling when others produce them for our benefit and pleasure.

Today there is no relationship really between turning the volume dial on your radio up or down and the state of affairs that results. Electronic music is composed almost exclusively in this way. The composer sits in front of the dials governing his amplifiers and oscillators, but the tiny pantomimic dancing of his fingers bears little relationship in physical terms to what he may be producing in sound. Will the consequences of this schizophonic development be positive or negative? I leave you this debate. "Schizophonia" (its inventor says) is supposed to be a nervous word.

(click) Well here we are again with the pops tops and the

Big Boss with the hot sauce t'spin 'em for ya (*bloop-blip-bleep*). Get set for the nation's choices at 5:10 p.m. this happy afternoon in your town right after this impooooooooortant message . . . .

THE SOUND ENVELOPE

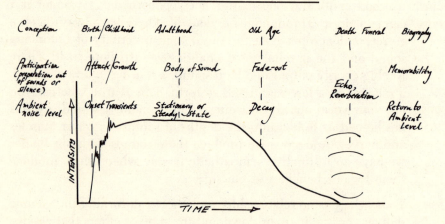

THE SOUND OBJECT

Listen!

Listen to the sound of your own eyelashes fluttering!

What else can you hear? Each of the things you hear is a sound object. The sound object may be found anywhere. It is high, low, long, short, loud, soft, continuous, or discrete.

Sound objects may be found inside musical compositions and outside musical compositions.

"Bring an interesting sound to school" is an exercise I often give to a class. And they find sound objects at home, in the street, or in their imaginations.

Let us understand the sound object as one completely self-contained acoustic event. A unique event. It is born, it lives, it dies. In this sense we may speak of the biological life of the sound object.

Often the sound object occurs circumjacently to other sound objects. In this sense we may speak of the social life of the sound object.

When we speak thus, we speak metaphorically, for in reality sound consists of dead mechanical vibrations. It is an anthropomorphic preference which inclines us to speak of music in such big metaphors as the act of bringing sounds to life and giving them social existences.

Sound objects may differ in numerous important ways through variations in: (1) frequency (pitch); (2) intensity (loudness); (3) duration; and (4) timbre (tone color).

In older forms of music discrete sound objects called 'tones' were used. Considered abstractly it was noted that tones appeared relatively isomorphic, that is they tended to resemble one another in their prime qualities—like bricks.

When we practice scales we tend to think of tones isomorphically—like bricks.

Big bricks:

Little bricks:

Often when we do our theory exercises we tend to think of tones in this way. In an isomorphic system tones live mechanical rather than biological or social existences (if they live at all).

Compared with such a "rational" theory of music, the multifarious sounds of the new music we have been studying may seem "irrational." On the other hand, traditional music theory underestimated the anarchic differences there are between different tones and tone-groupings through its addiction to the playing of scales and insistence on textbook graffiti. Great composers and performers certainly understood that the expressive potentials of tones are not all the same when played in different registers, or by different instruments, or when attacked and released differently, or with different durations, or with different degrees of loudness.

Supporting the intuitions of master composers and performers, recent work in acoustics and psychoacoustics (from Helmholtz on) has helped to make us all aware of the fascinating variety of the world of sounds and the drama of their social life together.

At the most abstract level there are the studies of mathematical acoustics. Not all of these studies are relevant to the ear. But the sound object is an acoustic event, the features of which can be perceived by the ear. By embracing and subsuming the "tone" of traditional music, the sound object now replaces it as the term by which we describe the cosmogenic acoustic event. From sound events are soundscapes built.

Every sound object is enclosed in an ectoplasm which we call the sound envelope. Inside is a vibrant existence which we may divide into various stages of bioacoustic life. The different stages may be given different names depending on how one wishes to view them, but the divisions of the envelope remain more or less the same. I have shown them together on a graph (p. 142).

Preparation

To begin at the beginning.

Every sound has a manner of preparation (the pianist raises his hands, etc.) which is a mimetic advance signal. If it does not have this (a radio suddenly switched on behind one's back) it surprises us as much as would a birth not preceded by pregnancy. The mimetic preparations for a piece may extend right out to the conductor's dressing room. Ceremony, ritual, theatrics.

Attack

Elsewhere I have called the attack the "ictus," that is, the instant of sound-impact. It ought to be a traumatic experience. The still air is cut with pristine sound. For an instant there is total confusion.

The onset behavior of sound is a fascinating object for study. When a system is suddenly excited a great enrichment of the spectrum takes place giving a sound a rough edge. Technically this is called onset transient distortion. When a sound is attacked more slowly less of this sudden excitement is present and an even tone quality emerges. Any instrument can attack smoothly or sharply; but some instruments have a natural tendency to "speak" more quickly than others and thus have more dissonance in their attack. (Compare the trumpet and violin).

In classical ornaments such as the *acciaccatura* were devices for emphasizing onset transient distortion. A nervous twitching at the head of a note. Addition of spice. *Piquer les dormeurs.*

Stationary Sound

Doesn't exist. In a sound everything is on the move. Nevertheless there may appear to be a period in the midlife of a sound in which nothing

is changing (same frequency, same volume etc.) and to the naked ear
the sound seems unprogressive and stationary. It would be useful exercise for students to try and measure the duration of what they assume
to be the stationary period of different sounds—that is, that portion
separate from onset and decay characteristics. Some sounds have simply
no stationary condition at all but consist entirely of attack and decay:
harp, piano, all percussion instruments.

The most stationary sounds are those of mechanical engines: cars,
air conditioners, power mowers, jets, etc. A few internal undulations do
not compensate for what is essentially a boring life.

Decay

The sound wearies; it dies away, perhaps to be followed by new sounds.
There are rapid decays and imperceptibly slow decays. It is biologically
natural for sounds to decay.

(The sound of the air conditioner does not decay. It receives trans-
plants and lives forever).

Reverberation

W. C. Sabine, the acoustician, has defined reverberation technically. It
is the time that elapses from the instant a sound source is switched off
until its energy decays to one millionth of its original strength (a drop
of 60db). As far as the ear is concerned it is the time it takes for a
sound to melt and be lost in the ambient sounds of the room. Obviously
the reverberation of the room affects the music played in it. Thus music
written for cathedrals (with a reverberation time of 6–8 seconds) is
slower than that written for the modern, dry recording studio in which
sounds must be quickly forgotten to make way for new ones.

Death and Memory

A sound lasts as long as we remember it. Who, having heard it, has ever
forgotten the opening modulation of *Tristan*, haunting the imagination
forever? Unforgettable sounds, like unforgettable stories give rise to
mythology.

The affectionately remembered sound joins hands with the anticipa-
tion of new sounds to form a loop which we call an appreciation for
music.

Sound Morphology

The form and structure of sounds.

Each single sound has its own internal morphology. Much of this can be heard by the ear when listening is carefully educated.

For the ultimate morphological study of sound objects we must go to the laboratory, or at least to the literature of those who have worked in the laboratory.*

But you may also, accepting the work of acousticians, still continue to believe in the poetry of sound. Scientific investigation does not prevent each sound from having its word-metaphor.

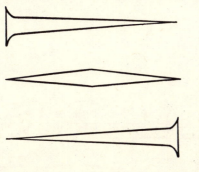

A sudden inspiration (The staccato note discharges energy in all directions.)

A nervous life (function of the trill: to sustain onset transients)

Calisthenics, limbering up but getting nowhere.

Finally on the move.

A serene life of reflection—Tao, Buddha

Pictographs for sounds may be useful. Even the elementary class ought to be able to draw, analyze, and classify sound objects by the pictography of their envelopes. Thus:

A precocious sound object

A well-balanced sound object (natural growth and decay)

A healthy sound object refusing to surrender to the decrepitudes of age, cut down suddenly at the height of his powers

---

* In this respect I would refer interested readers to the most interesting study by Fritz Winckel, entitled *Music, Sound and Sensation*, New York, Dover Books, 1967, from which I have borrowed numerous thoughts. Winckel works scientifically and the findings of his book may be useful to any musician in corroborating his intuitions.

Anyone can do this. A time-scale can be drawn across the bottom of the page to show the relative duration of the sound object. Relative pitch can be indicated by height; tone color by texturing or coloring the envelope, and so forth. Then the class can set about to analyze all the continuous, interrupted, gliding, steady, long and brief sounds of nature and of their lives.

The Society of Sound

We have been speaking of the lives of single sounds. But these are merely fragments in the larger social life we call composition.

A social psychologist, suspecting that music had discovered something important, asked me to speak to his class about *harmony*. Looking into compositions from the point of view of social systems could be a fascinating exercise. A composition as a pageant of humanity. Each note as a human being, a breath of life.

Some music is sociable with lots of harmonious hobnobbing (Mozart); some is full of belligerent antagonisms (Schoenberg); while some reveals the entanglements of a population explosion (Ives).

Let us look briefly at a detail in the social life of Richard Strauss's *Heldenleben*.[38]

Two noble lives in conflict; who will be victor, who vanquished?

They become belligerent enemies.

Confrontation at sword-point

But later they discover they have similar ideas and finally join hands in friendship.

Classical music prefers happy endings.

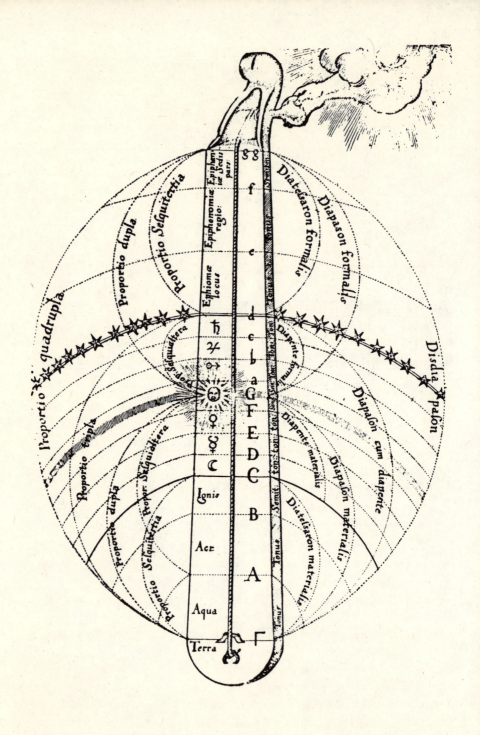

"The tuning of the world" from Robert Fludd's
Utriusque Cosmi Historia illustrates the continuing
desire of man to find harmony in his environment.

THE NEW SOUNDSCAPE

It would be pleasant to conclude that all soundscapes might prefer happy endings. Or that some might prefer quiet endings. Or that a few might just end.

From somewhere in the middle of the development section of the world soundscape, let us listen carefully to the themes and try to assess where they are carrying us.

Taking Cage's definition of music as "sounds around us, whether we're in or out of concert halls," Part III has been an attempt to persuade music educators that the most vital "musical" composition of our time is being played on a world stage. If we could reverse the figure-ground relationship, the cloistered hour a week we call the music lesson would be quite displaced by a much bigger music lesson—the very cosmic symphony we have tried to shut ourselves away from.

Music is, after all, nothing more than a collection of the most exciting sounds conceived and produced by successive generations by men with good ears. The compelling world of sounds around us today has already been investigated and incorporated into the music produced by today's composers. The task of the music educator is now to study and theoretically comprehend what is happening everywhere along the frontier of the world soundscape.

In the introduction I suggested that we may now have entered an era in which the prevention of sound may well be as important as its production. It may be that we already have too many sounds in the world for them all to be heard to advantage. It may be that some are ugly, boring, or simply unnecessary. Speculate, for instance, on the millions of identical motorized lawnmowers chewing their way over the acreages of suburbia. You may notice that one does not hear the sounds of the birds very clearly behind their mechanical moan. Or consider unmuffled power saws or electrified kitchen gadgetry: could not their plangency be dimmed? Of course. For the cost of a ticket to a concert a manufacturer could attach a muffler to any of these.

Motors are the dominant sounds of the world soundscape. All motors share one important feature: they are low-information, high redundancy sounds. That is to say, despite the intensity of their voices, the messages they speak are repetitive and ultimately boring. There is a hypnotic suggestibility about motors that makes one wonder whether, as they invade our lives totally, they may not mask out all other sounds, reducing us in the process to acquiescent and dopey bipeds indolently fumbling about in a mute hypnotic trance.

Just as the sewing machine gave us the long line in clothes, so the motor has given us the flat line in sound.

What effect do environmental sounds have? Consider, for instance, two composers, one living in the 18th century and the other in our own. The former travels everywhere in a carriage. He can't get horses hooves out of his mind, and so he becomes the inventor of the Alberti bass. The latter travels everywhere in his own sportscar. His music is remarkable for its drones, clusters, and whirring effects. (These may merely be idiosyncratic thoughts).

No sound contains less interesting information than that of an airplane. Its only embellishment is the Doppler effect. Compare this with the rich and characteristic sounds of the vehicle it replaced; the steam engine. A train made an informative noise: the whistle, the bell, the puffing of the engine with its sudden and gradual accelerations and decelerations, the squeaking of the wheels on the tracks, the rattling of the cars, the clatter of the tracks.

Or compare the aircraft with the object it imitates: the bird. The arabesque of the sedge-warbler, for instance is so intricate that a hundred hearings would not begin to exhaust its fascination for us. Even the separate notes of the song-thrush are more tuneful than any machine man has thrown into the air. But not so loud, of course. We hold the world's record for that.

If I am insisting rather on sky-sounds it is because these themes are going to dominate the next movement of our world symphony. I once drew a picture of a city of the future on the blackboard for a group of architecture students and asked them what the salient features of this environment appeared to be. There were seven helicopters in the sky of my drawing; yet no student found this particularly salient. I (exasperatedly): "Have you ever *heard* seven helicopters?"

The big sound sewer of the future will be the sky.

Already this is evident. Soon every home and office in the world will be situated somewhere along this new expressway. In recent years some municipal governments have begun to show an interest in the control of nuisance sounds (barking dogs, etc.); but this unimaginative legislation is pathetic when any number of thunderous things can happen in the sky over our heads without restriction as to how frequently or how loudly they may happen.

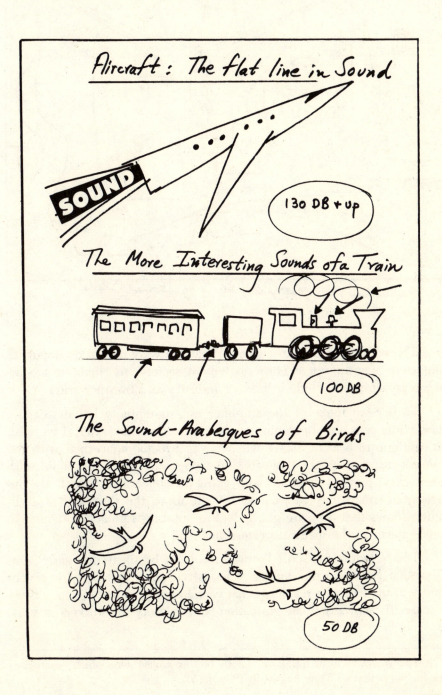

Question: What will the sky sound like?

The whole world is an airport. What are we going to do about it? Objective of a musicians noise abatement society: to eliminate all unnecessary sounds, including those of industry and transportation.

Earlier we spoke of the amplifier as a potentially lethal weapon. The evidence is now beginning to come in and it shows that if we wish to continue to hear at all we will have to become concerned with the forensic aspects of this "musical" development. Research done with teen-agers, playing in bands and going to concerts at which the intensity of sound may easily pass 100 db above the threshold of audibility, shows that they are going deaf in numbers significant enough to cause alarm in the medical profession.*

I have before me some literature put out by the Workmen's Compensation Board on the danger of industrial noise and how to prevent injury to the ears as a result of what is colloquially called "boilermaker's disease." It shows that ear protection is mandatory for workers in sonic

---

* Numerous articles have appeared recently on this subject. One which summarizes the finding is that in *Time*, August 9, 1968, p. 51.

environments less loud than the sound produced by the bands which play at my school on occasions too frequent to count. "We have succeeded in almost totally conquering boilermaker's disease," a research worker of the Workmen's Compensation Board proudly announced at a recent conference.

Such then are the emphatic leitmotives of the world symphony: aircraft, amplified guitars, the sounds of warfare and power machinery. These are the big blocks of sound, the flat lines of sound, the lethal weapons which now dominate the composition. They demonstrate the crudity of its orchestration.

Next the lesser leitmotives: the ubiquitous radios and television sets, the sounds of street traffic, the telephone (which Lawrence Durrell describes in *Justine* as "a small, needle-like sound") the sounds of plumbing, of furnaces and air conditioners. These are the jabber-sounds.

And here in the center of it all, like a viola in the finale of a trumpet and drum allegro, are the sounds of our own voices. We no longer sing in the streets of our cities. Even speaking is often a strain. What should be the most vital sound of human existence is little by little being crushed beneath sounds which we may quite accurately call "inhuman."

Portions of the world symphony have already been played and will not be repeated: the steam engine, the horse-drawn carriage, the cracking of whips (which Schopenhauer found so agonizing) the coal-oil lamp. Yes, what did the coal-oil lamp sound like? You will think of others.

A class of elementary school children was given the phrase: "As quiet as . . ." and was asked to complete it with all the hushed similes that perhaps only a class of elementary school children can find behind the cacophony adults are hardened to accept as necessary to the progress of civilization.

Birds, leaves, the cries of animals, varieties of wind and water. Where do these enter into the contemporary world sonograph?

Will there by any more pianissimo movements?

Will there soon be an adagio section?

And so to end with an assignment: Keep a world sound diary. Wherever you go take note of what you hear. We are all in the world symphony. What is not yet apparent is whether we are merely part of its apparatus or the composers responsible for giving it form and beauty.

I have tried to show how the rich universe of sound around us could be the object for a new kind of musical studies, a program that would carry the participants across the party-lines of the conservatory curriculum and sweep them out into the shifting shapes of what we might call the "middlefields" between many different disciplines.

But if we wish to apply thought to the nerve of what is happening today, where else would we go?

Much has been left open for further development, and active student's will add their own ideas, correcting whatever errors they detect as they plunge deeper into the fields of science, social science, and art from which to form the working principles of a whole new theory of music, a theory in pace with the imaginative leaps of the artists who are today carrying music in bold, new synergies quite beyond whatever the dictionaries of the past thought it to be.

The universe is your orchestra.

Let nothing less be the territory of your new studies.

EPILOGUE

All this is a long way from the piano. For the past two hundred years the piano has been the focal point of all musical studies: the piano as *Ersatz* orchestra, the piano as tool of accompaniment, the piano as commanding and heroic soloist in its own right, the piano as archsymbol of a distinct era of music making and of the institutions concerned with its promulgation.

Today, the pianos in suburbia are slumbering.

The fingers of the young have turned elsewhere—to the guitar, the saxophone, the potentiometer. And the piano begins to look like a decorated hearse.

Ah yes, it is true that a few small hands still learn to play *Mistress Mary* for the music festival. *Et puis?*

"What! sixteen and *still* studying the piano," said an aunt once to a young French girl, who happened to be helping with this book.

Today, the pianos in suburbia are slumbering.

The piano is a drawing room instrument, the sociologist Max Weber pointed out, an amusement devised for the North European winters. All the great piano compositions were written by Northerners. Out of the blood-spitting cold they came to warm their well-kept fingers on the fiery keyboard. The Southerners, whose drawing rooms dissolved into gardens, preferred portable instruments, the guitar, the mandolin, instruments you could remove to shady groves or moonlit patios.

Today again the concert hall has moved.

The new orchestra is the universe.

The piano concerto is a ghost in its midst. And there is something spooky about the institutions in which many pianos sit.

But let us forever cherish a few great pianos in our company. Your treasure-museum is of great beauty. You will not be forgotten, but will forever enchant us with the reveries of your memorable *amours*.
Tell us

> how Mozart tickled you,
> how Beethoven boisterously caroused with you,
> how Schumann kept you up late at night,
> how Listz rode you like a wild stallion,

how Debussy painted you blue,
how Stravinsky mistook you for a stop clock,
and how John Cage snapped your garters.
Breathe history into our ears.
For the activity has moved elsewhere, and you are too big
to be carried there . . . .
Farewell slumbering piano . . . .
You have stated your case well.
Let now others state theirs.

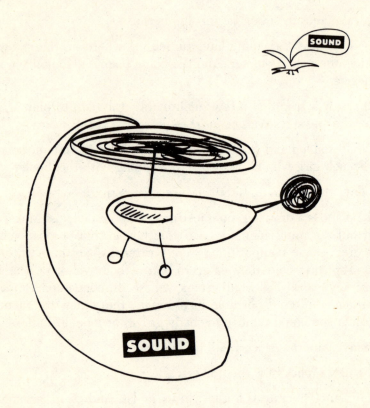

NOTES

1. Nikos Kazantzakis, *Report to Greco*, New York, Simon and Schuster, 1965, p. 189.
2. Pascal, *Pensées*, ed. Ch. M. des Granges, Paris, Garnier Frères, 1964, p. 131.
3. John Cage, *Silence: Lectures and Writings*, Middletown, Connecticut, Wesleyan University Press, 1961, pp. 8 and 191.
4. Hermann von Helmholtz, *On the Sensations of Tone*, trans. Alexander J. Ellis, New York, Dover Publications, 1954, pp. 6 and 7.
5. Max Gunther, "The Sonics Book," *Playboy*, May 1967.
6. *Ibid.*
7. Gunther Lehmann, "Noise and Health," *The Unesco Courier*, July 1967 (issue titled "Noise Pollution").
8. Gunther, *op. cit.*
9. *Ibid.*
10. Evelyn Waugh, *Mexico, an Object Lesson*, Boston, Little, Brown & Co., 1939, pp. 28–31.
11. Gunther, *op. cit.*
12. O. Schenker-Sprungli, "Down with Decibels!", "Noise Pollution."
13. Constantin Stramentov, "The Architects of Silence," "Noise Pollution."
14. Arthur Schopenhauer, "On Noise," *Studies in Pessimism*, ed. H. E. Barnes, trans. T. B. Saunders, Lincoln, Nebraska, University of Nebraska, 1964.
15. Stramentov, *op. cit.*
16. Schopenhauer, *op. cit.*
17. Leo L. Baranek, "Street and Air Traffic Noise—and What Can Be Done About It," "Noise Pollution."
18. Schenker-Sprungli, *op. cit.*
19. Schopenhauer, *op. cit.*
20. G. L. Fuchs, "Cordoba (Argentina) Takes Noise Abatement by the Horns," "Noise Pollution."
21. Schopenhauer, *op. cit.*
22. Fuchs, *op. cit.*
23. Gunther, *op. cit.*
24. Schopenhauer, *op. cit.*
25. "Noise Pollution."
26. Schopenhauer, *op. cit.*
27. Fuchs, *op. cit.*
28. Stramentov, *op. cit.*
29. "Noise Pollution."
30. *Ibid.*
31. Lehmann, *op. cit.*
32. Gunther, *op. cit.*
33. Lehmann, *op. cit.*
34. "Noise Pollution."
35. Boethius, *De institutione musica*, quoted in *Source Readings in Music History*, Oliver Strunk, New York, W. W. Norton & Co., 1950, p. 84.
36. Shakespeare, *The Merchant of Venice*, V.i.
37. Johannes Kepler, *Harmonice Mundi*, ed. Caspar and v.Dyck, Munich, Gesammelte Werke, 1938, Chapter 3.
38. Richard Strauss, *Heldenleben*, Eulenburg Edition, pp. 162, 163, 191, 197, 214, and 215.

Part IV
WHEN WORDS SING

This fourth part is about voices — human voices — audible human voices. I write it jubilantly and in desperation. It records experiences I have had on numerous occasions in different places with children and adults. The voice was the only instrument employed. The human voice singing, reciting, chanting, intoning, sometimes in the most unlikely ways, but always in a lively and emphatic fashion, little by little overcoming inhibition after inhibition to find the personality of each individual voiceprint.

Just as the architect uses the human body to provide the module for his living structures, so too it is the human voice together with the human ear that must provide the standards in any discussion of the acoustical environment salubrious for human life. Tragically, we have not yet realized this.

Researchers have noted that there is much more colorful modulation in the voices of primitive peoples than among us. Even in the Middle Ages the voice was a vital instrument. Reading was then performed out loud; one felt the shape of the words with the tongue. In the Renaissance everyone sang as indeed they do in all less "developed" cultures today. We did not need McLuhan to tell us that just as "the sewing machine . . . created the long straight line in clothes . . . the linotype flattened the human vocal style." For centuries we have heard nothing but bespectacled muttering.

I have not begun with traditional singing. If anything we leave off at about the point this begins. (The qualified teacher can go on easily enough from there.) My purpose was to work with raw vocable sound, to start all over again like the aboriginal who doesn't even know the difference between speech and song, sense and sonority. I wish I could sing this part, and chant and whisper and bellow it. I want to get it out of its print sarcophagus. It needs to be played on the human instrument. In the Middle Ages it would not have been necessary to urge this — but today it is — so I urge you to perform this part with your voice.

Out loud.

VOICEPRINT

Sit quietly, attentively. Close eyes. Listen. In a moment you will be filled with a priceless sound.

In Mantra Yoga the disciple repeats a word over and over like a charm, sonorously feeling its majesty, its charisma, and its dark narcotic powers. When the Tibetan monk recites "OMmmm OMmmm OMmmm," he feels the sound surge through his body. His rib-cage wobbles. His nose rattles. He vibrates.

With a deep resonant voice begin to repeat:

OMmmmmmmm OMmmmmmmm OMmmmmmmmm

Feel its vibratory thrust. Hypnotize yourself with the sound of your own voice. Think of the sound rolling out of your mouth to fill the world. When the word "Om" is uttered the beginning of the "o" will be 120 feet away in all directions around you before the "m" begins.

OMmmmmmmm OMmmmmmmm OMmmmmmmmm

This is your voiceprint. You have said nothing. You have said every-thing. One needs no words. The reed in your body has informed you. You are alive.

Exercises

1. Take your own name. Repeat it over and over until it gradually loses its identity. Lull the sense of it to sleep, hypnotize it until it no longer belongs to you. Now that it is merely a quaint sound object hanging in front of you examine it thoroughly with your ears.

2. Charm other words in this way. The Mantra Yoga disciples knew how meditation and auto-hypnosis can assist in clairaudience. We can learn this secret from them.

MELISMA

"Melisma" is the Greek word for song. In Western music it usually means an extended vocalization on one vowel or consonant—a jubilant outburst. Let now the reed of your voice express itself. Let it go free. Discover its scope, its expressive potentials. Discover the shapes of the things you can draw with your voice. Use your imagination and produce:

1. The highest sound of which you are capable
2. The lowest sound
3. The softest sound
4. The loudest sound
5. The smoothest sound
6. The roughest sound
7. The funniest sound
8. The saddest sound
9. A stern sound
10. A boring sound
11. An interrupted sound
12. A rhythmic, repeated sound
13. An unrhythmic sound
14. The highest sound again
15. Now suddenly, the softest
16. Gradually modulating to the funniest

(You laugh at your voice. Good. Listen to the sound of your own voice laughing at itself.)

If you have a tape recorder, tape your voice performing the above exercise. Listen to the curious vocal warble that is you. Then play it back again and try to counterpoint it with your live voice performing opposite effects to each of those on the tape.

See what your voice makes of these shapes. Try to perform each of them.

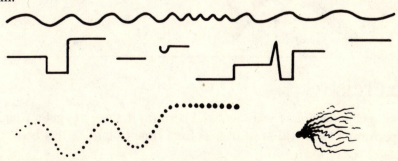

Exercise

Draw some other shapes for yourself and perform them.

In the following picture I intend a composition for solo voice. Try to perform it. What do you make of the high, low, continuous or interrupted shapes, the dark shapes or those that explode or wiggle or drip? There will be as many different realizations of my piece as there are singers. It is a piece of infinite possibilities.

Exercise

Draw a composition of your own and perform it. Or try to get a friend to perform it. You will need friends from time to time in this book.

NATURE CONCERT

The first time I tried the following exercise was at a summer camp in the Laurentian mountains of Quebec. A crowd of 80 amateur musicians of all ages from 6 to 60 gathered in the spacious assembly room one evening after dinner.

I gave them a problem.

> Using only your voices, create a composition based on the sounds of nature. Make your imitations as convincing as possible.
> Everyone must participate and the piece should have some sense of form. You have fifteen minutes.

The assembly was divided into groups of about 6 to 8 performers each. Out they went into the forest or by the water and began to experiment with their voices.

The idea for such an exercise, it should be added parenthetically, was suggested by a statement in Marius Schneider's article "Primitive Music" from *The New Oxford History of Music* (Vol. 1, p. 9), where he writes: "One must have heard them to realize how extremely realistically aboriginals are able to imitate animal noises and the sounds of nature. They even hold 'nature concerts' in which each singer imitates a particular sound (waves, wind, groaning trees, cries of frightened animals), 'concerts' of surprising magnificence and beauty."

When our musicians returned each group had to perform their composition while the others listened (eyes closed). A critical discussion was to follow each performance.

The first group got up and gave us a barnyard concert: cows mooed, horses whinnied, dogs barked, pigs oinked. Everyone laughed hysterically. Then the second group got up and gave us—another barnyard concert. The laughter was less uncontrollable this time. When the third group got up and gave us (predictably?) yet another example of barnyard jabber—at least of sorts, for I think they added cats and birds—there wasn't any laughter at all. Now we could begin work.

Which of the three performances had been the most convincing? When this had been decided, the two losing groups were sent out again to come up with something better.

Next group. A new theme at last. Their theme was a summer storm. Silence. Then the wind blew, gradually becoming more ferocious. Raindrops began to fall, tiny at first and sporadic, then larger and more intense. At the height of the storm, lightening with thunder on its tail. At length the storm abated, the rain dribbled away, the wind died, and birds came whistling their high inscrutable tunes. It was indeed a concert of "surprising magnificence and beauty."

They demurred at first when I asked them to write it down, but at length they did so and it came out something like this:

The tone of the experiment had now been set and the succeeding groups had something to emulate (or suffer the consequences of the most severe criticism by their colleagues and banishment to the forest to improve their offering).

The "summer storm" group, however, still wasn't satisfied. Most of their sounds pleased them but—"thunder," that was indeed difficult to produce with the human voice.

Try it and you'll see.

Exercise

A soundscape is a collection of sounds heard in a given place. A soundchronicle is a collection of sounds heard in a temporal sequence, perhaps dramatic, perhaps telling a story without words. With your voices construct elaborate soundscapes and soundchronicles.

THUNDER-WORD

How *do* you produce thunder with your voice? James Joyce tried it. In *Finnegans Wake* we find the following fantastic word-concoction:[1]

BABABADALCHARAGHTAKAMMINARRONNKONN-
BRONNTONNERRONNTUONNTHUNNTROVARRHOUN-
AWNSKAWNTOOHOOHOORDENENTHURNUK!

As Joyce was a poet with a genius for sound it will be worthwhile analysing his thunder-word. I have divided it into two syllables to help in its reciting—for you have to get the feel of it in your throat.

By comparing the words for thunder in a few common languages we note that they all have a rather grumbling sound and that Joyce borrowed from them.

B A|B A|B A|D A L|C H A R A G H|T A K A M|-

M I N A R|R O N N|K O N N|B R O N N|

T O N N E R|R O N N|T U O N N|T H U N N|-

French German   Italian   English

T R O V A R R|H O U N|A W N|S K A W N|-

Portugese   Swedish

T O O|H O O|H O O R|D E N E N|T H U R N U K|!

Swedish:	aska	French:	tonnere
Danish:	Torden	Spanish:	trueno
Dutch:	donder	Portugese:	trovao
German:	Donner	Italian:	tuono

The frequency with which certain letters occur, or do not occur, in Joyce's thunder-word is significant.

"A" appears 12 times (mainly at the beginning of the word).
"R" appears 11 times.
"N" (counting the digraphs as one sound) appears 11 times.
"O" appears 8 times, mostly at the middle and end of the word.

"U" if you pronounce it as "oo," appears 8 times, mostly towards the end of the word.

"T" appears 5 times.

"K" appears 4 times.

"B" appears 4 times.

All others appear less frequently than this.

The five primary sounds are "A," "R," "N," "O," and "U." All are continuous sounds that can be drawn out by the voice. The secondary interrupted sounds are abrupt: "T," "K," and "B." It is interesting also that the liquid "L" and the sibilant "S" appear only once each; they are obviously not very useful for expressing thunder.

The onomatopoeic theory of the origin of language contends that language arose in imitation of the sound of nature. As it is not true of all words, many linguists doubt that onomatopoeia is the real or only origin of our habit of speaking. Nevertheless, many of our most expressive words have the onomatopoeic quality—as poets know.

Exercises

1. Read Joyce's thunder-word aloud, inflecting it broadly to imitate the event it celebrates.
2. With several voices build a polyphony from it, using some voices to sustain or repeat certain characteristic sounds.
3. Improve Joyce's word.

THE BIOGRAPHY OF THE ALPHABET

Every sound casts a spell. A word is a bracelet of voice-charms. Individually considered, its letters (phonemes) tell the attentive listener a complicated life-story. Pronounce each of the following sounds phonemically, as it would appear in a word, listening, listening. I tell what I can of their story and leave the reciter to add his own discoveries. We are not interested here in phonetic dogma, but in colorful metaphors that unlock secrets.

"A"   (Pron. ah) The most frequent vowel-sound in English. Elemental. *Ur*-sound. If the mouth is wide open you can't produce any other sound. Together with "m" as "ma" it is the first word spoken by millions of infants.

"B"   Has bite. Combustive. Aggressive. The lips bang over it.

"C"   (Pron. k) Muffled, underground explosion of the vocal chords.

"D"   Sharp, attacking, tongue-thrust.

"E"   (As in *wet*) A tight, constipated sound. Best to keep it short. Unpleasant when sustained (R.M.S's opinion).

"F"   Soft friction of cotton or felt rubbed. Compare with "th." As both both are relatively high-frequency sounds they are sometimes not passed with fidelity by the narrow frequency-band of the telephone. The telephone says "fankyou."

"G"   Gutteral, brash in a solar-plectic sort of way.

"H"   Breath of air. Especially effective in Arabic where it is pronounced as an explosion from the chest. In the medical word for bad breath "h" figures importantly (Halitosis).

"I"   (Pron. ee) Highest vowel. Thin, bright, pinched sound, leaving the smallest cavity in the mouth. Hence useful in words describing smallness: *piccolo, petit,* tiny, wee.

"J"   Sound of metal striking cement. Jaded jingle. When sustained, "jjjjjjj," it suggests a motor needing oil.

"L"   Watery, luscious, languid. Needs juice in the mouth to be spoken properly. Feel it drip around the tongue. Feel the saliva in lascivious lecher."

"M"   In the Phoenician alphabet "mem" originally stood for calm sea, the sea then being the fundamental tone in all maritime soundscapes. Today it might mean calm motor, the motor being the fundamental in all contemporary soundscapes. But consider also the murmer of the bees in Tennyson's "The Princess":

The moan of doves in immemorial elms,
And murmuring of innumerable bees.

"N"   The feminine of "M"?
"NG" Nasal. "N" with a headcold. On the other hand "ngs" may suggest the silver resonance of the viol string under bow, as Ezra Pound knew precisely when he wrote:

And viol strings that outsing kings.

"O"   The second most frequent vowel in English, it suggests roundness and perfection. Consider the sound of children's voices singing in the dome of a cathedral as heard by Verlaine:

Ô ces voix d'enfants chantant dans le coupole!

"P"   Pip, pop, pout. Combustive, comical. Listen to the soft popping of the pipe smoker.
"R"   Rippled in French, trilled in Italian, it suggests recurrence or rhythm. The English make it a masterpiece of ugliness by scraping the vocal chords over it; hence choir boys are taught to pronounce it "aw." In the American midwest it has obviously been influenced by the sound of the tractor and combine.
"S"   The highest-frequency phoneme (8,000–9,000 cps.). In the days of snakes and serpents it reminded one of those things: for instance, the hissing sibilence of Hell in Milton's "Paradise Lost":

. . . thick-swarming now with complicated monsters. . . .
Scorpion, and Asp, and Amphisbaena dire,
Cerastes horned, Hydrus, and Ellops drear,
And Dipsas . . . .

"SH" White noise. Full frequency-spectrum of random sound.
"T"   On a typewriter all letters sound like "T"-tttttttttt.
"TH" (As in that) The sound of a pencil writing. Compare with "th" (as in thing) which might be the soft brushing of charcoal drawing.
"U"   (Pron. oo) Dark vowel, lazy, corpulent. Notice the ripening of vowels in this line by Swinburne:

From leaf to flower and flower to fruit.

It can also have a reverberant or tunnely quality. It reminded Virgil of the cooing of pigeons:

tua cura, palumbes . . . turtur ab ulmo.

"V" The flat line in sound. A motor with a muffler. The adequate muffler should make a motor sound like "fffff."
"W" "Ooah." Pronounce it slowly. The long "oo" and the snapped *sforzando* cutoff make it a scary ghostlike sound.
"Y" "Eeeah." Reaction to the ghost.
"Z" Sound of bees; sound of small aircraft. In the English language "z" appears about 0.7 times per 1000 letters. Airplanes are more frequent.

Then there are the many digraphs. There are those like "TS" or "TZ" that sound "foreign"; those like "SL" that sound disgusting (slimy, slippery, slut, slum), and so forth.

I leave the reciter to embellish the story further. . . .

Exercises

1. Write the biography of the letter-sounds in your own name.
2. Which letters (phonemes) would be the best to express the following subjects: mystery, terror, sadness, gaity, machine-gun fire, bombs exploding, a puddle, wind, a lawn mower, a headache.
3. Louis Aragon wrote a poem called *Suicide*. It went:
   abcdefghijklmnopqrstuvwxyz.
   Discuss what he meant.
4. The ancient Rabbinical scholars used to call consonants the skeleton of the world and the vowels its soul. Why?

ONOMATOPOEIA

From a consideration of the letter (phoneme) as a sound-object in isolation, let us again consider whole words. To begin:

> Discover some watery-sounding words.
> Discover some metallic-sounding words.
> Discover some bumpy words.
> Discover some shaggy words.
> Discover some syrupy words.

Some words have continuous or repeated sounds to suggest repeated movement; some are short and sharp to suggest a sudden or arrested action. Discover some of each.

Now pronounce your list out loud. Let your tongue dance around each word in imitation of the event or quality it suggests. Repeat each a dozen times, exaggerating and musicalizing it more and more to bring out its word-soul.

Splash, SSSplash, SplaSHSHSH, SplAAAsh

Onomatopoeic words are magnificently sonorous because poets invented them. But all words are not so. Does the word "gold" glitter? Is the word "war" adequately ugly? (Who do you suppose invented these words?)

Some words that may not be strictly onomatopoeic today retain vestiges of color. *Troubleshooter* has restlessness; its sharp consonants struggle against one another. The word *Bell,* despite the long "l" and the sharp attack of the "b," is perhaps not the most imaginative word for this subject. A student once suggested a substitute: *Tittletatong.* Obviously more colorful, it has tinkle at the beginning and reverberative spread at the end. One might look up the word for "bell" in several different languages, including some oriental. Having done this one comes to the conclusion that inventors of such words actually listened with some care to this sound.

Many words have an explosive feel about them. The word "explosion" itself (when emphatically pronounced) seems to crash out of itself. You will easily be able to think of other explosive words.

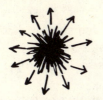

The opposite is "implosion." Just as in modern painting it is harder to find implosion than explosion shapes (for "action" art is the art of exclamation!) it will be harder to find implosive words, words that start grandly but then duck in at their close. One clearly implosive word is *Spuck,* which Joyce uses in *Portrait of the Artist as a Young Man* to describe water being sucked down the lavoratory sink.

Let us consider the word *Sunshine.* First sound: "s"; highest frequency, dazzling. The "sh" following is full-frequencied, a broad band of sound, and thus suggests a fuller spectrum of light. The vowels are brief and neutral. The two "n's" reflect and attenuate the cosmic flashes of the "s," much perhaps as a planet or moon reflects the sun's light—a palpable glow. Thus, a whole cosmos is expressed in the word *Sunshine.*

I always thought the word *Moonlight* was also quite suggestive of its meaning. The soft opening of the "m," the round attenuated "oo," the liquid "l" (moonlight on water)—all these things made up for the slight discontinuity of mood at the close of the word. I was once explaining this to a grade seven class when to my surprise they disagreed with me. So they were given an assignment: Create a more suggestive word in a private language to substitute for "moonlight."

Here are some of their words:

LUNIOUS
SLOOFULP
NESHMOOR
SHALOWA
NU-U-YUL
NOORWAHM
MAUNKLINDE
SHIVERGLOWA
SHEELESK
MALOOMA
SHIMONOELL

Two years later I was to set these words to music—but, more of that later.

Exercises

1. "Here is a flaky-sounding word," a grade-seven student said, and he pronounced: *"Theekfa."* Can you invent some more?
2. In your own private language invent words for: raindrops, insects, war, bells.
3. Arrange the words for raindrops in a descending order from the highest (smallest) to the lowest (largest) according to their sound. A conductor passes his hand across the room so that everyone enunciates his word when the conductor's finger passes him. Listen to the tickertape of rain, falling on roofs, falling in water, falling on streets, falling in rain barrels. (Add a solo voice improvising the "blues" because of the wet weather.)
4. Bells come in all sizes too. Pronounce the words you have invented to bring out their specific sonorous qualities. Is your bell small, large, simple, complex? Draw a picture of your bell. Now chant or sing the sound of your bell. Every one must know that your chanting refers to the picture of your bell and not someone else's. Build a polyphonic chorus of bells.
5. Invent a whole private "onomatopoeic" language.
6. Foreign languages are also pure music. Listen to foreign languages: German, French, Chinese, Arabic, etc. Discuss which are beautiful, which ugly, which happy, which sad, which melodious, which strident. Why?
7. After listening to each of the foreign languages try to imitate it with your own voice, observing as many of its salient features as you can.
8. Even harder: Start to speak a nonsense language, spontaneously inventing as you go. Gradually modulate to predominantly soft sounds, then to hard sounds, then to pure vowels, then to dipthongs, then to total consonants, etc. Record your voice. Check your success.

VOWELS

Vowels, said the ancient Rabbinical scholars, are the word's *soul*, consonants its skeleton. In music it is the vowels that give the composer an opportunity for melodic invention, while consonants articulate rhythm. A phonetician defines a vowel as the peak sonority of each syllable. It is the vowel that provides wings for the word's flight. Consider the role of the vowel in this (or any other) piece of vocal music:

(Ambrosian Chant: **Antiphonale Missarum,** p.208)

We have spoken of the vowels as high or low, having different pitches or frequencies. The following chart shows this more exactly. The bands of frequencies which give each vowel its particular *timbre* or color are called "formants." The two important formants given in the chart (high and low for each vowel) result from the cavities of the mouth (high formant) and the pharynx (low formant).

Vowel sound	Low frequency	High frequency
e (eat)	375	2400
a (tape)	550	2100
i (tip)	450	2200
e (ten)	550	1900
a (father)	825	1200
o (tone)	500	850
u (pool)	400	800

Different vowel sounds are produced with the tongue in different places. You will be able to determine how the cavity of the mouth is changed in size by the position of the tongue as you experiment producing the above sounds.

This is not to be a technical book and the above chart is included for one principal reason: to clear up a misunderstanding concerning singers. Sometimes singers are accused of inarticulate pronounciation in the high register of the voice. While the vowel formants are somewhat adjustable, there are definite limitations beyond which the particular vowel desired can no longer be produced. At 1000 cycles we notice that pure vowels are no longer pronounceable because their low formant is below this frequency. You can verify this by trying to pronounce all the vowels while singing the highest note of which you are capable. This means that as a soprano begins to approach high C, the vowel sounds are simply no longer distinguishable, thus the words cannot be pronounced. Here the composer is guilty; the singer guiltless.

But we wish to think of the vowels more poetically. The poet Arthur Rimbaud saw the vowels as different colors:

A   black
E   white
I   red
O   blue
U   green

In a similarly subjective way we might *hear* the vowels as different tones in a scale:

An exercise would then consist of singing different texts to the vowel scale. Here is a brief example, using the Swinburne phrase quoted earlier:

Whole songs could be composed with the vowel scale. Such exercises would also clearly reveal the aural delicacies of great poetry, though more notes would be required in the scale to do justice to all the shadings of dipthongs, etc.

In some languages, called *tone languages*, the position and the inflection of the vowels is very important. Chinese is a tone language. As it is largely monosyllabic it has few word sounds with which to represent a vast number of things and ideas. Thus different pitches and inflections are used to distinguish between homophones. In the Chinese of Peking four tone differences are employed.

1. high pitch
2. high and rising
3. low and rising
4. high and falling

In the same way, variations could be added to the vowel scale by letting certain vowels rise or fall in pitch. Thus:

or:

An infinite number of variations (glides, embellishments, melismas) are possible so that the composer or singer would have to choose from a number of possibilities each time each vowel was encountered in a text. In this way the psychographic curve of each word's soul would be revealed.

Some languages have a large number of vowels and others have very few (only 2 or 3). One assumes that in a language with very few vowel sounds little singing is possible. A language with no vowels would be a boneyard.

L...NG...G...W...TH...N...V...W...
L...S...W...LD...B...B...N...Y...RD.

Exercises

1. Sing your favorite songs, paying careful attention to the role of the vowels. But try singing them totally eliminating the consonants and see what happens. Discuss.
2. Construct a language with no consonants, just vowels.
3. Using the vowel scale, set your language to music.
4. Invent different vowel scales, some using glides or intervals or ornaments or melismas, and create songs for them.
5. Forget the vowel scale. Using your free imagination, try setting a text to music in such a way that each word's soul is brought to life by the psychographic curve of your melody.

THE PSYCHOGRAPHIC CURVE OF THE WORD'S SOUL

Where the word stops, there starts the song, exultation of the mind bursting forth into the voice.

Thomas Aquinas, *Comment in Psalm., Prolog*.

To set a word to music only one obligation is necessary: work up from its natural sound and meaning. A word should swell with sensual pride in song; it must never be scrabbled through clumsiness.

Pronounce.

Listen.

Compose.

The drama producer Stanislavsky used to make his actors repeat a word forty times with forty different inflections and justify each interpretation before allowing them to utter it on stage. It would be a useful habit for everyone using language to cultivate.

"Here is a text," I told my class. "I want you to draw the psychographic curve of its soul in song. It is an expressive text, a dramatic text, a visual text."

DEPOSUIT   POTENTES
(He hath put down   the mighty
DE SEDE   ET   EXALTAVIT
from their seats   and   exalted
HUMILES.
the meek.)

Some students wrote melodies, others used the flash of penline in an action script that gave mere contour. It didn't matter, as long as they could perform it before the class.

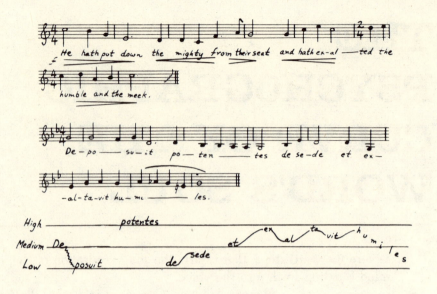

By comparing our various settings we were able to see how effective each of us was in breaking the words out of their grey coffins of print. "Deposuit," "potentes": such words should be pounded out. "Exaltavit": it must defy the laws of gravity. "Humiles": a humble but not a lily-livered expression. After we had discussed the beauties and deficiences of our settings for some time, I played the class Bach's setting of the same words from his *Magnificat*.

For those who didn't read music I put the melody on graph paper:

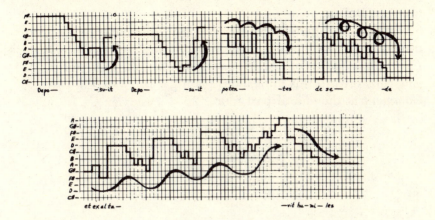

The question now is: what did Bach do to this text that none of us thought to do? It is not hard to discover the genial touches, for instance the whiplash at the end of the cascade of "deposuit." Or the powerful but falling setting of "potentes," like a mightly potentate bouncing downstairs on his rump. The neutral words "de sede" are turned into a echoing swirl of the fall. With the word "exaltavit" we begin to climb upward, not all in one burst like a rocket, rather like a bird, arching each trajectory of flight higher until the summit of the melody is reached, to fall and fold smoothly into the relative major of "humiles."

A recording of this aria was played and everyone compared his own setting with Bach's melody. No further comment was necessary. No amount of jabber from the music teacher could have established Bach's genius so emphatically with the class.

Exercises

1. The word Credo means "I believe." With this word you sum up all your beliefs and convictions, religious, social, moral. It is the real you, your whole *raison d'être* for living. Set the word Credo to music. Later you may wish to compare Bach's setting in his *B Minor Mass* or those of other composers.
2. A poem by Giuseppe Ungaretti called Morning consists of one cosmic line:
      M'illumino d'immenso (I am filled with immense light)
   —suggesting an immense illumination of the spirit in the morning

light. Any English translation fails to do justice to the psychographic curve suggested by the words of the original Italian. Set it to music in Italian.

3. Study Claudio Monteverdi's *Mentre vaga Angioletta*, a virtuoso display of pictoral vocal writing, from his Eighth Book of Madrigals. (There is a fine recording on Vanguard BG 579.) I give the English words to this miraculous madrigal in *Texts Without Comment* at the end of part four.

PIANISSIMO SECRETS

"What is the softest sound you can produce with your voice?" I often ask a class, and usually they whisper. "Softer," I say, "I can still hear you." And the notes of their whisperings fade to almost inaudible twitchings of the lips. Very well, if this is the softest sound of which we are capable, let us say something about it.

THE PSYCHOLOGY OF THE WHISPER

The whisper is secret. It is a privileged information. It is code, not intended for everyone. The whisper is aristocratic and unsociable. It is ominous. It is to be feared. Those for whom it is not intended instinctively want to understand it, therefore they listen harder. A work which began with a whisper would immediately possess the whole audience. They would be eavesdroppers on a private ceremony. A sense of privilege would prevail.

Downtown, no one whispers.

THE PHYSIOLOGY OF THE WHISPER

The whisper is the result of a turbulent stream of air passing through the vocal cavities but lacking the resonance produced by the vibration of the vocal chords. A word whispered with the finger on the throat, doesn't vibrate. When the vocal chords are not employed the acoustic effects are constant and almost invariable; that is to say, whispered speech cannot be inflected; it cannot be sung. Any deviation of even a few semitones is almost impossible as one will discover when he tries to whisper the words of a song to the melody. If the tune is to be preserved, the pronunciation must be distorted.

Some consonants, such as "h" "f" "s" and "sh" are always unvoiced. Such sounds have the natural intimacy of the whisper but they are poor singers. They are sneaky sounds—the Secret Service of the alphabet. Note the frequency of such sounds in some foreign words for whisper:

hviske (Danish) kvisa (Old Norse) hwisprian (Anglo-Saxon) Flüstern (German) chuchoter (French) susuran (Spanish)

Exercises

1. Invent some more words for whisper.
2. Carry on a class in which only whispering is permitted and assess the result.
3. Consider the opposite of the whisper. The opposite of the whisper is the scream. Experiment with the powerful excitement of screaming. Discuss its psychological and physiological makeup.

SOUND POEM

Whispers and screams. How many inarticulate vocal expressions are there? How many interjections and ejaculations; puffs, groans, whistles, laughs, roars?

Sometimes I cover the blackboard with expressions like those below and then have the class perform them as they are pointed out. With two or three conductors pointing to various expressions and a divided class, the complexities of vocal sound which might result are inexhaustible.

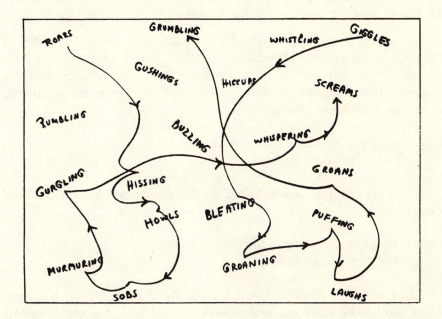

The more civilized speech becomes, the fewer the ejaculations and interjections, the less ripple and curve it assumes when spoken. The linguist Otto Jespensen has conjectured the reason for this. "Now it is a consequence of advancing civilization that passion, or, at least, the expression of passion, is moderated, and we must therefore conclude that the speech of uncivilized and primitive men was more passionately agitated than ours, more like music or song."[2]

I have just been listening to two tape recordings I made of Miranda, age seven. In the first she reads a story from her reader; in the second she makes up a scary story of her own. The first sounds flat and stupid. I wish you could hear the second.

Once there was a little old man. He wanted to get a piece of
volcano rock. So he got all his hiking equipment ready. Then
he hiked up the mountain. It took him twenty years. When he
got to the top he took off the lid. Ooooahoooo! Inside there was
a ghost and he mo—aned and he gro—aned. The man ran away
as fast as he could and he said, "I'm never going to
climb volcanos again!"

Miranda recites her unusual story with intense emotion. Words like
"moaned" and "groaned" are so highly inflected and attenuated they
are almost chanted. The "Oooooahooo' is a pure glissando melody.
Miranda knows that words are magic invocations and can cast spells.
So she exorcises them with music. Of course her teachers will correct
all this in another year or two by muzzling her to the printed page.

Primitive peoples also often have magic invocations, the sense of
which is unknown or unimportant, but which have spell-powers in their
sounds when chanted. Here, for instance, is a magic song from the
Yamana tribe of Tierra del Fuego. No one knows its meaning though
it is sung with great passion.

ma-las-ta xai-na-sa
hau-a la-mas ke-te-sa[3]

Another example of a meaningless charm invocation from the Ved-
das of India:

Tanan tandina tandinane
Tanan tandina tandinane[4]

In Christian Abyssinia the priest chants aloud the dead language
Géez though he does not understand it. In China too the Buddhist
priest does not understand the Pali of the Buddhist canon. In such cases
the meaning of speech is sacrificed to sonority; the words hold beauties
of inarticulate emotion. In the West the linotype has flattened out
human vocal style.

How do we break language out of its print sarcophagus? How do
we smash the grey coffins of muttering and let words howl off the page
like spirits possessed? The poets have tried. First the Dadaists and
Futurists, and now the Concrete poets of our own time. Hugo Ball's
Dadaist poem (ca. 1916):

gadji beri bimba
glandridi lauli lonni cadori

gadjama bim-beri glassala
glandridi glassala tuffm i zimbrabim
blassa glassasa guffm i zibbrabim . . . .

Some of the Dadaists and Futurists experimented with visual effects, trying to lift their word-messages out of the silent embroidery of the print-line, as the following excerpt from a poem by F. T. Marinetti shows.

Marinetti's poems—particularly the book *Mots en liberté* from which the above example comes—could easily be performed as solo or choral compositions. But let us construct a sound poem of our own and perform it as a chorus.

For the following, I am using some very simple conventions. They are these:

1. Let the size of the letter or word dictate its dynamics.
2. Let the position of the letter or word (high or low on the page) dictate its general pitch.
3. If a word is broken or followed by a wavy line, let it be sung.
4. If a word or letter is hand-written let it be intoned or chanted.

5. If it is interrupted on the page let it be broken.
6. If it explodes, let the voice explode over it.
7. If it is written in dotted lines, let it be whispered.
8. Follow the graph for the relative duration of the effects.
9. Let your imagination govern any other visual effects employed.

Exercises

1. Construct some other sound poems and perform them. (How could colors be used to make them more dramatic and expressive?)
2. In Berlioz's *Faust* the demon's chorus sings the following meaningless text:

> Has! Irimiru Karabra
> Tradi oun marexil firtru dinxé burrudixé
> Fory my dinkorlitz
> O mérikariu! O méviexé!

Graphicalize and perform it as a diabolical sound poem.

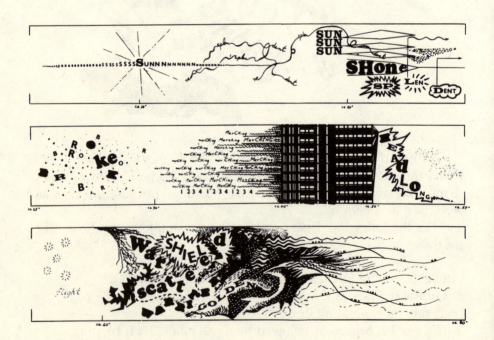

189

WORDS AND MUSIC

Let us take a moment out for reflection. Up to this point we have been stressing the similarities between words and music, their primal and melogenic unity. But are they identical? Are there no differences?

There are and they cannot be ignored. Most prose, for instance, does not sing. I am not overwhelmed by the musicianship of the gentlemen who composed this evening's paper. I notice few vocal pyrotechnics in the editor's column. Clearly other things are more important here. How do we best describe the differenc between music and these other things?

Language is communication through symbolic arrangements of phonemes called words.

Music is communication through arrangements of tones and sound objects.

Ergo: Language is sound as sense. Music is sound as sound.

In language words are symbols standing symbolically for something else. The sound of a word is a means to another end, an acoustic accident that can be dispensed with entirely if the word is written, for then the writing conveys the word's essence and its sound is totally absent or unimportant. Printed language is silent information.

In order for language to function as music it is necessary first to sound it, and then to make of those sounds something festive and important. As the sound comes alive the sense withers and dies; it is the eternal Yin and Yang principle. If you anesthetize words, for instance the sound of your own name by repeating it over and over until the sense of it slumbers, you arrive at a sound object, a musical pendant living in and for itself, quite independently of the personality it once designated. Foreign languages, too, are music when the listener understands nothing of their meaning. Similarly, a Merz poem by the Dadaist Kurt Schwitters is music.

BöwörötääzääUu pögö böwörötääzääUu pögiff

To the old argument of whether it is important to understand the words of the singer, we may now say that as speech becomes song the verbal sense must die. In the following chart I have plotted the stages by which this may be said to happen.

190

MAXIMUM SENSE

MAXIMUM SOUND

1. Stage speech (deliberate, articulate, projected)
2. Domestic speech (unprojected, slangy, sloppy)
3. Parlando (slightly intoned speech; sometimes used by clergymen)
4. *Sprechgesang*—sung speech (the moving curve of pitch, duration and intensity assuming relatively fixed positions) Schoenberg used 5- and 3-line staves to indicate Sprechgesang
5. Syllabic song (one note to each syllable)
6. Melismatic song (more than one note to each syllable) In 14th-century music single syllables are often attenuated through whole compositions
7. Vocables (pure sounds: vowels, consonants, noise aggregates, humming, screaming, laughing, whispering, moaning, whistling, etc)
8. Electronically manipulated vocal sounds (may alter or transform them completely)

Item 8 should more accurately be assumed to cover a wide range of distortions, some minimal, some total. In general our tolerance for speech distortions has jumped dramatically since the invention of electro-acoustical methods of sound transmission. The signal (voice) to noise ratio on a taxi radio or a walkie-talkie may be very poor but those trained to listening to these instruments have no difficulty in making sense from them. In time such speech may be considered more natural than living human speech, just as already today recorded music is more natural than live music.

Must language and music be mutually exclusive? Or can they be held together in an equapoise that satisfies all the requirements of each?

This was the art of *motz el son*, the troubador's art. It was also the art of plainsong, the singing of liturgical prose. But has this delicate balance between words and music been lost since the Middle Ages? Will it ever be discovered again?

The Sphinx shakes his head.

Exercises

1. Study the words and melodies of plainsong.
2. Study the words and melodies of Provencal songs (and read some of the many articles Ezra Pound has devoted to this subject).

CHOROS

Whether the ancient Greek dramas were totally sung or were only sung in part we do not know. But we do know that the choruses were sung or chanted by a group; the very word *choros* means to sing in a circle.

The Greek *choros* performed two important functions: it narrated portions of the drama that took place elsewhere or at other times (the flashback technique in film can be compared here) and it acted as an articulate spectator, moved with him by the pathos of the action, to cry out in joy, scorn or sympathy. This passionate expression was accomplished by means of choral music—alas, we know not precisely how today. Therefore, we have to re-create on our own.

A group of university students were performing Sophocles' *Antigone*.

STUDENTS: How can we perform the choruses?

SCHAFER: Can any of you sing?

STUDENTS: No.

SCHAFER: No?

STUDENTS: No.

SCHAFER: Well, let's look at the first chorus.

> Sunshaft of the sun
> Most resplendent sun
> That ever shone on Thebes
> The Seven Gates-of-Thebes:
> Epiphany you broke
> Eye of the golden day:
> Marching over Dirce's streams
> At dawn to drive in headlong flight
> The warrior who came with shields
> All fulminant as snow
> In Argive stand at arms
> Scattered now before the lancing sun.

SCHAFER: What is the theme here?

STUDENTS: A battle in the sunlight.

SCHAFER: And what then are the key words?

STUDENTS: Sunshaft, sun shone, Gates, Thebes, golden day, marching, drive, headlong, flight, warrior, shields, Argive, arms, scattered, lancing, sun.*

SCHAFER: So we will want to create the tumult of this battle just by our voices. How? First let's set the cosmic scene of the battle. Let's get the sun. Notice how often the word sun and its adjectives are repeated. The poet obviously wanted the battle to scintillate under this flashing sun. The creation of this sunscape must therefore be worked out with great care.

So we began to work out sun sounds. The sibilance of the word could be exploited to suggest the merciless piercing of the lances of the sun on the arms of the warriors: Sssssssssssssun. The first word of the text, "sunshaft" gives the secret. It is night. Then suddenly the first sunshaft of dawn glints across the horizon and strikes the opposing armies, poised for the charge. How to create this striking image with our voices?

Silence. Darkness on stage. As the lights very slowly come up an imperceptible hissing begins and grows louder and louder, reaching a ferocious intensity as the lights come up brightest.

Then the sunshaft breaks into many rays of bright daylight. For this we had all the girls sustain a high full vocal cluster on the syllables "un" and "aft" as the boys sounded the full-frequencied spectrum of "sh" in growing and wading waves. Something like this:

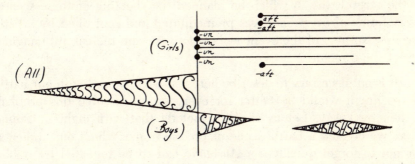

Later we were to dramatize this scene by having the chorus lie flat on the stage on their backs and slowly move their arms and legs out spread-eagle fashion.

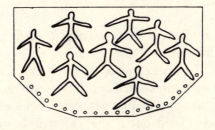

---

* The reader may notice that we have already used some of these words as the text for our Sound Poem.

Over this choric texture soloists rose from the floor and intoned the next few lines in a kind of *Sprechgesang* or sung-speech, overlapping and holding the significant vowels and consonants that would emphasize the alert and spine-tingling situation.

On the word "marching" the armies began to approach one another, at first cautiously, then with increasing speed, with "headlong flight," until the individual warriors could be discerned, rushing into the fray with clashing shields and arms. The counterpoint became frantic and pugilistic. But it was never careless, never sloppy. For the strategy of a charge is planned, and warriors are highly skilled in their business.

I referred the class here to another battle scene from art, that of the battle on the ice in Serge Eisenstein's film *Alexander Nevsky*, for Eisenstein has written copiously (in *The Film Sense* and elsewhere) on the careful way in which he planned the shooting of these scenes. Every frame of every shot was premeditated and controlled by artistic purpose. Nothing of the event wobbled away from the careful imagination of the director.

It is not necessary to describe here just what we did with our battle chorus; for it would be better for every group to solve this problem in their own way. Let us simply conclude that with eight untrained voices we created a battle scene of precise frenzy which our audience was not to forget quickly, for *Antigone* had to be repeated by public demand.

Exercises

1. Any Greek drama will provide wonderful texts of many varying moods, suitable for choral work. Try some.
2. Shakespeare, too. Analysis of Shakespeare's King Lear (3.2. 1-7). Here there are four sentences. Each has a different tempo and different types of sound. The first suggests brief and violent gusts of wind. The second is built on "r" and "s" sounds, and evokes the sound of savage rain. The third, full of immensely varied vowels

and clashing consonants fulminates with the flash of lightening, while the fourth booms with thunder. Using the appropriate phonemes together with pure sounds suggesting a storm, a class could easily build up a polyphonic accompaniment for this text.

> Blow, winds, and crack your cheeks! rage! blow!
> You cataracts and hurricanoes, spout
> Till you have drenched our steeples, drowned the cocks!
> You sulphurous and thought-executing fires,
> Vaunt-couriers to oak-cleaving thunderbolts,
> Singe my white head! And thou, all-shaking thunder,
> Strike flat the thick rotundity of the world!

CHORIC TEXTURES

There are times when one thing is sung or said and there are times when many things are sung or said. Thus we have, on the one hand, *gesture*, the unique event, the solo, the specific, the noticeable; and on the other we have *texture*, the general aggregate, the mottled effect, the imprecise democracy of conflicting actions.

A texture may be said to consist of countless inscrutable gestures. They are like the one-celled bacteria which are perceptible in masses or cluster formations only. Thus we treat the sound events in a texture statistically.

One of Zeno's paradoxes applies here: "If a bushel of corn turned out upon a floor makes a noise, each grain and each part of each grain must make a noise likewise, but, in fact, it is not so."

The aggregate sound of a texture is not merely the simple sum of a lot of individualistic sounds—it is something different. To understand why elaborate combinations of sound events do not become "sums" but become "differences" would take us into the field of the physiology and psychology of pattern perception—but we cannot embark on such a purpose here.

Because they are treated statistically the precise notation of the details of a texture is less important than general questions of density and coloration. The Impressionist painters knew that a suggestion of green brushstrokings would be enough to produce leaves. So in music, many composers have similarly used only approximate notations or graphic devices to indicate textures of sound, leaving the conductor to fix the weight, density, dynamics, coloration, and the other qualities of specific effect.

Accordingly I shall indicate the textural categories below by means of approximate visual effects, leaving the class to work out the details, much as we did in our discussion of the bamboo chime texture analysed in the second part *Ear Cleaning*.

CHAOS

The first texture to consider is *chaos*. Chaos is the *Urgeräusch*, the sound of the universe before creation; and if the Second Law of Thermodynamics is correct, we may assume that it is the sound to which everything is gradually being returned. For this law says that in a closed system (the Universe) entropy (the random element) tends to increase so that all energy gradually becomes more diffuse and purposeless. Such a development is a very long way in the future.

Today a lot of chaos can nevertheless be heard in indeterminate music. One might assume that chaos is easy to achieve. This would be false, for to sustain chaos is exceedingly difficult. Such a soundscape would have to be random in every way—no two gestures could be identical. For man, who is fundamentally antientropic, that is, a random-to-orderly creature, this is an alien concept. The opposite of chaos would be a controlled, homogeneous, single unison note. The unison note and chaos share one important feature: they are both boring, neither goes anywhere. A chaotic texture consisting of limitless, self-contradictory gestures may be full of animation but it is self-cancelling so that the ultimate effect is one of frenzied neutrality—total static animation.

COMBUSTIONS

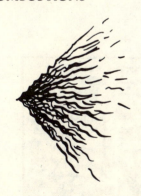

What is a *combustion*? A sudden explosion of chaos. Example of a combustion: a sneeze! The first feature of any combustion is its sudden start. This is then followed by more or less violent chaotic activity, which gradually fades out. The more suddenly a combustion is attacked, the more startling its power. A combustion could be formed of one kind of sound or of many kinds of sound.

How would you produce an explosion of gunpowder employing voices? Of flying glass? Of an angry crowd? Of a happy crowd? The kinds of vocal combustion possible are unlimited.

CONFUSIONS

The difference between a confusion and a chaos is that a confusion is intentional and it. is controlled. (Hence we draw a delimiting line around it.) A confusion is intentional disorder to throw logic into relief. Passion versus intellect. The successful composition is a combination of both. Text for an experimental vocal confusion:

TUMULTUOSSISSIMAMENTE.

Word fragments and raw vocables combined in a jungle-texture.

TUMULTUOSSISSIMAMENTE

CONSTELLATIONS

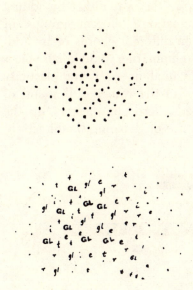

A *constellation* suggests stars, pinpoints of activity surrounded by spaces. Here the texture is rarefied. The sounds of a constellation, therefore, are short, pointed, and exposed. They should fulminate; they should glitter. The word glitter itself, "g" "l" "i" "t" "e" "r" could be the text of a vocal constellation.

CLOUDS

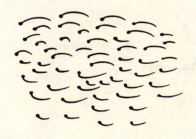

The *cloud*, by contrast, is more diffuse and fuzzy. Its sounds overlap, hang on in the auditory memory with real or imagined reverberation. Even the attacks of sound may be mollified by tapering. The object would be to give a blurred quality to the overall sound. Try working out such an effect to these words: ". . . dimples the water." (Here care will have to be taken to muffle the sounds of the words themselves, which are rather sharp.)

BLOCKS: SLABS

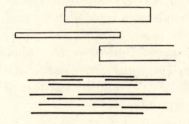

Blocks or slabs of sound are sustained chords or clusters. Sonorities can be built up in this way either by adding or eliminating different groups of voices on different chords or by adding or eliminating individual voices on individual notes. Extra plasticity is given to the rather dull sound of sustained chords or clusters by the careful use of dynamic shadings.

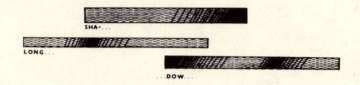

SHA-...

LONG...

...DOW...

WEDGES

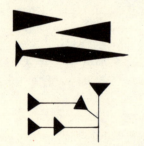

A chord or texture may appear to "grow" in size as a result of its dynamics. It may also grow by the gradual addition of more tones. Choric textures of this sort might be called *wedges* after cuneiform writing which is angular and shaded in this way. A text for vocal experimentation might therefore come from the Babylonian cuneiform.*

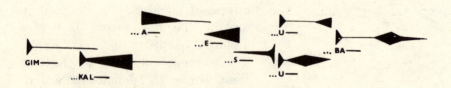

GIM— ...KAL— ...A— ...E— ...S— ...U— ...U— ...BA—

---

* (See *Texts Without Comment* at the close of this part for more Babylonian words.)

CONTOURS

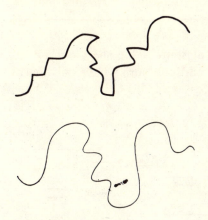

All these textural effects stand in contrast to what we may call the *contour*, the main melodic thrust, of the composition. The contours of a composition, whether melodies or simple counterpoints, or solo effects of any kind, will always predominate to give each piece its own special shape. But the choric textures of which we have been speaking will help produce the basic climate of sound against which individual contours and gestures may arise.

Exercises

1. Using voices create a choric texture to suggest mist; to suggest rain; to suggest a stream; a waterfall; a river; an ocean. Compose a piece of "Water Music" by looping together this itinerary of water sounds.
2. The following remarks of Leonardo da Vinci might be helpful in studying the different textures of running water.

> Of the different rates of speed of currents from the surface of the water to the bottom. Where the water is swift at the bottom and not above. Where the water is slow at the bottom and swift above. Where the water is slow below and above and swift in the middle. Where it is slow in the middle and swift below and above. Where the water in the rivers stretches itself out and where it contracts. Where it bends and where it straightens itself. Where it penetrates evenly in the expanses of rivers and where unevenly. Where it is low in the middle and high at the sides. Where it is high in the middle and low at the sides. Of different slants in the descents of the water.

What we are really considering here is species counterpoint, the combination of melodic lines moving in different directions and at different tempi. Although often misunderstood, counterpoint is really the study of rhythm. By translating da Vinci's analysis of water flow into exercises in sound we emphasize the original etymological relationship between "rhythm" and "river." Try constructing part-compositions for each of da Vinci's ten different types of water flow.

HAIKU

Japanese Haiku poems could make ideal sources for short choral improvisations using elements of textures and contour. I have set one of these as an example.

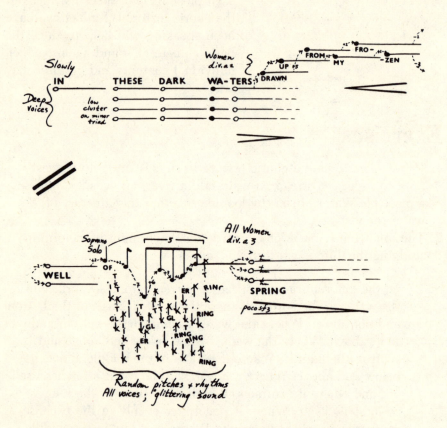

Let student groups work out settings for some others.

MOUNTAIN-ROSE PETALS
FALLING, FALLING,
FALLING NOW...
WATERFALL MUSIC
                    Basho
SEAS ARE WILD TONIGHT...
STRETCHING OVER
SADO ISLAND
SILENT CLOUDS OF STARS
                    Basho

MIRROR-POND OF STARS...
SUDDENLY A SUMMER
SHOWER
DIMPLES THE WATER
                    Sora
SILENT THE OLD TOWN...
THE SCENT OF FLOWERS
FLOATING...
AND EVENING BELL
                    Basho

SIGHT SINGING

I often give a class this problem: You have one note. Make up a composition with it. All I ask is that you don't bore me.

In the course of seeking ways to keep their one-note compositions interesting, they discover rhythmic articulations, changes of tonecolor and dynamics, the functions of rests, echo effects—any number of fundamental musical principles.

One day an eighth grade class and I had been working on a unison note for about half an hour. But things were bogging down.

STUDENT: This is sure a flat piece.

SCHAFER: What's the flattest part of the world you know?

STUDENT: Manitoba.

SCHAFER: All right, let's call the piece Manitoba.

ANOTHER STUDENT: But, Manitoba isn't this flat. I was there.

SCHAFER: What breaks the flatness?

STUDENT: Grain elevators.

SCHAFER: Sure, and trees and barns and rivers, and so on.

I suddenly had an idea to construct a little exercise in which the various visual events to be seen above the Manitoba horizon might become different intervals above a sustained note. Since each object was higher or lower on the horizon, each would have to be a different interval.

1. Fence   up — 2
2. Farmhouse   up + 2
3. Tree   up — 3
4. Barn   up + 3
5. Silo   up p4
6. Elevator   up × 4
7. Bird   up p5 (moving in a melisma over several notes)
8. River   down — 2, + 2 (rippling)

The following picture was drawn on the board and while the class sustained the horizon note solo voices had to sing the word for any of the visual events pointed out at the appropriate interval. This bizarre little piece was actually later performed on a concert with wry humor by the class.

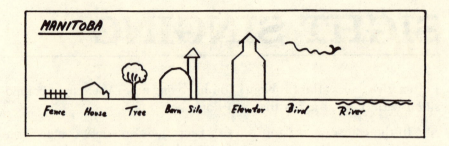

I later explained what we had done to some of my university students. A few months after that I received the followng letter from one of them.

> Dear Murray:
> I think we're doing some exciting things in music. Some
> of the students think I'm nuts, but they are enjoying music.
> I've adapted your Manitoba idea in one class to fit the
> Social Studies course—at the moment a fleeting glance
> at Egyptian and Mesopotamian civilizations. Result:

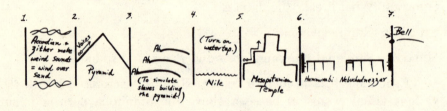

Exercise

Make up other sight-singing exercises on the skylines of the world.

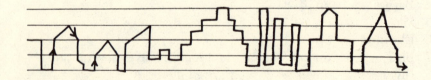

MOONLIGHT

And finally, here is a study-piece for youth choir. It is an ear-training exercise, for the singers must learn to pitch all the notes by interval from the preceding notes. As a text I used the onomatopoeic words for moonlight invented by seventh grade students (See Onomatopoeia, p. 172). I have suggested a few bells might add dulcimer splashes of color (moonlight on water?) to the choral sound. Obviously moonlight calls for a very soft interpretation, but those places where the lines grow thicker, it could be a little louder.

Why do I call it *Epitaph for Moonlight*? Because I doubt whether a group of young people today asked to produce synonyms for moonlight could find inspiration so easy as did my young poets in 1966. The moon as a numinous and mythogenic symbol died in 1969. It is now merely a piece of property—and moonlight will soon rhyme with neon.

The moon is dead, I saw her die.

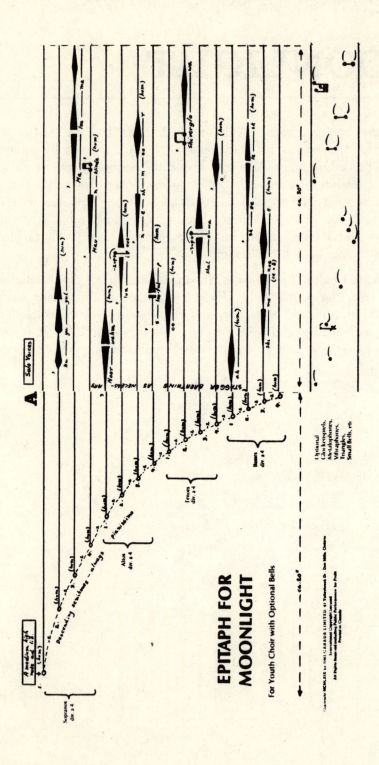

EPITAPH FOR MOONLIGHT

For Youth Choir with Optional Bells

206

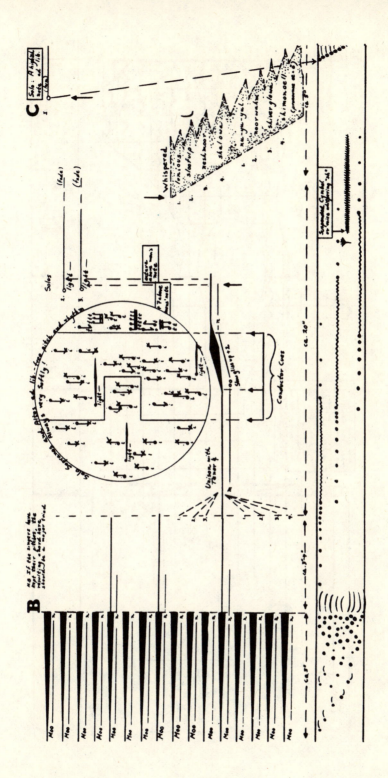

207

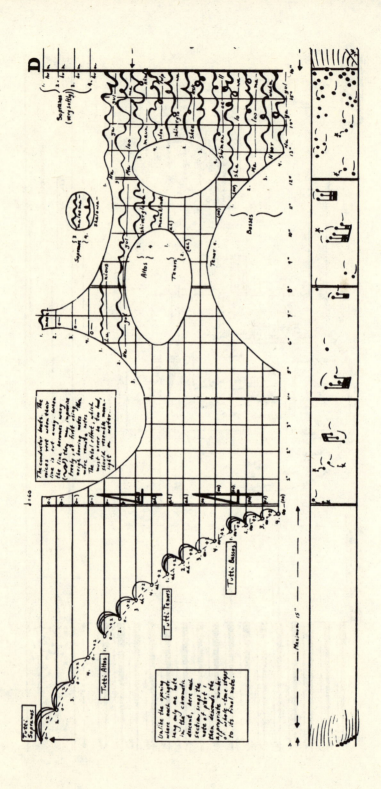

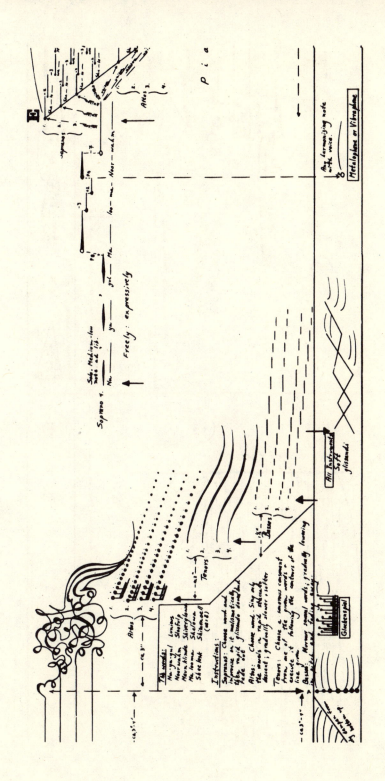

209

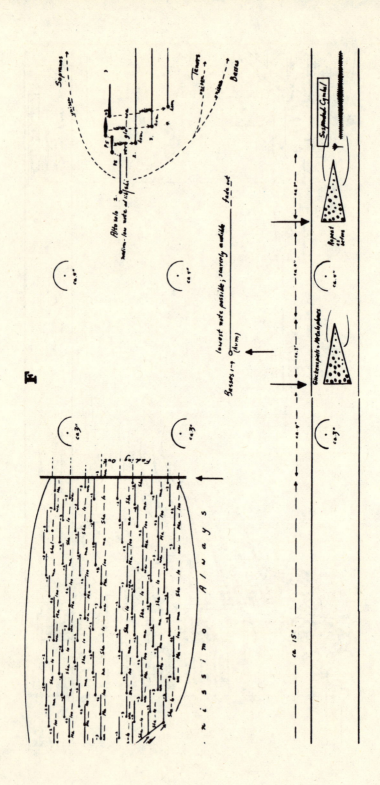

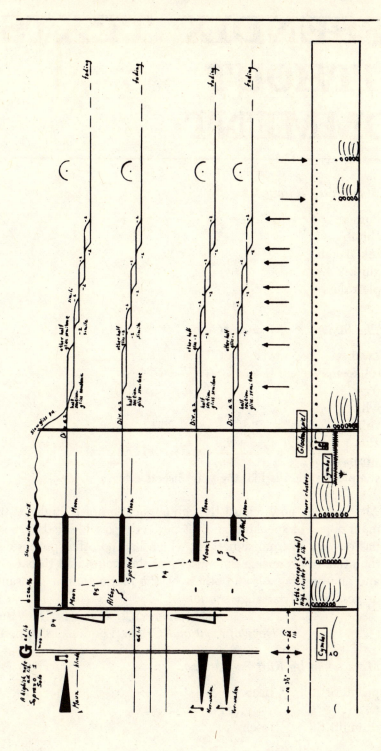

APPENDIX: TEXTS WITHOUT COMMENT

War-Words (Grade 7)

Pugnicunarious
chinib
zeklakoom
glutz
pletride

The Sibilence of Insects (Grade 7)

Zwat
schkeemow
trrsk
whist
chirrup
zllt
sipsip
shelpleck (sounds like the way insects crawl)

Although we now regard the communication of thought as the
main object of speaking . . . it is perfectly possible that speech
has developed from something which had no other purpose
than that of exercising the muscles of the mouth and throat
and amusing oneself and others by the production of pleasant
or possibly only strange sounds.
> —O. Jespensen, *Language: Its Nature,
> Development and Origin*, London, 1959, p. 437.

Merz poem by Kurt Schwitters

priimiitittiii   tisch
tesch
priimiitittiii   tesch

```
 tusch
priimiitittiii     tischa
tescho
priimiitittiii     tescho
tuschi
priimiitittiii
priimiitittiii
priimiitittiii     too
priimiitittiii     taa
priimiitittiii     too
priimiitittiii     taa
priimiitittiii     tootaa
priimiitittiii     tuutaa
priimiitittiii     tuutaa
priimiitittiii     tuutaatoo
priimiitittiii     tuutaatoo
priimiitittiii     tuutaatoo
priimiitittiii     tuutaatoo
```

Poetry is the art of pantomimic dancing with the tongue.
  —Sir Richard Paget, *Human Speech*, London, 1930, p. 202.

Raindrops (University students)

p
pta
petetata
tliptliptlip
bleepblop
pittapitt
betebetebetebete
drimpollillins
plimniblemay
lapluttop
dook
pairleedroms
tilapitatu
cudabulut
ipdes
pelak
schplort
thipthipwoosh

Just as in literature transmitted to us poetry is found in every
country to precede prose, so poetic language is on the
whole older than prosaic language; lyrics and cult songs
come before science . . . .

—Jespensen, op. cit., p. 432

Short peyote song of Arapaho Indians [5]

ye no wi ci hay
yo wi hay
wi ci hay
yo wi ci no
wi ci ni
(repeat from start)
wi ni wi ci hay
yo wi hay
wi ci hay
yo wi ci ni hay
yo wi ci ni hay
yo wi how
wi ci hay
yo wi ci no
wi ni no wa.

Babylonian personal names: from Cuneiform tablets at Telloh

AABBA AADDA AAZZI AAHAMATA AAKALLA AAMÊ
AARHAAŠ AELA AEIGIDÚ AURUGIŠTA ABAÀGANNA
ABAALLA ABA ENKI ABABBA ABBAABBA ABBAURU
ABBAGI ABBAGINA ABBADUGGA ABBAKALLA
GIMKAKUDDA GIMKAZIDDA GIMKALAEŠUBA
GIMKARAGGAN GIMKAREGAL GIMKI GIMKIA
GIMKIDABAR GIMKIDARKAGIMKIQUALO GIMKIRAM
GIMKURDAM GIMMUGUB GIMNE GIMNIGINNIGGIM-
NIGSALMAL GIMNILATTA GIMNINAKI GIMNINI
GIMŠAG GIMSADAP GIMSALNAGUNI GIMSAG
GIMŠKHARBINI UDURNA ÚDURRUGAR UDUKUMMA
UDULU UDGUBARKU UDDURBA UDZABARUBURI
UDNEGARŠAGGA UZZAAN UZZAKI URABBA UREANNA.

We may perhaps draw the conclusion that primitive languages in general were rich in all kinds of difficult sounds. . . . It is a well-known fact that the modulation of sentences is strongly influenced by the effect of intense emotions in causing stronger and more rapid raisings and sinkings of the tone. . . . Now it is a consequence of advancing civilization that passion, or, at least, the expression of passion, is moderated, and we must therefore conclude that the speech of uncivilized and primitive man was more passionately agitated than ours, more like music or song. . . . These facts and considerations all point to the conclusion that there once was a time when all speech was song. . . .

—Jespensen, *op. cit.*, p. 419.

Sing of the wrath of Achilles . . . .
—Opening of *The Illiad*, Homer.
Arms and the man I sing . . . .
—Opening of *The Aeneid*, Virgil.
I beg thee to employ exuberance of diction in they recitation of these pleasant tales.
—Harun Er-Rashid to the story-teller; *Thousand and One Nights*.

"Bird Songs"[6]

Spotted Woodpecker — *tchack*
Whitethroat — *week-week-week-week*
Treecuper — *see-see-see-sissypee*
Hawfinch — *Deak . . . waree-ree-ree Tchee . . .tchee . . .*
   tur-wee-wee
Greenfinch — *wah-wah-wah-wah-chow-chow-chow-chow-*
   tu-we-we
Crossbill — *jibb . . . chip-chip-chip-gee-gee-gee-gee*
Reed-Bunting — *Zee-zee-zee-zurr*
Grey-Wagtail — *Ge-ge-ge-ge-ge-ze-ze-ze-ze*
Nuthatch — *tchirrr* (rolled "r") *pee-pee-pee-pee-pee*
Great Titmouse — *ze-too, ze-too, p'tsee-ée, tsoo-ée, tsoo-ée*
   ching-see, ching-see, deeder-deeder-deeder
   deeder, biple-be-wit-se-diddle
Blue Titmouse — *dee-dee-dee-deedeidderee; pwee, pwee-tee,*
   tee, tee, tee: se-se-se-did-e-did-e-did-e-dit
   tsee-tsee-tit-it-it

Coal Titmouse — *chee-dee, chee-dee, chee-dee; did-dee, did-dee; terrukee, terrukee; weecho, weecho*

Crested Titmouse — *chee-killarree theek-ur-ur-urr*

Willow Titmouse — *tchay-tchay-tchay Eees-aig, aig, aig, aig*

Marsh Titmouse — *Ching-ching-ching-ching ching tow-ow-ow-ow*

Goldcrest — *Err-èèder-èèder-èèder-eezeezee*

Pied Flycatcher — *Tchéetle, tchéetle, tchéetle diddle-diddle-dée; tzit-tzit-tzit, trui, trui, trui*

March Warbler — *za-wee*

Red Warbler — *tuk-tuk-twirr-twirr-twirr*

Sedge-Warbler — *tchissick*

Wood-warbler — *dür-dür-dür- dür it-it-it-it-it*

Chiffchaff — *zip, zap, zip, zap, trirr-trirr*

Mistlethrush — *tre-wir-ri-o-ee; tre-wir-ri-o-ee-o; tre-we-o-wee-o-wee-o-wit*

Cuckoo — *cuck-cuck-oo; coo-coo-cuck; cuck-cuck-cuck-oo; wuff-wuff-wuff; grorr-grorr-grorr*

Bittern — *Boomp*

Corncrake — *crex-crex, krek-krek, rerp-rerp*

Common Snipe — *tik-tik-tik-tuk-tik-tuk-tik-tuk chip-it; chick-chuck; yuk-yuk*

Our cries of pain, fear, surprise, anger, together with their appropriate actions, are more expressive than any words.
—Darwin, *Descent of Man*, Chapter 3.

Where the word stops there starts the song, exultation of the mind bursting forth into the voice.
—Thomas Aquinas, *Comment. in Psalm.*, Prolog.

A verse without music is a mill without water.
—Folquet of Marseilles (d. 1231).

. . . we will never recover the art of writing to be sung until we begin to pay some attention to the sequence, or scale, of vowels in the line, and of the vowels terminating the group of lines in a series.
—Ezra Pound, *ABC of Reading*, New York, 1960, p. 206.

It then turned out . . . that I had never done greater justice to the poet than when, guided by my first direct contact with

the sound of the beginning, I divined everything that obviously
had to follow this first sound with inevitability.

> —Arnold Schoenberg, *The Relationship to the Text,*
> Blaue Reiter catalogue, 1912.

It is natural in an art form which is concerned with the
human voice that none of its many possibilities should be
ignored, so that in opera the spoken word too—whether
unaccompanied or melodramatic—should occupy the same
position as the sung word: from recitative to parlando,
from cantilene to coloratura.

> —Alban Berg, *Die Stimme in der Oper, Musikblatter
> des Anbruch,* X Jarhrang, Nov-Dez., 1928, Heft 9/10, Wien.

English text of Mente vaga Angioletta *from*
Claudio Monteverdi's Eighth Book of Madrigals
Angioletta delights all
sensitive spirits with
her singing.
The spirit of music takes hold of
sonorous voices and shapes them into
voluble life in masterful harmony,
turning aside, then urging on with
interruptions then a repose,
slowly, quickly,
sometimes murmuring
in deep sound alternating flights
with repose and peaceful sighs.
Now suspended in a free line,
now pressing down,
now breaking,
now reining in,
now as a vibrant arrow,
now moving in circles,
quivering and variable,
firm and full.
O miracle of love, the
heart responds.

Debussy discussing the chorus for his projected opera Le Diable
dans le Beffroi:

What I should like to achieve is something more scattered
and split up, something both more nimble and intangible,

something apparently inorganic, and yet with an underlying control—a real human crowd in which each voice is free and in which all the voices combined nevertheless produce the impression of an ensemble

—E. Lockspeiser, *Debussy*, Vol. 2, London, 1965, p. 146.

On the blackboard a student had written:

PREVENT LOCKJAW/OPEN YOUR MOUTH.

Poetry is when words sing.

—Six-year-old boy.

NOTES

1. James Joyce, *Finnegans Wake*, London, 1939, p. 3.
2. Otto Jespensen, *Language: Its Nature, Development and Origin*, London, 1959, p. 419.
3. C. M. Bowra, *Primitive Song*, London, 1962, p. 58.
4. *Op. cit.*, p. 59.
5. Bruno Nettl, *Music in Primitive Culture*, Harvard, 1956, p. 23.
6. E. M. Nicholson and Ludwig Koch, *Songs of Wild Birds*, London, 1946.

I wish to thank Jean Mallinson and Brian Fawcett, who read the text with poets' ears.

Part V

THE RHINOCEROS IN THE CLASSROOM

Above my desk I have written some maxims for educators, to keep myself in line. They are these:

1. *The first practical step in any educational reform is to take it.*
2. *In education, failures are more important than successes. There is nothing so dismal as a success story.*
3. *Teach on the verge of peril.*
4. *There are no more teachers. There is just a community of learners.*
5. *Do not design a philosophy of education for others. Design one for yourself. A few others may wish to share it with you.*
6. *For the 5-year-old, art is life and life is art. For the 6-year-old, life is life and art is art. This first school-year is a watershed in the child's history: a trauma.*
7. *The old approach: Teacher has information; student has empty head. Teacher's objective: to push information into student's empty head. Observations: at outset teacher is a fathead; at conclusion student is a fathead.*
8. *On the contrary a class should be an hour of a thousand discoveries. For this to happen, the teacher and the student should first discover one another.*
9. *Why is it that the only people who never matriculate from their own courses are teachers?*
10. *Always teach provisionally: only God knows for sure.*

The following essays are embellishments on these themes.

INTRODUCTION

Over the past decade I have had the opportunity of meeting countless music educators and teachers of the circumjacent arts across my own country of Canada, throughout the USA, in England, Australia, New Zealand, Germany, and Austria. Numerous lecture tours have made it possible for me to meet sympathizers, opponents, and sceptics; energetic and radiant teachers; timid and apathetic teachers; excellent teachers and bad teachers. At conferences and on tours I have met some whose work has carried them in unusual directions, and I have learned from them.

During this decade the teaching profession has demonstrated greater attunement for change. At first there were merely a few sparks of energy: the early work of Peter Maxwell Davies and George Self in England, that of the Manhattenville Project people in the USA, and by no means least, the work of uncelebrated "originals" in out-of-the-way places everywhere. Today we have a sizeable illumination, so that a few glintings have even transpierced the educational establishment, and there are now a few training colleges where some newer things are known. All the figures mentioned have one thing in common: they have tried to place creative music-making at the heart of the curriculum.

Our cities are less mulishly blatant in their denunciations. What was at first dismissible as the aberration of a few Young Turks has persisted to engage the imaginations of larger numbers of people, and is no longer dismissible. This is a more benign time, and it should be used to advantage to assess the value of the newer methods. I have drawn together these essays on music and the other arts—or more precisely, music growing to meet the other arts—with the hope of making my own thought-paths better known to educators interested in the serious discussion of ideas; for it was with the intention of defining a rationale for my actions that I went home after various experiences with students and argued these essays into existence.

A question often raised over the years at lectures and workshops has been "Where does it all lead?" and I suppose after ten years one ought to have an answer. But the easiest answer to give will be the hardest to take, and will not win many new converts to creativity.

"Where does it all lead?" the principal had asked after one of our more daring sessions, and looking desperately around the class at the debris, I fixed my eye on him firmly and said: "Anarchy, anarchy."

A totally creative society would be an anarchic society. The possibility of whole societies becoming self-actualized remains, nevertheless, slight, due to a persistent terror of original acts of all kinds. It is easier to remain Mr. Smith than to become Beethoven.

It deserves to be pointed out in passing that some other approaches to the subject are related to equally provocative social models. For instance, the orchestra or band, in which one man hectors sixty or a hundred others, is at best aristocratic, and more frequently dictatorial. Or what about the choir in which a heterogeneous collection of voices is brought together in such a way that no single voice is permitted to assert itself above the homogeneous "blend" of the group? Choral singing is the most perfect example of communism ever achieved by man.

The music class is always a society in microcosm, and each type of social organization should balance the others. There ought to be a place in the curriculum for individual expression; but the curriculum as previously conceived provided no opportunity for this, except in as much as it imagined its objective to be the training of virtuosi, in which case it generally failed.

The main thrust of my work has been in creative music-making, and while it is distinguished from the mainstream of education, which has been concerned above all with improving the executive abilities of young musicians, neither activity should be considered a replacement for the other. The trouble with specializing in digital celerity on an instrument is that the mind tends to get sluiced off in the process. It has been disappointing to observe large numbers of young people engaged in impossible attempts to jiggle their hands faster than Horowitz. (There was even a time in recent history when the virtuoso paradigm affected the appreciation of music, and one was supposed to have a Ph.D. even to know how to listen!) Fortunately the limitations of human aptitude are putting an end to these ambitions. On the other hand, there has arisen an equally disappointing tendency, particularly in America, to substitute for impossibly high standards none at all. The introduction of pop music in the classroom is an example of this slovenliness, not because pop music is necessarily bad, but because it is a social rather than a musical phenomenon and is therefore unsuitable as an abstract study, which music must always be if it is to remain an art and a science in its own right.*

---

* This is a controversial subject, but my contention is that musicianship, sociology and the money business do not benefit by being jumbled together—which is to say that it is impossible to analyse a pop song until it is ten years old, by which time why bother?

Different degrees of intelligence require different goals. Most of my work has been with ordinary rather than exceptional young people, yet I have still not met a child who was incapable of making an original piece of music. Humanity struck right down the middle may never be capable of appreciating the best of Bach or Beethoven, and most people could waste their lives trying to perform them eloquently. The genius syndrome in music education often leads to a debilitation of confidence for more modest achievements. Perhaps some of the most striking musical devices may be the result of the limitation of human intelligence rather than inspiration. For instance, it is commonly assumed that the medieval organum (singing in parallel fourths and fifths) came into existence when certain members of the singing group mispitched the notes of plain-chant. Similarly, it is conceivable that the canon came into existence when certain voices lagged behind the lead voices. If this is true, we might conclude that organum was the invention of the tone-deaf while the canon was the invention of the slow learner.

I am merely trying to point out that music education, geared down to the average human intelligence, may have its own rewards; and certainly it would be more appropriate for places like schools where average human beings congregate.

We must keep returning to the beginning. What are the basic ingredients of music? What are the pristine elements out of which it can be structured, and what are the expressive potentials which the human being or group possesses to realize these ends? I have gone back to these elementary questions. Perhaps I have never moved beyond them. Most of the things discussed in this book do not require elaborate resources—just a few sounds, a few voices. Elaborate audio-visual tools were avoided, perhaps not consciously, but somehow because they seemed unnecessary.

Critics have often pointed out that as I am a classroom teacher only avocationally, I have never actually worked with one group of children long enough to determine whether an approach such as mine stands a better chance of raising the competence of the profession or even of producing a greater number of musical epicures than other methods.*

---

* A series of eight sessions with 12-year-old children was recorded in the film *Bing Bang Boom* by the National Film Board of Canada, and this did at least lead us up to a point where the class composed and performed its first piece of music. Equally important, from the point of view of demonstrating my abiding belief that the teacher's first task is to plan for his own extinction, was the fact that while at the opening of the film I am the central figure, asking questions and devising stratagems, by the end I have become almost invisible, while the class has taken over its own destiny, criticizing the composition and planning new works.

This is a justified criticism. I make no special claims. I have entered classrooms and worked with young people because I like to do so as frequently as time permits. As I grow, my philosophy of music education changes. I have tried to prevent it from becoming a method out of sheer fear of boring myself. What is taught probably matters less than the spirit with which it is imparted and received. I have entered classrooms where hideous pieces of music were being performed well, have witnessed the enthusiasm there, and have left without an ill thought, vastly preferring such experiences to the other type where beautiful music is ripped to shreds by a grimacing teacher and sulking accomplices.

The best thing any teacher can do is to plant the spark of a subject in the minds of students, so that it may grow, even if the growth takes unpredictable forms. I have tried to make the enthusiastic discovery of music precede the ability to play an instrument or read notes, knowing that the right time to introduce these skills is when the child asks for them. Too often teaching is answering questions which nobody asks.

Mistakes have been made. I have often failed, and have allowed myself to be observed failing in public. Of course I have not tried to fail, but it is in the nature of experimental work that it should sometimes fail, for the moment an experiment succeeds it ceases to be an experiment. If the edge of the art is to grow we must live dangerously; which is why I teach my students that their failures are more useful than their successes, because a failure provokes further thought and self-criticism. A successful person, in any field, is often a person who has stopped growing.

Sometimes we do not know which is a failure and which is a success. What the teacher thinks has been a failure may be considered a success by a student, though the teacher may not know this until months or years later.

Some classes are complete puzzlers. I recall once giving a class of 12-year olds the assignment: "Music exists in time. I don't know what time means. Communicate the experience of time." This is a task I had often set for university students and the results had always been interesting. I had not then studied Piaget's work on time conceptualization in children, and it was clear when they came back the next day that the assignment was beyond them. Still, I wanted to find out how far their sense of time extended, and so I asked them how long the longest imaginable piece of music might be. "Two hours," said one boy. "Do you think you could play a two-hour piece of music?" He thought he could, so I asked him to choose his instrument. He chose a bass drum and started booming. That was the end of that class. We all listened to him for fifteen minutes, then the bell rang and the class went home for lunch. "How much longer?" he asked faintly at 12:30. "About an hour," I said, and he went on beating. At about one o'clock two of his chums returned early and brought him some chocolate milk. Then, as encouragement, they started beating along with him. Most of the class drifted in early to find out what was happening. When the two hours were up, the drummer collapsed on the floor. The principal heard about the experience and later asked me: "What did you do that for?" He was always asking abrupt questions to put one on the defensive. "Well," I replied, trying to summon up confidence, "it may be that education is merely the history of all the most memorable events in our lives. And if that is so, all I can say is that this was one lesson Marty will never forget."

A STATEMENT ON MUSIC EDUCATION

NOTE: One of the more memorable days in my life occurred in Moscow in October 1971 when I stepped up to give one of the inaugural papers in the section "The Training of Young Musicians" at the Seventh International Music Congress of the International Music Council of Unesco.[1]

The general air of somniferousness that prevails at all conferences was intensified by the mid-afternoon sun and a décor the color of clotted blood. When, as you will see below, I clapped my hands to illustrate a point, several of the delegates fell off their chairs. One other effect also proved unusual. In order to illustrate how much more dependent Beethoven was on his ears than his eyes I remarked that "Beethoven did not, as is commonly supposed, lose his hearing—he lost his *vision*." I don't know what the translators did with this elliptical though harmless remark, but they must have made it sound very powerful, for afterwards several delegates, even some who had missed the original speech, came up to enquire about the source of this new medical evidence concerning Beethoven's eyesight.

Every teacher ought to be allowed to teach idiosyncratically, or at least to infuse his teaching with his own personality. I am going to speak to you today about some personal ideas. From your own experiences you may be able to amplify, correct or challenge them.

My work in music education has been concentrated mostly in three fields.

1. Try to discover whatever creative potential children may have for making music of their own;
2. To introduce students of all ages to the sounds of the environment; to treat the world soundscape as a musical composition of which man is the principal composer, and to make critical judgments which would lead to its improvement;
3. To discover a nexus or gathering-place where all the arts may meet and develop together harmoniously.

To this I would add a fourth field which I am just beginning to explore: the uses to which oriental philosophies can be put in the training of artists and musicians of the West. I will speak of these in that order.

CREATIVE MUSIC-MAKING

I would like to think all teachable subject-matter can be broken down roughly into two classes, according to whether it satisfies the instinct for gaining knowledge or for self-expression.

History is a knowledge-gaining subject, and it consists (perhaps wrongly) of the transmission of a body of facts from the teacher's mind to those of the students. I see music as predominantly an expressive subject, like art, creative writing, or making of all kinds. That is, it ought to be this, though with a heavy emphasis on theory, technique and memory work, it becomes predominantly knowledge-gaining. While we encourage self-expression in the visual arts (and hang the products in art galleries as a testament to the exciting perceptivity of our young) the parallel in music is usually little more than to memorize "Monkey in the Tree" for some year-end social display. (One may also have learned a lot of lies about the lives of the great—and invariably dead—composers, and one will have drawn half a million treble clefs.)

The teaching of visual arts is well ahead of the teaching of music. There is in music, for example, no equivalent to the Basic Course which Johannes Itten developed for the first-year students at the Bauhaus, a course which has been widely duplicated all over the world. This was a course in free expression, but taxed creatively by the progressive limitation of choice, so that the student was led almost imperceptibly into contact with the great, elementary issues of visual expression. We can profit from the experience of art teaching. Could music not be taught as a subject which simultaneously releases creative energy and trains the mind in the perception and analysis of its own creations?

The big problem with education is one of tense. Education traditionally deals with the past tense. You can only teach things that have already happened. (In many cases they happened a very long time ago.) It is the tense questions that has kept artists and institutions apart, for artists, through acts of creation, are concerned with the present and future rather than the past. Education is neither news nor prophecy, neither present nor future. To perform, to interpret music, is to engage in a reconstruction of the past, which may certainly be a desirable and useful experience.

But could we not spend some of our energies in teaching to make things happen? Is this not a question worth considering? The only way we can turn the past-tense subject of music into a present-tense activity is by creating. Marshall McLuhan has written: "We are entering a new age of education that is programmed for discovery rather than instruction."

In a knowledge-gaining subject the teacher has all the answers and the student has an empty head—ready to assimilate information. In a class programmed for creation there are no teachers at all: there is only a community of learners. The teacher may initiate a situation by asking a question or setting a problem; after that the role as teacher is finished. One may continue to participate in the act of discovery but no longer as a teacher, no longer as a person who already *knows* the answer.

I emphasize this again: in a class programmed for creativity the teacher must plan for his own extinction. And I will add parenthetically that it took me several years before I felt comfortable doing this. I lead off a class by asking a question or setting a problem. These are of a special type; they must allow for as many solutions as there are students in the class. The class must become an hour of a thousand discoveries, and the secret is in the question asked. Types of questions:

1. Silence is elusive: try to find it.
2. Write down all the sounds you hear.
3. Find an interesting sound.
4. Find an interesting sound consisting of a dull thud followed by a high twitter.
5. Find a sound which passes by you from south-west to north-east.
6. Let five sounds inhabit two minutes.
7. Place a single sound in a profound container of silence.

You will notice that these problems are progressively limiting. They force the student to concentrate harder. But they always permit unlimited solutions.

Sometimes I begin a course by leading the students into a room filled with percussion instruments. The first lesson is brief: "Get acquainted with these instruments. I'll be back tomorrow to see what you have discovered." The next day I return and ask some questions. Have they discovered the reverberation time of the vibraphone? Have they discovered how many shades of sound they can produce from the tam-tam using different sticks and brushes? Have they discovered the function of the pedal on the tubular chimes? If not, they have not done the assignment. I leave again.

When they are relatively familiar with the types of sounds possible from the instruments available, we begin improvisation and composition sessions. I divide them into small groups. Everyone in the class must compose at least one piece and must conduct it. Sometimes students find it more convenient to write their piece down in graphic or pictographic notation. Colors are also popular. Anything is permitted so long as the intention can be communicated to the other members of the performing ensemble. But little by little throughout the course I impose regulations in order to force the students to concentrate harder. The whole course is gradually propelled towards the final assignment, which is this: "You have one tone.* Compose a piece with it. All I ask is that you don't bore me."

That, as you can appreciate, is an extremely difficult assignment.

THE SONIC ENVIRONMENT

A second phase of my work as music educator is concerned with the sonic environment in which we live. I do not wish to confine the habit of listening to the music studio and the concert hall. The ears of a truly sensitive person are always open. There are no ear-lids.

I have found that one can also perform valuable ear-training exercises employing the sounds of the environment. How, precisely, are you listening at the moment? (Schafer claps his hands.)

What was the last sound you heard before I clapped my hands? What was the first sound you heard after I clapped my hands?

How good is your aural memory? What was the highest sound you heard in the past ten minutes? What was the loudest? And so forth.

I often ask my students questions like the following:

(a) How many airplanes have you heard today?
(b) What was the most interesting sound you heard this morning?
(c) Who has the most beautiful speaking voice in your family? In the class? Etc.

Sometimes I have students make collections of interesting sounds throughout a building and write them down on a map so that others can find them and listen to them too. One of my students has been discovering all the unique sounds of the Vancouver soundscape, the sounds you would hear in no other city in the world. She plans to give her collection to the tourist bureau so that visitors interested in more than "sight-seeing" can discover also what a rich acoustic experience Vancouver presents to the curious ear. Another student is making a collection of disappearing and lost sounds, all the sounds which formed part of the sonic environment but can no longer be heard today. She is carefully recording these sounds, cataloguing them with elaborate notes. Perhaps they will be of interest to some museum of the future.

---

* "Tone" (North America); "note" in English usage.

The sonic environment of any society is an important source of information. I do not have to tell you that the sonic environment of the modern world has been getting louder and probably uglier. The unrestrained multiplication of machines and technology in general has resulted in a world soundscape, the intensity of which is continually rising. There is now recent evidence to demonstrate that modern man is gradually going deaf. He is killing himself with sound. Noise pollution is one of the great contemporary pollution problems.

Anyone interested in music should be interested in these facts. If we all go deaf there will simply be no more music. One way to define noise is to say that noises are sounds that we have learned to ignore. We have been ignoring them so long that they are now completely out of control.

My approach to this problem is to treat the world soundscape as a huge macrocosmic composition. Man is the principal creator of this composition. He has the power to make it more or less beautiful. The first task is to learn to listen to the soundscape as a piece of music—to listen to it as intensively as one would listen to a Mozart Symphony. Only when we have truly learned how to listen to it can we begin to make value judgments about it. Which sounds do we like? Which do we want to keep? Which are unnecessary? Are some of the more delicate sounds being threatened by the larger or more brutal? For instance, my students discover that they cannot hear the sounds of the birds when a helicopter or motorcycle passes by. The solution is implicit. If we want to continue to hear birds at all we will have to do something about the sounds of helicopters and motorcycles.

This is a positive approach to the noise-pollution problem, and I regard it as the only one which has a chance of being successful. It must be initiated by musicians, for we are the architects of sounds, we are concerned with making balances and arrangements of interesting sounds to produce desired aesthetic effects.

A MEETING PLACE FOR ALL THE ARTS

I want now to suggest an even more radical idea. The longer I am involved in music education, the more I realize the basic "unnaturalness" of existing art-forms, each of which utilizes one set of sense receptors to the exclusion of all others. The fantastic demands made to achieve virtuosity in any of the art-forms have resulted in abstract accomplishments to which we can rightly apply the term "unnatural," for they in no way correspond to life as we experience it on this earth.

Beethoven did not, as is commonly supposed, lose his hearing—he lost his *vision*. It is the painters, whose works hang in the silent vaults of the museum, who lost their *hearing*.

For the child of five art is life and life is art. Experience for a child is a kaleidoscopic and synaesthetic fluid. Look at children playing and try to delimit their activities by the categories of the known art-forms. Impossible. Yet as soon as those children enter school, art becomes art and life becomes life. They will then discover that "music" is something which happens in a little bag on Thursday morning while on Friday afternoon there is another little bag called "painting." I suggest this shattering of the total sensorium is the most traumatic experience of a young child's life.

A class of 6-year-old children is asked to imitate birds and fly about the gymnasium. "Tweet-tweet-tweet" go some of them as they spread their wings. "Quietly, children," says the teacher. How limply fly the muzzled birds! So a piano is brought in and teacher plays the *Swallow Song*. Thus begins the twitterboned balletics of the dancing class. The parents come to admire our pedagogical accomplishments. The children have become so "artistic."

Why was the sensorium shattered? Why do we not have simply one multitudinous art-form in which the details of perception corroborate and counterpoint one another as they do in life? Perhaps you are thinking I am going to say that the whole development of separate art-forms was a mistake from the start. I am not going to say that: not exactly.

We separate the senses in order to develop specific acuities and disciplined appreciation. Music is a collection of elegant acoustic events and the study of music is useful and desirable as a means of cultivating aural acuity.

But a total and sustained separation of the senses results in a fragmentation of experience. To perpetuate this state of affairs throughout a lifetime may be unhealthy. I would like us to consider once again the possibilities of synthesis of the arts.

I have no particular philosophy of education, but of one thing I am growing unyieldingly convinced. In the first years of school we should abolish the study of all the arts. In their place we should have one comprehensive subject, perhaps called "media studies," or better "studies in sensitivity and expression," which would include all yet none of the traditional arts.

Yet, at a certain point we could still separate out the individual arts as separate studies, though always bearing in mind that we are doing so in the interests of developing specific sensorial acuities. This would be the middle period of study. Ultimately, having cleaned each of the lenses of perception, we might turn to a reconfiguration of all the art forms into the total work of art again—a situation in which "art" and "life" would be synonymous.

Wagner's idea of the *Gesamtkunstwerk* was noble but premature. Such a concept cannot be comprehended by the graduates of conservatories and ballet schools. But today there is renewed interest in mixed media among the young. I believe the time is approaching when we will be forced to design study programs to achieve a new integrity in art —and in life.

I promised to speak at the conclusion of these thoughts of the ways in which my own thinking is beginning to be influenced by oriental philosophy. This is not easy, for our experiments in this field are not yet conclusive. But one thing oriental philosophies can teach us is a reverence for stillness, for the calm soundscape in which a little gesture can become big because it is uncrowded by competition.

It is paradoxical that in the West the moment we produced hi-fi sound-systems for the reproduction of sound, the general soundscape slipped into a lo-fi state—that is, one in which the signal-to-noise ratio is about one to one. It then became impossible to distinguish wanted sounds from mere accidents and sonic jabberware. In a story by the Argentinian writer Borges the hero dislikes mirrors because they multiply people. I am becoming suspicious of radios for the same reason.

In the West, silence is a negative concept, an embarrassment to be avoided. In some oriental philosophies, indeed in Christian mysticism, silence is a positive and felicitous state in itself. I would like to regain that state in order that a few sounds could intrude on it and be heard with pristine brilliance.

In our classes we have been trying to employ some yogic relaxing exercises as a preparation for the listening and creating experience. Little by little the muscles and the mind are relaxed to a point where the whole body becomes an ear. This may take some hours, but at the conclusion, students have told me, they have heard music as never before.

When the Japanese calligrapher paints, he sits motionless for what seems to be an eternity; then he picks up his brush and with a deft movement of the wrist, fastens a perfect symbol to the page. He has been mentally mastering that movement for a lifetime. He doesn't fumble.

I would like to see us stop fumbling with sounds and begin to treat them as precious objects. After all, no two sounds are the same, and once uttered a sound will be lost for ever—unless we remember it. To me, ultimately, music is nothing but a collection of the most fascinating and beautiful sounds made by people with good ears and affectionately remembered by humanity.

ANOTHER STATEMENT ON MUSIC EDUCATION

Any discussion of music and education will be an attempt to answer four basic questions: Why teach music? What should be taught? How should it be taught? Who should teach it? Here are my feelings on these questions.

WHY TEACH MUSIC?

It has not been easy to secure a place for music at all in the context of public education systems in many countries today; and even where it does exist, it is usually strongest in the primary school, fading away progressively as the child grows.

Many school administrators have no music in their bellies. It is not easy to show these people that great minds of the past have assigned to music an educational role of the highest significance, unless they have read the writings of Plato, Aristotle, Montaigne, Locke, Leibnitz, Rousseau, Goethe, Shaw, and others, which is by no means likely. But the cultural "guilt complex" which prevents unmusical people from expelling music entirely from the curriculum also forces them into a justification of its presence without adequately understanding why it should be there. Excuses are invented, the most common being that music promotes social well-being: "Singing and playing together can bring understanding and goodwill." What is really being said here is that music-making is good citizenship. Brass bands and competitive music festivals are the traditional means of bringing about this herdesque happiness, without, of course, the peculiar social models on which they are based being recognised for what they are.

Arguments are often advanced to justify music on moral grounds. Luther, Milton, and Burton all strongly advocated music on the grounds that it makes good and gentle men. But we may fairly certainly say that this argument collapsed when Beethoven was adopted by the Nazis—who were not gentlemen. Music may help to promote many things: sociability being one of them; grace, ecstasy, religious or political fervor and sexuality being a few others. But in itself music is fundamentally amoral. It is neither good nor bad, and there is no conclusive evidence of a relationship between human character and aesthetic preferences.

Perhaps this represents a decline in the efficiency of music. Plato attributed such strong moral powers to music that he was obliged to outlaw a good deal of it from his *Republic*. Similarly,

> We recall that in the legendary China of Old Kings, music was accorded a dominant place in state and court. It was held that if music throve, all was well with culture and morality and with the kingdom itself. The music masters were required to be the strictest guardians of the original purity of the "vulnerable keys." If music decayed, that was taken as a sure sign of the downfall of the state. . . . No sooner were those wicked notes struck in the Royal Palace than the sky darkened, the walls trembled and collapsed, and the kingdom and sovereign went to their doom.[2]

We might like to see such power restored to music. There is a faint echo of it still in totalitarian states, where the utterances of artists are feared by politicians. In the West there are no risks associated with art, and so we must ask ourselves again: Why do we have music in our schools?

The answer is simple. Music exists because it uplifts us. Out of our vegetable bondage we are raised to vibrant life. Some people (following philosophers such as Schopenhauer and Langer) believe music to be an idealized expression of the energies of life and the universe itself, and there is little doubt that this notion can be given concrete expression in an appealing and convincing manner, as has already been done by Dalcroze and a few other figures.

Thus we can demonstrate that the practice of music can assist the child in coordinating the motor rhythms of the body. The *andante* walks (from It. *andre* = to walk). Music can run, jump, hobble, and swing as well. It can be made to synchronize with bouncing balls, with waves, and horses hooves, and with hundreds of other cyclic or regenerative rhythms of nature and the body. Singing is breathing. The universe vibrates with a million rhythms, and man can train himself to feel the pulses. The physiological bond between these impressions and man's expression of them has ben beautifully caught in Pierre Schaeffer's phrase "One listens with the hands") (*On écoute avec les mains*). The sounds we hear immediately compel us to respond, to reproduce them on instruments of our invention.

Music exists so that we may feel the echo of the universe vibrating through us. To catch these vibrations we need a bold music—mind-stimulating, heuristic, imaginative—a music in which the mind and body join in acts of self-discipline and discovery. To justify music fundamentally on any grounds other than its importance to intellectual, muscular and neural stimulation and coordination leads to problems which can only be solved in the long run in unmusical ways.

WHAT SHOULD BE TAUGHT?

We have two obligations here. Obviously any society will have a repertoire of past musical experiences which it will want to keep alive. In the West we have been quite assiduous in realizing this objective, even though the repertoire we have kept alive is often not as broad historically as it might be. In the interests of putting our own culture into perspective, the music of other cultures should also be studied, a matter which is only beginning to receive attention.

But we have another obligation, and that is to continue to expand the repertoire. Here we have fallen down miserably. It is a question of tense. If the achievements of a society are all in the past tense, it is in serious trouble. This is why it is always necessary to keep alive the exploratory instinct for creative music-making. Education could become news and prophecy; it need not be limited to lighting up the tribal history. I do not mean that we should merely shovel music by contemporary masters into the classroom. Rather, I am concerned that young people should make their own music, following whatever inclinations seem to them right. For this to happen the teacher has to be very circumspect about when and how he or she interferes. The hardest thing the teacher may have to learn is to keep quiet and let the class struggle—especially when he thinks he knows the right answer.

The American painter William de Kooning was once asked about how past traditions had influenced his work. He replied: "The past doesn't influence me. I influence it." Quite right, for the past is only illuminated by the light of present activity. No one is permitted a total view of the past. As our present activities change, so does our perspective on the past; and so, too, do our perceptions and skills. For example, let us look at two models of the history of Western music, both very different from the traditional model on which our present system of music education is founded.

One of the illustrations in Robert Fludd's *Utriusque Cosmi Historia* of 1617 is a diagram entitled "The Temple of Speculative Music," and it shows how the study of music was divided in his day. Here we find the division of the monochord, the church modes, the proportions, the study of counterpoint, and so on, all neatly schematized in order that the liturgical music of the seventeenth century could be executed properly (*See Model* A).

Model A

This model is rather violently juxtaposed with one prepared by a first-year university student entitled "History of Western Culture Music." It was prepared as a guide for the student himself in teaching school music, and each block was to receive an equal amount of time in the curriculum. The distinctions in the area the student knows and loves best are very subtle indeed. The rest lies in darkness (*See Model B*).

Model B

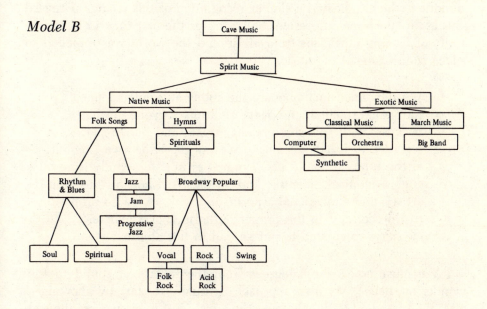

Everything in history which bears on the present is useful. Anything which doesn't is paleography and will require the attention of musicologists. It is their job to revivify neglected traditions—for the "rearguard" can also be a growing edge of the art. But the real nerve of music must remain present-tense creating, and it is to this subject that I have devoted most of my personal attention. The exercises I employ fall naturally into three groups.

1. Listening
2. Analysing
3. Making

I have discovered that listening exercises need not necessarily be limited to making discrete judgments about the sounds we find inside the time and space containers of compositions and concert halls. A solfège can be worked up on any available sounds from the environment as well. The main thing is that sounds should not only be listened to but should also be analyzed and judged. If, for instance, we are listening to the sound of leaves rustling and a bulldozer drives by, the teacher should not miss this opportunity to point it out as an example of bad orchestration, equally as egregious as when, in classical music, a viola is made to struggle against a timpani. In part three, *The New Soundscape*, I noted that we have now entered an era in music history when we may have to be as much concerned with the prevention of sound as with its production. In 1969 the International Music Council of Unesco passed a motion which indicated a similar recognition of this change. I regard this as an epoch-making resolution since, for the first time in history, a unity of leading musicians from all around the world was impelled to place silence ahead of music.

> We denounce unanimously the intolerable infringement of individual freedom and of the right of everyone to silence, because of the abusive use, in private and public places, of recorded or broadcast music. We ask the Executive Committee of the International Music Council to initiate a study from all angles—medical, scientific and juridical—without overlooking its artistic and educational aspects, and with a view to proposing to Unesco, and to the proper authorities everywhere, measures calculated to put an end to this abuse.

We must proceed by degrees from the felicity of sound to the wonder of silence. My own approach is usually to start by allowing a class total freedom to do whatever they wish. But in art we are allowed only one free gesture; all the rest is discipline. Thus little by little I try to tax the imagination by introducing whatever rules seem to be implicit in the first free action, just as Johannes Itten did in his extraordinary "Basic Course" at the Bauhaus. We start with freedom, but then, little by little we concentrate on craftsmanship and economy. We might call this contracting into abundance. The ultimate assignment would be a single gesture in a container of silence, which is prepared for by weeks or months of concentration and training.

Once when I was guest-teaching an unusual situation developed which forced us to concentrate very hard, employing limited means. I found myself in one of those open-style schools in which the only sound-proof room is the toilet. As I entered the classroom the teacher said: "I hope you are not going to make a lot of noise." She had already had complaints from the adjacent classes. The walls went up about eight feet and over the gap, between there and the ceiling, the voice of another teacher could be heard: ". . . now if the radius of the circle is multiplied by . . ." etc.

The situation called for an unusual assignment, and so I told the class that I would like us all to work together to devise one sound which would be so astounding that the mathematics teacher would be compelled to stop and listen to us. "He never stops," volunteered a student. "All the more difficult for us," I replied, and we set to work We thought of many sounds, and when at last we agreed on the best one, we tried it out, then stopped breathlessly to see what would happen. Over the wall we heard ". . . then the solution to the radius problem will be. . . ." "We failed," I concluded reluctantly. "But we'll try again tomorrow."

HOW SHOULD MUSIC BE TAUGHT?

I have been discussing education programmed for experiment and discovery. In such a situation the teacher must become accustomed to being a catalyst to whatever might happen in the class, rather than dictating what must happen.

It is my very strong feeling that in the future we might expect to experience a withering of the teacher's role as an authority-figure and focal point in the class. In truly creative work of any kind there are no known answers and there is no examinable information as such. After providing some initial questions (not answers), the teacher places herself in the hands of the class and together they work through problems. I have given explicit accounts elsewhere of my own experience along these lines. It is enough to mention here that by making "music" with sheets of paper, by inventing our own private onomatopoeic language, by collecting sounds at home and in the streets, by improvising in small groups, and by doing all the other things we did, we did nothing that anyone couldn't do once ears had been opened. This was the exclusive skill demanded.

Sometimes techniques from other disciplines can be usefully employed in music education. From social psychology we can learn a good deal about group dynamics. The problem here is to measure the assignment given with the appropriate number of people likely to realize its completion. I have discovered that for the kinds of heuristic problems I like to set, groups of seven to nine persons are optimum. This allows for free discussion, and it also permits a leader or conductor to cue and coordinate the entire group in an improvisation or exercise. I never appoint leaders, but let them arise naturally from the ranks. The trick is to devise varying assignments for the groups, so that at one time or another each member will discover naturally that he or she possesses the requisite skill to lead the group.

We live in an interdisciplinary era, and it often happens that a music class can spill out into a session in another subject. I never resist this when it happens. For instance, in forming groups I often ask the class to divide itself into, say, four groups of equal numbers. This generally takes some time. I put a clock on them and tell them to hurry up. On one occasion with 12-year-olds this took twenty minutes to accomplish. I then asked them how long they supposed it would have taken had I divided them myself. "Maybe twenty seconds." "Does this then suggest to you any difference between democracy and dictatorship?" "Dictatorship is faster!" "And therefore better." "No!" And we launched into a discussion of why not.

Sometimes a model from another subject can be successfully adapted to music education. I have used models from theatre, dance, the visual arts, communications theory, electronics—even from baseball.

One summer Bill Allgood and I were teaching musicianship at a summer camp in Maryland. We found it hard going; nothing we did really fired the students' interest. Then we had an idea: musical baseball. We divided them up into two teams. The fielding team was to place men on the bases and in the outfield. Each student took his instrument. The pitcher played a motive at random, consisting of from one to as many notes as there were players on the team. The batter had to imitate it exactly on his instrument. Each failure was counted as a strike. If he succeeded it was equivalent to hitting the ball. It was then up to the appropriate fielder (say the second-base man if the motive had consisted of two notes) to field the ball by repeating the same motive. If he succeeded the batter was out. If he failed, he had a hit. We worked out all sorts of little refinements, but that was the general shape of the game. We spent days playing it—and of course improved our ears remarkably in the process.

WHO SHOULD TEACH MUSIC?

Traditional music: professionals. No compromises here. Professionals only. Music as a complex discipline embracing theory and performance must be taught only by those qualified to do so. No compromises. We would not allow a man who had attended a summer-school course in physics to teach it in our schools. Why should we tolerate this with music? Is music any less involved with complex acts of discernment? It is not. Can the seismographic control over muscle and nerve-energy demanded for musical performance be acquired in a few weeks? It cannot. It is not enough, therefore, to say that the education authorities are satisfied to have music taught this way. *We* are not satisfied! If we are not satisfied we must change the system until we *are* satisfied.*

Only the student with high musical qualifications and aptitudes should be encouraged to undertake the extensive training program necessary for the teaching of music in the traditional sense. No compromises. We reject the current notion that the teacher should be some sort of Renaissance hero, equally proficient at fifteen skills. We may always be short of qualified music teachers, but better short of good things than smothered with bad. Perhaps the itinerant music teacher is the only solution for the less populous areas of the country, unable to maintain qualified music teachers on a permanent basis.

By qualified music teacher I mean not only someone who has attended a university or music school specializing in the subject, but also the professional musician who has earned a living and a reputation through proficiency in a keenly competitive profession. At the moment one of the black spots in school policy (at least in North America) is the systematic exclusion of such people from teaching. The professional musician would bring a devotion and a competence to music education that even a university education has no guarantee of producing. Music education is a matter to be undertaken by musicians, the best we can get, wherever we can get them.

The great Swiss music educator Dalcroze has written: "Under an ideal social system, everyone will make it his duty to dispense his art and learning freely about him; every true musician, both composer and artist, will devote an hour daily to the giving of music lessons for the benefit of the public—then, and not until then will the problem be solved."

We will want to preserve the good things from the past and develop some good things of our own. In the discovery of new things virginity of intellect has its advantages. It may be possible, therefore, or even desirable, when searching for recruits for the teaching of music in the "present tense" to accept precisely those people who, possessing a love for the subject, do not possess the qualifications demanded of the

---

* In the North American school system, elementary-school teachers are usually required to teach all subjects. The colleges of education thus offer them minimal training in music education. When I was teaching elementary teachers in the Faculty of Education at Simon Fraser University, the amount of time provided for the music program was three hours per week for four months. This is typical of most colleges. This fact needs to be understood for a true comprehension of the following paragraphs. It was because I knew "music" could not be taught effectively within these limitations that I devised the *Ear Cleaning* course as a substitute.

traditional teacher. Their unprejudiced innocence may be useful in making discoveries of new techniques and approaches. The faculty of education or the teachers' college with a full program in music education will have no opportunity to give student teachers enough skill and information in the subject to make them confident and inspiring music teachers in the traditional sense. Here a special alternative is necessary, and this is where I believe some of the things I have been advocating can be of special value. Knowing nothing, we should attempt, in the short time available, to discover all we can about sound —its physics, its psychology, the excitement of producing it in the throat or of finding it in the world outside ourselves. You will say these teachers will not be teaching music. Perhaps not. But their simple exercises in sound-sensitivity may be of more value than all the drivel they would otherwise communicate in the name of an art they have no right to teach. Supposing they managed in their classes to clean out enough ears that all over the country a militant protest arose to combat the accumulating sewage of sounds in our daily environment, would that not also be a good thing? Perhaps even a better thing than slobbering over Mozart *noch einmal*?

I would append here a strong feeling I have that the collapse of specialisms and the growth of interest in interdisciplinary undertakings should not go unnoticed by those engaged in any kind of music education. Throughout the twentieth century the arts have demonstrated a strong susceptibility to fusion and interplay. I suspect it is only a matter of time before media studies are undertaken in the classroom, when the various individual arts are let out of the little bags in which they were placed so long ago, to indulge in an interplay that will be exciting and strengthening. Dalcroze was certainly much in advance of his time when, around 1900, he developed his eurhythmics, by which training in the temporal art of music was drawn into synergy with the activity of body movement in space.

The danger with these synaesthetic exercises is that an over-indulgence in them brings about a confusion of the senses, and unprofitable piling-up of resources rather than an acuity of sensorial experience. This is the problem with most of the multi-media art-forms today. The extended study that Kandinsky makes of the single dot in his book *Point and Line to Plane* needs to be duplicated in the other arts (in music, for example, with the single tone*) before we dare embark on complex combinatorial undertakings. It is the most elementary forms

---

* *Or* "note."

of any art—the matrix forms—to which we must return each time we wish to step out in a new direction. Only when they are purified and clearly apprehended will it be possible to embark on a new program of integrated studies.

It is doubtful whether traditional departments of music are the places to cope with "present-tense" musical education as I have been outlining it here, for the study demands talents from which they have tried to keep themselves immune. Then other more suitable places must be found to carry on these studies. And before long it may occur, even to universities, that they are desirable, necessary, inevitable.

A NOTE ON NOTATION

About 200 junior high school students were present one sunny afternoon in Toronto in 1966, and I told them they were going to have a word-association test. As soon as they were given the word, they were to write down the first thing that came into their minds. The word was "music."

45 students wrote "notes."
25 students wrote "sound(s)."
23 students wrote the name of an instrument other than the piano.
16 students wrote "piano."
12 students wrote "composer" or gave the name of a composer.
11 students wrote "teacher" or "Miss —."
9 students wrote "melody" or "tune."
8 students wrote "staff."
6 students wrote "music paper."
7 students mentioned records or recording stars.
6 students wrote "music paper."
6 students wrote "school."
The remainder gave an assortment of associations from "love" and "peace" to "boredom."

These results staggered me. I had, of course, suspected that the material of music would compete uncomfortably with the spirit of the art; but when nearly a third of the students react to the subject by writing "notes," "staff," or "music paper," an arrangement of teaching techniques is urgently needed.

Music is something which sounds. If it doesn't sound, it isn't music.

I have always resisted music reading in the early stages of education, for reading too easily encourages a departure to paper and blackboards, *which are not sound.*

How much time in music education is spent in silent exercises—in the penmanship of clef-drawing, or in otherwise acquiring silent knowledge of things about which silent knowledge is neither useful nor desirable?

Conventional musical notation is an extremely complicated code, and years of training are necessary for its mastery. Until it is mastered, it is an impediment to confidence. It is debatable whether we have these years to squander in a public education system. Ideally what we want is a notation that could be mastered in ten minutes, after which music could be returned to its original state—as *sound*.

In Iran a blind master teaches a group of six students to play the santour. He plays a highly embellished phrase and nods at one of the students. The student repeats it. If he does so accurately, the teacher plays another phrase and nods at another student. If he makes a mistake the teacher repeats it and nods at him again. Often the student anticipates a phrase being dictated by the master and a complex heterophony results. The class lasts two hours. Not a word is spoken. Not a note is written down.

We live in an entr'acte between eras. While countries like Iran are nudging into the era of literacy, the West is entering the age of the second illiteracy.

Television replaces the textbook, and the tape-recorder is replacing the musical score. Whether conventional notation will survive this shock is not yet known, but the rapid breakup it is undergoing at the hands of today's *avant-garde* composers suggest that it needs total reappraisal. For the moment, however, we will have to contend with a multiplicity of systems, and the whole matter should give the educator much food for thought.

Musical notation consists of two elements: the graphic and the symbolic. The history of Western music shows that at first the graphic tended to predominate. The dimensions of time and pitch were plotted along the vertical and horizontal axes of the page, and the Greek diacritical markings ´` and ^ were employed to indicate movement: up, down, and up and down, respectively. Later, symbolic conventions began to become more pronounced: the use of clefs, filled-in and open notes, accidentals, key signatures and editorial markings such as *p*, *f*, *ritardando*, etc. There is no analogue between these signs and the things they indicate; they are simply symbols agreed on by convention as being suitable to suggest certain musical maneuvers. Often graphic and symbolic features exist in close relationship, though they can be separated. For instance take these two notes ○ •. The first precedes the second in time because it comes before it on the space of the page (graphic). But it is not the size or shape or length of the two notes that distinguishes their duration; it is a convention that black notes are shorter than white ones (symbolic).

Sometimes our notational system has two signs for the same thing, one which is graphic and the other symbolic, for instance, the word *crescendo* and the sign <. In general we may say that in conventional notation the symbolic elements are more highly organized and therefore tend to predominate. The difference between symbol and graphic notations is that the former gives more precise information, while the latter indicates the general shape of the entire piece. If he or she knows nothing about notation, the fledgling musician will almost invariably devise one which is more graphic than symbolic in character. He wants to indicate the total form of his composition; he has not yet learned to be concerned with details.

I never discuss notation at all to begin with. When the matter eventually comes up I let the class struggle with it for a while. By that time they are already composing pieces, which may be vocal, or conceived for simple percussion instruments. As the students usually work in smallish groups, they can manage these first exercises by discussing

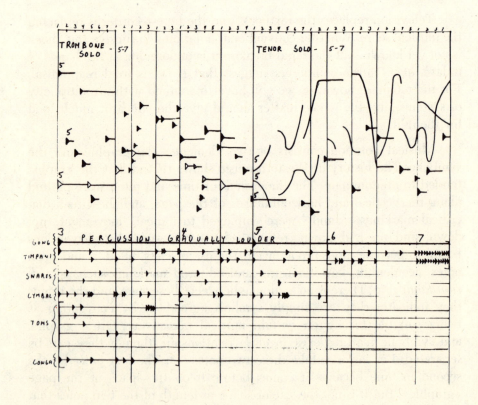

An example of a student's notation.

in advance what they intend to do. As the assignments grow more elaborate, the time approaches when a written score seems inevitable, and so I let them devise their own, using any means they wish. These first scores are always very colorful but usually quite unsuccessful. Nevertheless, it is interesting to see what information they contain: is it pitch that concerns the students most, or rhythm, or tone-color? Different students react in different ways, but few manage to take all the parameters of musical expression into consideration on their first tries. By showing them what has been neglected they are led into a deeper consideration of the total experience of music-making. This is accomplished by taking a score and giving it to an alien group for performance, then enquiring of the author whether the interpretation came up to expectations. We then try to determine which features of the music were missed out, and another attempt is made to render the notation more precise.

In this way an interest in music theory begins to develop. This is the moment to introduce conventional musical notation, which is probably still the most adequate system for the communication of most musical ideas. Once students have discovered this their desire to master it grows rapidly.

I have often wondered whether there could not be developed some more satisfactory transition from the exotic notations my students first produce to the conventional system. The great beauty of the early work of George Self[3] is that by using a very few of the basic signs of traditional theory he manages to give us a system which permits relatively free expression of ideas without violating conventional theory. I have proved to myself that Self's method can be taught to 6-year-olds in fifteen minutes in such a way that at the end of that time any child in the class can write and perform a little piece of his or her own invention. The rudiments are these: one line gives three classes of pitches, high, medium and low, above, on and below the line; there are two types of notes—black for short notes and white for long notes; there are two dynamic distinctions—*forte* and *piano*; and barlines are employed to indicate conductor's cues. All the potentials for *any* type of musical expression have been introduced in embryo.

It ought to be possible to develop further from here. For instance, by the addition of one more line, five pitch-zones would be available, giving us a pentatonic system; or with two more lines we could have a modal system of seven notes. By adding two leger lines and two clefs in various positions we could then have modes beginning on F, D, A in the treble clef and A, F, C in the bass clef. Transposition could scarcely be made more effortless than this.

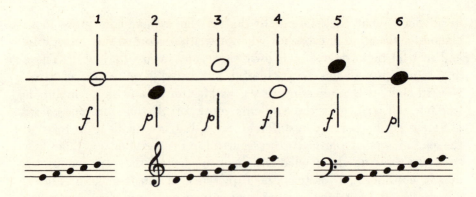

To be useful notation must be objective. Subjective notations may look attractive, but unless they can be communicated to others the composer will suffer some unhappy surprises. A special task of music educators ought to be to invent a new notation, or notations which, without departing too radically from the conventional system, can be quickly mastered in order that the devilment of penmanship exercises may never again be allowed to displace the purr of live music-making.

Examples of notations by students will
often be strange and colorful.

THE MUSIC BOX

A few years ago educational kits became fashionable in North America as partial replacement—along with television, films, and tapes—for the textbook. It was part of a genuine attempt by some educators to unfasten the curriculum so that it could be better manipulated by teacher and student to suit individual requirements.

In my lifetime I have seen the principle features of education and environment shift places. When we were young the things we studied were quite strictly controlled. We memorized a good deal: poetry, dates, maps, and tables. Everything was programmed and predictable. Our out-of-school environment, on the other hand, was quite free. We had a ravine to play in and it was there that we built tree-forts, made caves, went fishing or played cowboys, sought, invented and discovered, quite unmolested by teachers or parents.

Today it is otherwise. The modern urban child inhabits an environment in which the imagination is kept prisoner. The streets of his city are laid out with Euclidian strictness, and his spare time is divided between organized games and entertainment cycles such as television serials. As a reaction against the disciplines of the external environment, education is now becoming a quest for discovery. The classroom walls are coming down. Children are now being urged to move about freely, to invent on their own, to find a hobby or to use their imagination in unorthodox ways—exactly what we did in the fields of our youth.

Education today is antienvironment still, but in precise opposition to the days when the school bell, the pointer, and the strap used to represent military headquarters in the unruly countryside of trees and ponds, pony-rides and snowstorms.

The object of any media kit, therefore, is to introduce a little entropy into the classroom. But like many misunderstood tools, kits were soon being mass-produced in styrofoam settings by Madison Avenue hucksters, whose minds were about as open as traps, which is to say that they were not forms of possibilities at all but only new forms of authority, as rectilinear as a book.

If one is going to invent a kit for the modern classroom, the first thing it ought to be is a cunning mess. The human being is fundamentally antientropic, that is, he or she is a random-to-orderly arranger. Thus if we wish the idea of order to occur in the mind of the child, we should start with a little chaos. This is how our ancestors proceeded to produce

Gothic cathedrals, pyramids, and Japanese gardens out of the random environment in which they found themselves. Confronted with information that is already packaged, the child cannot invent; it can only memorize or, in extreme cases, reject and destroy.

But the impression of disorganization of the media kit must be an illusion, for in reality the kit, while incomplete in itself, must reveal its completion in the incentives its contents suggest. In this sense we may speak of possibilities, lurking beyond the material itself, waiting to be discovered; and the measure of a good kit is the distance separating the original contents, which may be modest, from the imaginative outsweep they suggest to the kit's users.

In 1969 an invitation came from the Ontario Arts Council to participate in the preparation of a media kit for music education. For about two months I worked with numerous others (Harry Freedman, Harry Somers, Linda Zwicker, and my brother Paul) to produce a kit of calculated disorder called *The Music Box*.[4]

First we divided the vast subject of music into several areas, then we set to work trying to discover materials and ideas for each of these areas. Our general categories were:

1. Instruments and Sound-Makers
2. Tapes and Records
3. Musical Scores
4. Articles, Pamphlets and Booklets
5. Idea Cards
6. Lead-out Items (to suggest connections with other subject areas)

The completed box contained nearly 300 items, so I will mention here only a few from each category, to give some idea of what we tried to cover.

1. *Instruments and Sound-Makers*
   Conventional
   - bells
   - pellet drums
   - tambourines
   - erh-wa (Chinese stringed instrument)
   - wood-block
   - Japanese flute
   - etc.
   Unconventional:
   - a sheet of paper on which was written: "This piece of paper is a musical instrument. How many sounds can you make with it?"

- a stethoscope, for listening to one's heart, one's stomach, or the walls of buildings
- balloons, to be filled with sugar, rice, or pellets, etc.

2. *Tapes and Records*
   - a tape of random electronic sounds with a splicing kit, to create tape compositions
   - an LP of a Chinese opera
   - an old 78 r.p.m. pop record from a junk store, etc.

3. *Musical Scores*
   - undeciphered Babylonian cuneiform inscription believed to be musical notation (in the hope that some youthful cryptologist might succeed in doing what no Assyrologist has yet been able to do)
   - Mozart's stochastic composing method for writing a limitless number of minuets by throwing dice and selecting from a stock of phrases
   - some oriental notations
   - numerous *avant-garde* scores, particularly those with a high graphic content
   - an example of sheet music from the 1890's entitled "A Kiss Through the Telephone"

4. *Articles, Pamphlets and Booklets*
   An assortment of printed material dealing with music history, appreciation, acoustics, tape-recorders and electro-acoustics, noise pollution and hearing conservation, together with pictures of musical instruments, broadsides and programmes of old local concerts, ancient reviews from local newspapers, etc.

5. *Idea Cards*
   These were intended as triggers to touch off discussion-groups or initiate individual projects. Much of the material for these cards was drawn from my own previous booklets. Here are a few examples that will not be found there, though they move in the same way and are intended to draw the reader into the participation of their solutions.

You have four tones* and one minute

Try to walk absolutely silently. Listen to the huge sounds you make.

Using only your voice and *non-speech* sounds tell a class-mate: (1) where you have hidden a certain object; (2) your impressions of a holiday; (3) your impressions of some mutual friend; (4) how you feel about this exercise.

---

* In English usage, "notes."

A composer once took a recording of a symphony and by re-recording it several times he reduced it to a single click. Q. How did he do it?

Find a three-dimensional object. "Sing" it as you move around it.

With your voice describe the sound a shovel makes:
(*a*) in clay
(*b*) in gravel
(*c*) in sand
(*d*) in snow

If concert halls were shaped like this

or this

or this

instead of this

What kind of concerts would we have?

Sing a steady *glissando* up one octave lasting precisely ten seconds.

Bring a high, thrilling sound to school. The next day bring a dark, gloomy one, then an explosive one, etc.

In a private language create a word to describe the sound of walking
(*a*) in fresh snow
(*b*) in hard-packed snow
(*c*) in slushy snow

Improvise a solo and record it. Play back the tape. Add a live improvisation in counterpoint.

Can you think of a sound that has been going on continuously for the past fifteen minutes, even though we haven't been listening to it?

The sound of a flag flapping in the wind .

The sound of the tallest building in your town falling down.

Turn this room into an orchestra.

Dead matter grows when new particles are added on the *outside* of old particles, like a snowball.

Living matter grows when new particles grow *between* the old particles.

Q. Is music dead or alive?

The sound of fingernails on glass .

If Chopin is

and Bach is

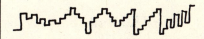

— what are Beethoven, Debussy, and Stockhausen?

All the pianos in suburbia are slumbering.
Go and wake them up.

Let us establish an archive of disappearing sounds. How many of these can you record on tape?
- quill pens on paper
- hand-operated lawn-mowers
- street-cars*
- butter being churned
- hand-rung school bells
- treadle sewing-machines
- horses on cobblestones
- the quiet explosion of old cameras
Can you think of others?

---

* Trams.

6. *Lead-out Items*

- a seashell
- an audiogram
- a stroboscopic disc
- a kaleidoscope
- a pair of rubber thongs with ribbons (for dancing?)
- a pair of dark cardboard glasses for listening in darkness
- clear 16-mm. movie film and equipment for drawing on the film
- schematic for building a sine-wave oscillator
- schematic for building a transistor-radio jammer
- schematics for building musical instruments
- a set of ear-plugs

Once *The Music Box* was in a penultimate state we experimented with it in four different schools for several months. All teachers found it exhausting to work with, for there could be as many projects going on at once as there were students. Another difficulty was that many of the items in the *Box* were soon destroyed or lost. This was, of course, predictable, and we were careful in our introductory notes to make the teacher and students aware that the *Box* was to be regarded as perpetual process, to which they should continually add ideas and materials of their own. We even suggested that a class might consider making up a box of their own for presentation to another class.

It is not appropriate for one of the authors of *The Music Box* to have the last comment, and so I close with two statements by others. The first is a letter from one of the first teachers to experiment with the *Box* to a prospective future user.

Dear Valerie,

I must begin by apologizing for waiting so long to write you. There have been so many things to keep me busy that it's amazing I even have time to teach. (You no doubt know the feeling well.) I'll try and answer your questions and add some things which I think you'd also be interested in as I write.

First, the multi-media "music box" is really helping me to formulate my own thoughts and purposes for music education. Namely that there is much more to discover in music than just learning to sing or play an instrument; not that I'm understating vocal or instrumental programs, but too often they can get us into narrow ways of dealing with music. Hopefully a good music program can contain vocal *and* instrumental work *and* activities which would evolve out of *The Music Box*.

I'm not intending to presume that *The Music Box* is the only way to get out of this narrow path, but it's working for me.

I said very little to the students about the box before it came to the school other than, "I've got a surprise for you next week." It was placed in the center of the room. I briefly commented on the fact that they could work by themselves or in groups and that several tape-recorders, record-players and film-projectors were available in the room if they needed them. At that, I just allowed them to delve into the box in groups and take out and have a good time with whatever they found interesting. Their initial reaction was one of great excitement. After about 45 minutes I yelled things to a halt and we had a good talk about where we should go from here. This was a most important discussion and I got immediate feedback about what they wanted to do and what extra equipment they needed for their particular activity. . . . Both the students and I felt that at least two or three of these exploratory sessions were necessary—even more for some students. The most important part of the program is *what do we do from here?* At the moment here are some of the activities that have evolved with three classes (a grade 7, a grade 8, and a grade 9 class).

1. Drawing on 16-mm. clear film with coloured markers (abstract art, animation, graffiti of all kinds)—lots of discovery here about number of frames per second, sound-tracks, etc.
2. Same as above with sound-tracks of their own.
3. Experimenting with all kinds of sounds. (I had the students who were interested go home and find the most interesting, exciting sound they could discover and bring it to school.)
4. Experimenting with sounds on a tape-recorder—slowing down and speeding up their sounds to produce new sounds and organizing their sounds as "compositions for tape recorder."
5. Making and using simple electronic apparatus (sound-generators).
6. A basic study, with the help of an oscilloscope, of the physics of sound.
7. Composing for voice(s), one or more instruments, instruments and/or voices, plus other sounds.
8. Composing as above but writing down their notation as dots, thin and thick lines, ascending and descending lines, etc., rather than writing conventional notes on the staff.

9. Composing—writing in the conventional manner.
10. Reading, discussing, and experimenting with the printed material in the music box.
11. Investigation of how a loudspeaker works.
12. Learning to play new instruments.
13. A study of music in other cultures and time-periods.

These are basically the activities which have evolved so far. Some of the students started working with one activity, stopped, and went back at a later date. Some are working all the time on their activity. Others were excited for two or three initial periods and haven't gone back since. Generally, at any one time, about 50 per cent of the class is working on activities which grew out of their experiences with *The Music Box*. Those who don't work with it make a small band or work in an ensemble group with me or a student conductor. This is really the only problem to date: that of having to be in so many different places at the same time. It really develops independence on the part of the students, since I can't be motivator, consultant, resource person, and conductor all at the same time in five or six different areas of the school. There's no question about it—it's easier to work with one band or one choir with all the students in front of you at the same time. However, the importance of what we're doing, I feel, demands flexibility, adaptability, and lots of energy on the part of the teacher.

At the moment, the program, in my opinion, is a very successful one, and as long as the students are free to make lots of choice of activities, they are having a great deal of fun discovering, learning, and experimenting.

Yours sincerely,

Exhausted Teacher

The second comment on the *Box* is taken from an article in a Toronto newspaper.

COSTLY CACOPHONY

It just doesn't do these days to be dogmatic about what is music or what is a musical instrument—a circumstance happily seized upon by the staff of the Ontario Arts council for its design of the Music Box. This is described, in the heady jargon of contemporary educators, as an unstructured, multimedia teaching tool. Brace yourselves, for we are about to open the lid: tapes, records, *avant-garde* music scores, booklets, old sheet music from around the world, a seashell, castanets, bells, kazoos, a tambourine, pellet drum, harmonica, length of chain, cheese grater and thimble, a Chinese erh-wa (don't ask us) and almost 300 other items of musical exotica.

The whole cacophonous package can be yours for $395, although it is obviously expected that most will go to schools. Maybe they are aimed at the music teacher who thought he had everything, rather than the parent who already thought he had too much.

Is there really any point in trying to have an educational spending ceiling while the Ontario Arts Council is plotting to raise the roof? (**The Globe and Mail**, 1 December 1971).

THRENODY

NOTE: It would be a misconception to think that because young people are less skilled than professionals in their executive musical abilities it is easier to compose music for them. One might say that the poverty of stimulating repertoire for the contemporary young suggests precisely the opposite. Many composers seems to find the technical limitations of youth groups beneath or beyond their abilities.

Of all my attempts in this form one of the most ambitious is *Threnody* (a religious piece for our time), which was written for and premièred by the Vancouver Junior Symphony in 1967. It is difficult to find a theme that will connect with today's youth. I wanted to find something that would engage their minds as well as their ears, their conscience as well as their musicianship. *Threnody* was one attempt to find a solution to these questions. The paper that follows first appeared in *Music*, May 1970, Vol. 4, No. 5

There are times when one is inclined to think the great days of religious music are over: The church was once the strongest patron of music; it was powerful and could afford the services of the very best musicians. The sumptuous religious music of Guillaume de Machaut and Monteverdi, of Mozart and Schubert, testifies to centuries of exceptional musical sponsorship. But since the time of Beethoven, such religious music as we have had has been brought into existence only rarely by the churches, and most of these works are performed in concert halls. Today an avowedly religious composer like Stravinsky has been deprived of his authentic patron, and the vibrant expression that he and others might have brought to the church has been rejected, often for flabby substitutes. God's taste seems to have deteriorated in recent years.

But despite the disinclination of the church to patronize the most contemporary or most ambitious forms of musical expression, composers have shown no equivalent disinclination to stop composing religious music.

I hope under religious music we may include everything with strong Christian ethics and humanitarian implications; for I was thinking, while writing the preceding paragraph, less of the delightful works of composers such as Benjamin Britten, with texts glossing aspects of the Bible or liturgy, and more of the many works by modern composers, in both the popular and the classical fields, which take up moral positions on contemporary problems such as war, racial discrimination and undignified human behavior of all kinds, for Christianity has solutions to these problems. The work of which I am about to write is one of this type. It has two main purposes in performance and only one is musical. Music is used here as the swiftest means of transporting the audience to the emotional-point where they realize the stupidity of war, of all wars, of all apologies for wars.

Threnody is an 18-minute work for youth. It is scored for youth orchestra, youth choir, five young speakers, ages 8 to 18, and electronic sounds. *Threnody* is an anti-war protest. The texts spoken by the speakers come from two documents: (1) eye-witness accounts by children and young people of the atomic bombing of Nagasaki on 9 August 1945; (2) comments and telegrams to and from the Potsdam Conference in July 1945 following the first successful test explosion by the United States. The first text is spoken by children; the second text by adult voices on tape. The opposition this creates is violent. For example:

> *Men's voices on tape:* "The test was successful beyond the most optimistic expectations of anyone. . . . There were tremendous blast effects. . . . The President showed me telegrams about the recent experiment. He was rather inclined to use the text as an argument in our favor in the negotiations. . . . The President was delighted and said it gave him his cue for the issuance of a final warning."

> *Children's voices:* "Five minutes later a girl came struggling up the road. Her clothes were in shreds and her hair was in disorder. . . . As I came near to Urakami I began to meet many injured people. They were stumbling along, weeping crazily. Their faces, necks and hands were blistered and on some of them I could see sheets of skin that peeled right off and hung down flapping."

Threnody is an uncomfortable work. I prefaced the score with a statement by the scientist Jacob Bronowski from his book *Science and Human Values*:

> When I returned from the physical shock of Nagasaki . . . I tried to persuade my colleagues in governments and in the United Nations that Nagasaki should be preserved exactly as it was then. I wanted all future conferences on disarmament, and on other issues which weigh the fates of nations, to be held in that ashy,

clinical sea of rubble. I still think as I did then, that only in this forbidding context could statesmen make realistic judgments of the problems which they handle on our behalf. Alas, my official colleagues thought nothing of my scheme; on the contrary, they pointed out to me that delegates would be uncomfortable in Nagasaki.

The music of *Threnody* is in a contemporary idiom, but it is always conceived for the age-group for which it was intended. Within a controlled framework there are numerous sections where the young singers and instrumentalists are given opportunities for thoughtful improvisations. "Thoughtful" rather than spontaneous because the improvisatory sections are always set in apposition to portions of the spoken texts, for which they must set an appropriate mood and illumination. In rehearsal I usually try to have the instrumental soloists and the speakers rehearse together, drawing the musicians' attention constantly to the character of the words they are accompanying. To perform *Threnody* properly one must take up an ethical position on the subject matter.

In all rehearsals of *Threnody* (and I have been present during the preparations for several performances involving different groups) one notes a devolving seriousness and intensity as the theme of the work gradually becomes apparent. Sometimes at first an air of levity prevails, occasioned partly by the peculiar graphics of the score, which contains some notational idiosyncrasies, and only little by little do the performers adjust to the gravity of the texts they are reciting and accompanying. You know they are asking themselves questions as they go along. Sometimes the youngest participants never realize the nature of the tragedy. Their innocent portrayals of the grizzly texts give the whole a poignancy that is hard to describe, but moving to experience.

I recall clearly the premièr in 1967 in Vancouver, given before an audience consisting largely of teachers and parents, people intimately involved with the destiny of the performers. There were tears. Afterwards there was no applause, just a strained silence, until one by one the listeners got up and left. I think it was only at this moment that the performers realized the full impact of the work themselves.

The dropping of those first bombs was an epochal event in history, a moment when humanity sensed for the first time, perhaps only dimly yet, that we now hold the power of total annihilation in our own hands. When I was asked to write a work for young people which would speak to them directly, I thought first of this terrible bequest. Significantly neither the title of the work nor most of the text fragments I chose to use mention the Nagasaki event specifically, and the work therefore continues to apply to Vietnam, to Biafra, to any demonstration of aggressive stupidity, to any holocaust.

Sometimes performance organizers feel the need to associate *Threnody* with a special event such as Remembrance Day, or to follow it with a discussion of the implications it raises. Clearly it is a musical sermon; it does not belong to the conventional concert program. In a 1969 Toronto performance it was followed by a discussion between the performers, the audience, and a panel including former Canadian Prime Minister, Lester B. Pearson, A Nobel Peace Prize winner, Robert Jay Lifton, the Yale psychiatrist and author of the book *Death in Life*, chronicling the after-effects of two Japanese atomic bombings, and Stanley Burke, the Canadian newsman who had recently resigned to devote himself exclusively to relief work for the victims of the Biafran war. I think it helped to provide an opportunity for the release of emotions summoned up by the performance, though numerous people left before the discussion, obviously not prepared to indulge in the casuistry of words.

A composer always hopes his music will circulate. I naturally have this hope, but of all my works I hope *Threnody* will travel the most, the farthest, and deepest. I literally want it to be performed to death. I want it to be performed until it is no longer necessary. Then I will burn the score.

AFTERNOTE: I recall saying something to this effect during our panel discussion in Toronto. Lester Pearson, who, I am sure, thought my view of war somewhat simplistic, afterwards said he would like to see the work performed during one of the ceremonies of the United Nations, and offered to discuss the matter with some friends there. The *engagé* artist always feels that if his work is strong and its message clear it may succeed in persuading men whose ambitions seem to be provoked by other considerations. I had almost forgotten Mr. Pearson's kind gesture when one day I received a letter from a certain UN ambassador who informed me that the work had been discussed by a number of people there, but that while they had found it moving, they were afraid that, should it be performed, it might make some of the delegates feel uncomfortable—a strange confirmation of Jacob Bronowski's statement about the disinclination of politicians to become transported by the emotion of compassion or tears.

The author speaks with performers during a performance of *Threnody*. (*Courtesy of* CBC Information Services)

DEPARTING IN NEW DIRECTIONS

It might begin somewhat like this:

Everyone is asked to write down the things they perceive. Ten minutes later, in discussing the lists, we note that while many have seen some interesting sights, few have heard anything remarkable, fewer still have touched, tasted or smelled anything at all. From this we conclude that for most people "I perceive" is synonymous with "I see."

We then spend considerable time trying to unclog all the sense-receptors. The class is piled with exercises and questions. How many senses are there? What about sensations of cold, heat, pain, pleasure? Do you discover any evidence in your body for a kinaesthetic or muscle sense? If not, stretch, flex muscles, expand flank. What about a visceral sense? Sit motionless and feel your lunch moving through the digestive tracts of your stomach; feel blood in your veins, nerves in your ears. Feel *malaise* and *élan* of muscle and viscera. Listen to the sound of your own eyelids fluttering; smell the skin of your hand; count the hairs on your arm.

Sit silently and receive the messages of the world.

It is the senses that give us information about the outside world and the welfare of our own body. The subject absorbs us in discussion.

"What about extrasensory perception?" asks a student. Here information is detected from the outside world, seemingly without the intervention of any known receptors. Brain-waves tuning in on an electromagnetic network. More animated discussion.

Often, we discover, we develop a keen awareness of a sense receptor by amputating some of the others around it. So the class is blindfolded and asked to touch their way around the room. At last we discover the texture of the chairs we've been sitting on with blunted rumps for some weeks. How long is this wall? You can't see? So *feel* it in slow motion with your hand registering every imperfection of the paint with seismographic delicacy.

I tell the class I have placed someone in the center of the room and ask them to describe him, using all their senses except that of sight.

How long is his nose? What is the texture of his hair? Has he changed his socks recently? Does he smoke? Is his skin salty? What else?

I ask the class to return tomorrow and bring five interesting textures to school. They are to leave their blindfolds on until they find their way out of the building. Gingerly they disperse.

Next day. Hundreds of furry, spiky, slippery, flaky, glossy, bristly, crinkly little objects are passed around with eyes closed. One student has brought some raw meat. Several girls scream at its touch, refusing to hold it.

The known escapes monotony by being made unknown; thus is the world revitalized.

I have brought a bag of apples, and I give one to each student, saying I want the apple to be apprehended as a mixed-media experience.

They smell the apple.

They feel its cool cheek.

They inspect its speckled geography as though it were the map of a favored country.

They rattle the womb-pod and listen to the loosened seeds dancing.

Then they bite . . . .

Five senses. As they munch, I read them a sonnet by Rilke:

> Full round apple, pear and banana,
> gooseberry . . . all this speaks
> death and life into the mouth . . . I sense . . .
> Read it from the face of a child
>
> tasting them. This comes from far. Is something
> indescribable slowly happening in your mouth?
> Where otherwise words were, flow discoveries,
> freed all surprised out of the fruit's flesh.
>
> Dare to say what you call apple. This
> sweetness, first concentrating, that it may
> in the tasting delicately raised,
>
> grow clear, awake, transparent, double-meaning'd,
> sunny, earthy, of the here and now—
> O experience, sensing joy—immense![5]

This is not an appropriate time for theorizing, and so we go on listening to ourselves eating our apples for the remainder of the hour.

Another day my colleague Joel Smith takes over. With his painterly fingers Joel holds up a small white sphere and asks the class what it is.

"An egg," someone says brightly.

"How do you know?" Joel asks. "What do you really see?"

"A white disc," another student volunteers. "A ping-pong ball." "No! A moon. A symbol of fecundity."

Joel is concerned with the relatively and multiplicity of reality. Holding the egg out over the floor he asks: "Now what?"

"You're going to drop it."

"Take a sheet of paper and draw this."

He drops it. It splatters on the floor.

We look at the drawings. Some show the egg suspended in Joel's fingers with the floor dangling beneath and radial lines of gravity shooting suspensefully between the two. Others show the egg in flight, plucked from Joel's fingertips by the energetic floor. Others show a split-second freeze before the carnage. Still others show the egg dashed into fluid and shell-splinters. Looking at the soft puddle, we are aware that a remarkable metamorphosis has been enacted before our eyes— but so quickly; it has hardly registered.

Quickly, Joel takes another egg from his pocket and dangles it tantalizingly above the floor. Alertly we give ourselves to the situation; this time we want to study the miraculous transformation more intimately.

He drops it.

It lands, bounces, then rolls away, a little shell-shocked but otherwise utterly intact. Hard-boiled. Joel Smith says laconically, "Reality is sometimes ambiguous."

Joel Smith is a painter. I am a composer. We have been teaching together as part of an experiment in which we have integrated visual arts and music at Simon Fraser University.* Each section of our first-year Communications course has been taken by a composer and a painter. Peter Huse and Bob Bigelow, with enviable intellectual zeal, have attempted to build a panaesthetic grammar, joining vision to hearing. Their practical experiments have led them to the development of pictographic notations for the new music which their class composes

---

* That is, 1965–71. Joel Smith and the others mentioned in this article fled when the Faculty of Education decided they preferred autoharps and painting snowmen to invention.

and performs. Doug Muir and Iain Baxter are more relaxed, oriental almost, with their group. Iain's mute, but highly rhetorical, nonverbal teaching is a natural complement to Doug's exercises in meditation and yoga as a preliminary to music appreciation.

I entered Doug Muir's class one day. The room was darkened. Everyone had their shoes and stockings off. They were breathing deeply, moving gently on instruction. Then they lay on the floor and listened to a variety of music on records. "The whole body is an ear," Doug kept reminding them.

Joel Smith and I sometimes never get beyond our elementary sensitizing exercises, never get into visual arts or music as such. When we do, we always try to remain vigilant for a nascent symbiosis, and then to build on it.

One day I had been discussing the canon. The canon is a musical procedure in which one voice follows another in strict imitation but delayed in time. It suddenly occurred to me that we could easily have a multimedia canon. So four students took up positions at four drawing boards, and another four stood in front of them. Those in front were instructed to make sounds with their voices, and those at the drawing boards were asked to translate their hearings immediately into visual patterns. As the first four vocalized, sometimes in surprising or entertaining ways, the second four dashed paint around their papers. The result was somewhat like an animated cartoon with phase shifting. Then we added four dancers who were asked to ignore the sounds they heard and concentrate on moving their bodies into the shapes they saw appearing on the page. Finally, four more students were given percussion instruments, and were asked to concentrate on reproducing the gestures of the dancers on their instruments. At first this quadruple multimedia canon seemed totally incoherent, but after half an hour it was amazing how adept the performers had become at the act of instantaneous and imaginative translation.

Sometimes a simple prop will serve as a means of translation from one sense to another: for instance a mirror. There is a well-known theatre exercise in which two people face one another, the one mirroring the shapes of the other's hands and body. This can be taken as an opener for a series of synaesthetic exercises. For instance, after moving in synchronization for a while I inform the class that the mirror I wish them to consider now has unique properties—it imitates every *sound* placed in front of it as well as every image. Every sound made by one participant must be reproduced exactly and instantaneously by the person opposite. The mirror talks; the mirror sings; the mirror makes strange noises—and always in unison with itself. On some occasions, with musicians, instruments are substituted for voices and students are trained to duplicate pitches as instantaneously as possible. The leader sounds a pitch, the mirror duplicates it; as soon as he does a new pitch is sounded, and so forth. On other occasions we have ended up on the floor facing one another in pairs across a long roll of paper. Starting from the center one student draws abstract patterns in slow motion while the student opposite produces a mirror inversion of the drawing simultaneously.

We have five senses to apprehend the environment. Yet we are so contemptuous of our abilities to touch, taste, and smell things that we have developed nothing at all approaching art for any of these sense modalities. One day I want to take all the possible art-forms compiled by Joseph Schillinger, the mathematician, and have a class create an art-work in each of them.

We already have some beautiful examples of mixed-media art in religious ritual. An example is the Catholic Mass. For the eyes there is the art and architecture of the cathedral; for the ears, the bells and chanting voices; for the nose, incense; for the mouth, the transubstantiation of the bread and wine; while the sense of touch is stimulated in many ways from the prayer beads in the hand to the stone against the knees in prayer. Yet all of these sensations are orchestrated in such a way that they never produce sensory overload.

There are numerous other examples of mixed-media rituals. Wine-tasting is an activity which, if performed correctly, brings all the senses into convergence. This is why the glasses must be touched together to bring beauty to the ear—the one sense which might otherwise be ignored.

From the very beginning of the Simon Fraser experience, we have been intent on developing technique and content for a new teaching which does not break the primal unity of the senses. Or rather, let us say, it has already been broken, and we are concerned with reconfiguring it again in natural fields of interaction.

This is not accomplished easily, especially by those, like ourselves, who have been rigorously trained in isolated art-forms; for, in the attainment of our virtuosity, we have been obliged to allow much of our perceptual apparatus to atrophy. But perhaps this very fact makes us all the more eager to regain a confluence of the senses.

In the first year there was the Sensitivity Course, which met on Saturdays, and to which numerous faculty members were invited. We would simply gather in the Theatre at 10 o'clock for a series of experiences, talks, and discussions, which went on until we got tired. When we wanted to study the eye we gathered together a physiologist to tell us about the physiology of vision, a psychologist to tell us about the psychology of vision, and a painter and an architect to share with us their insights into the aesthetics of vision. I recall we ended up that session arguing about whether Homer described the sea as 'wine-dark' because he was color-blind or because the pigment of the Aegean was different in his day.

A cosmetician and a pestologist came to our Sensitivity Course one day to discuss their work in the area of smell. The cosmetician sprayed us all with her perfumes and charmed us with her vitreous sales-talk. Then the pestologist demonstrated the rather different kind of stink-bombs on which he was working, in which poison fumes, when inhaled, kill insects. We ended this session by discussing possible ways of formulating a "smell-scale" for olfactory compositions, rather along the lines of that developed by Des Esseintes, the hero of Huysmans' novel *A rebours*. Further experimentation proved that "smell chords" consisting of three or four different aromas proved to be rather flat, but "smell-melodies"—in which a progression of several aromas is spread out, for instance on a forearm—were intoxicatingly effective.

How long will it be before we revive the olfactory delicacies described in the pages of the *Thousand and One Nights*? Often I have wondered whether it is possible to have an art-form at all without having a metalanguage by which the art-form can be defined and described. For instance, supposing we wished to have an art of smell. It would first be necessary for us to give names to all the smells so that we could arrange them into a system from which compositions could be created. Certainly our ability to describe aural and visual phenomena (i.e., to position them within a system) far exceeds our ability to describe tactile or olfactory experiences. And so music and painting are art-forms, and the other things are not, or at least not yet.

What lies before us now is quite clear. We must revivify atrophying sense-receptors by discovering new art-forms which involve them in exciting new ways. And we must discover the unifying feature of all the art-forms in order to achieve a higher synthesis.

Let the games of children be our model. To delimit them into known art-forms would be a useless exercise in taxonomy; and yet there is a unifying principle here, an integrity of intent and action.

Today we are searching above all for natural expression.

Official art is artificial.

We must reach out and invent new art-forms in the hope that this integrity, never absent in the games of children, may return to all of us.

The whole body is an ear: the author leads the class
in relaxation exercises, gradually inducing
concentrated listening.

CURRICULUM VITAE

Can creativity be institutionalized? This is a question which institutions hoping to get on the move should consider.

But most institutions do not wish to get on the move. Like monuments, they hope to live for ever by remaining stationary. They uphold traditions and usually act as if they are stuffed. We may call them reactionary or authority-bound, but they are dykes against anarchy and caprice. Only in violently changeable times do we dare question their functioning in public.

When I was young I went to a university to learn. I had no illusions about learning many new things there, and for a time I was content to learn old things. When this no longer remained interesting I tangled with some of my teachers and one day found myself sitting in the dean's office. The dean was a brooding Spenglerian German and he was very angry. He kept clenching his fists into little balls and squeezing himself. He told me I had to make a choice: either to stop disturbing the teachers or get out.

It was a brilliant crisp day in mid-winter. The sun was shining brightly and the snow was sparkling. I was just about to reply when I noticed the way the sun was shining through his ears. He had big ears— what the French call "les étoiles." I could see all the little blood veins in them.

A strange thing happened. I laughed. It was one of those nervous little laughing fits boys sometimes get before they are to be punished.

"Get out!" said the dean.

"Perhaps I've made a mistake," I suggested.

"Get out!"

That was the end of my formal education, and for many years I kept as far away as possible from all institutions, which I was certain were conspiracies against change ruled by pusillanimous Prussians who enjoyed squeezing themselves. Authority has always seemed to me to be the opposite of invention. It represents an unwillingness to learn. And so one seeks out mentors in other places, in books if necessary. My mentors shine transparently through my work: Ezra Pound, Paul Klee,

Wassily Kandinsky, and Sergei Eisenstein—great teachers because they were great learners.

When, years later, I entered my first academic institution it was through the back door and with extreme misgivings. As I grew more confident, however, I began to take on a sense of mission; I was determined that as a teacher I would not inhibit or destroy the youthful zeal of my students. I was not able to live up to that ideal entirely, of course, and experience has taught me to regard it as naive. Sometimes a teacher's function may also be to act as an abrasive against creative impulses—to resist talented students at times in a deliberate attempt to get them to investigate and defend the premises of their own intuitions.

I do not know whether my work is taken seriously or not. I have done a lot of guest lecturing in universities or schools and have been aware that I have often been brought in as a diversion from the tedium of routine. Schafer makes whoopee for a few days, after which the class gets back to the serious business of blowing the clarinet.

Still, one cannot resist the temptation of devising model institutions in which one would like to work. What I give here is intended only as one stream in an institution dedicated to the integrated arts. Nothing in this book is so tentative as my model curriculum, which is why it appears where it belongs, on the last page.

CURRICULUM OUTLINE FOR MUSIC

Daily opening exercises: (1) the singing of plain-chant; (2) contemplation; (3) eurhythmics.

First Year
Perception and Sensitivity (sound, vision, taste, smell, touch, movement, gesture, psyche and soma)
Ear Cleaning (learning to listen)
Creativity (free exploration to discover repertoires of sounds)
Acoustics I (basic acoustics)
History and Theory I (basic)
Voice Culture I (experimentation with the voice in poetry, song, elocution)
Instrument (by choice)

Second Year
Ear Training I (pattern perception)
Creativity (controlled creativity, working with set forms)
Psycho-acoustics

Noise Pollution
Media Studies I (intermedia workshop, eurhythmics, dance, etc.)
History and Theory II
Voice Culture II (choral singing)
Instrument (by choice)

Third Year
Ear Training II (study of the world soundscape)
Creativity (free-within-controlled composition)
Electro-acoustics
Electronic and Computer music
Media Studies II (film and television)
History and Theory III (exploration of an exotic musical
    culture)
Voice Culture III (composition with the voice, poetry, radio
    program, etc.)
Instrument (by choice)

Fourth Year
Two projects:

1. Personal (creative or scholarly)
2. Social (group or individual investigation of a socio-acoustic
    situation; i.e., work on the World Soundscape Project)

NOTES

1. First published in *The Australian Journal of Music Education*, No. 10, April 1972.
2. Hermann Hesse, *The Glass Bead Game*, New York, Holt, Rinehart & Winston, 1969; London, Jonathan Cape, 1970, pp. 28–29.
3. George Self, *New Sounds in Class*, Universal Edition, London, 1967.
4. Subsequently published by The University of Toronto Press.
5. *Sonnets to Orpheus*, I, 13, trans. M.D. Herter, New York, Norton, 1942.